Evaluation of World Bank Programs in Afghanistan, 2002–11

IEG WORLD BANK | IFC | MIGA

INDEPENDENT EVALUATION GROUP

Evaluation of World Bank Programs in Afghanistan, 2002–11

Contents

BOXES

FIGURES

TABLES

Acknowledgments

This evaluation of the World Bank's organizational effectiveness was prepared by an Independent Evaluation Group (IEG) team led by Anis Dani. The evaluation was carried out under the guidance of Ali Khadr (Senior Manager) and the overall direction of Caroline Heider (Director-General, Evaluation).

Members of the core team included Mary Breeding, Prem Garg, Gita Gopal, Min Joo Kang, Albert Martinez, J. van Holst Pellakaan, Stephen Pirozzi, Susan Stout, Clay Wescott, and Corky de Asis. Thanks are also due to Rebecca Paterson and Svetlana Markova for their support during the preparatory phase. The review of analytical and advisory activities (AAA) was coordinated by Prem Garg and the reviewers included Norman Hicks, Andres Liebenthal, Eugene McCarthy, John Nellis, Stephen Pirozzi, Salvatore Schiavo-Campo, and Christine Wallich, in addition to the core team. The beneficiary survey was carried out by CAERUS, the Facebook survey was managed by Bahar Salimova, and the survey of the Afghan civil service was undertaken by Lorenzo Delesgues. The background study on gender was conducted by Disha Zaidi under the supervision of Gita Gopal. The team also acknowledges the advice received from Geeta Batra on the recommendations and Management Action Record, Stephan Wegner in finalizing the findings on the International Finance Corporation (IFC) and the Multilateral Investment Guarantee Agency (MIGA), and William Hurlbut and Caroline McEuen in editing the report.

IEG is grateful to the numerous representatives of the government and development partners who provided valuable insights into the Afghanistan program. The team is also thankful to World Bank management and country team members, including both previous and current staff, working on Afghanistan, who provided valuable time, information and feedback on the country program to the evaluation team.

Peer reviewers are Basil Kavalsky (former World Bank Country Director), Ian Bannon (Sector Manager, Africa Region, Conflict and Social Development Unit), and Clare Lockhart (Chief Executive Officer, Institute for State Effectiveness).

Abbreviations

AAA	Analytical and advisory activities
ADB	Asian Development Bank
AISA	Afghanistan Investment Support Agency
ANDS	Afghanistan National Development Strategy
ARTF	Afghanistan Reconstruction Trust Fund
AUWSSC	Afghan Urban Water Supply and Sanitation Company
BPHS	Basic Package of Health Services
CAS	Country Assistance Strategy
CDCs	Community Development Councils
CGAP	Consultative Group to Assist the Poorest
CPE	Country Program Evaluation
DAB	Da Afghanistan Bank (Afghanistan Central Bank)
DABM	Da Afghanistan Breshna Moassese
DABS	Da Afghanistan Breshna Shirkat (power utility company)
DDA	District Development Assembly
DFID	U.K. Department for International Development
EIRP	Emergency Irrigation Rehabilitation Project
EQUIP	Education Quality Improvement Program
ESW	Economic and sector work
FCS	Fragile and conflict-affected state
FDI	Foreign direct investment
FMBA	First Microfinance Bank of Afghanistan
FY	Fiscal year
GDP	Gross domestic product
I-ANDS	Interim Afghanistan National Development Strategy
IARCSC	Independent Administration Reform and Civil Service Commission
ICT	Information and communications technology
IDA	International Development Association
IDLG	Independent Directorate of Local Governance
IEG	Independent Evaluation Group
IFC	International Finance Corporation
IMF	International Monetary Fund

ISN	Interim Strategy Note
JICA	Japan International Cooperation Agency
JSDF	Japan Social Development Fund
KURP	Kabul Urban Reconstruction Project
MAIL	Ministry of Agriculture, Irrigation and Livestock
MEW	Ministry of Energy and Water
MFI	Microfinance institution
MIGA	Multilateral Investment Guarantee Agency
MISFA	Microfinance Investment Support Facility for Afghanistan
MOCIT	Ministry of Communications and Information Technology
MOF	Ministry of Finance
MOPH	Ministry of Public Health
MRRD	Ministry of Rural Rehabilitation and Development
NDF	National Development Framework
NEEP	National Emergency Employment Program
NEEPRA	National Emergency Employment Program for Rural Areas
NERAP	The National Emergency Rural Access Project
NGO	Nongovernmental organization
NLTA	Nonlending technical assistance
NSP	National Solidarity Program
PEFA	Public expenditure and financial accountability
PFM	Public financial management
PRSP	Poverty Reduction Strategy Paper
PSD	Private sector development
Qatia	Audited Annual Appropriations Statements
SHEP	Strengthening Higher Education Project
TSS	Transitional Support Strategy
UNAMA	United Nations Assistance Mission to Afghanistan
UNDP	United Nations Development Program
USAID	United States Agency for International Development
UNICEF	United Nations Children's Fund
USTDA	US Trade and Development Agency
WHO	World Health Organization

Overview

Highlights

Despite extremely difficult security conditions, which deteriorated markedly after 2006, the World Bank Group has commendably established and sustained a large program of support to the country. The key messages of the evaluation are:

- While World Bank Group strategy has been highly relevant to Afghanistan's situation, beginning in 2006 the strategies could have gone further in adapting ongoing programs to evolving opportunities and needs and in programming activities sufficient to achieve the objectives of the pillars in those strategies.

- Overall, Bank Group assistance has achieved substantial progress toward most of its major objectives, although risks to development outcomes remain high. Impressive results have been achieved in public financial management, public health, telecommunications, and community development; substantial outputs have also been achieved in primary education, rural roads, irrigation, and microfinance—all started during the initial phase. Bank assistance has been critical in developing the mining sector as a potential engine of growth. However, progress has been limited in civil service reform, agriculture, urban development, and private sector development.

- The Bank Group's direct financial assistance has been augmented effectively by analytic and advisory activities and donor coordination through the Afghanistan Reconstruction Trust Fund. Knowledge services have been an important part of Bank Group support and have demonstrated the value of strategic analytical work, even in areas where the Bank Group may opt out of direct project financing.

- Contradictory advice and competing donor programs have compounded conflicting views among different government agencies, leading to a "missing middle" in the absence of agreement on subnational governance. Without viable district or provincial institutions, the investment in community organizations at the village level may not be sustainable, substantial project benefits notwithstanding.

- With the expected reduction of the international presence in 2014, sustainability of development gains remains a major risk because of capacity constraints and inadequate human resources planning on the civilian side.

To enhance program effectiveness, the evaluation recommends that the World Bank Group help the government develop a comprehensive, long-term human resources strategy for the civilian sectors; focus on strategic analytical work in sectors that are high priorities for the government; assist in the development of local government institutions and, in the interim, support the development of a viable system for service delivery at subnational levels; assist in transforming the National Solidarity Program into a more sustainable financial and institutional model to consolidate its gains; help strengthen the regulatory environment for private sector investment; and scale up International Finance Corporation (IFC) and Multilateral Investment Guarantee Agency (MIGA) support to the private sector.

Context

Security conditions pose a formidable challenge to Afghanistan's development and external partner support. Afghanistan has undergone a very tangible deterioration in security since 2006, including a spike in civilian casualties. This has affected the Bank Group's work through increased risks to staff, restrictions on movement, further constraints on supervision, and additional measures to deal with safety. Despite the extremely difficult context, the World Bank Group has commendably established and sustained a large program of support to the country.

Purpose and Approach

IEG's Country Program Evaluation (CPE) assesses the relevance and effectiveness of World Bank Group support to Afghanistan and some of the key risks to sustainability of development outcomes. The CPE covers the period FY02–11 and aims to inform implementation of the FY12–14 Interim Strategy Note and the preparation of the subsequent Country Assistance Strategy (CAS).

Following IEG's approach to evaluating Bank Group programs in fragile and conflict-affected states (FCS), the standard methodology for CPEs (appendix B) has been applied to Afghanistan. Emphasis has been placed on learning lessons to strengthen the Bank Group program in Afghanistan and inform programs in other FCS.

Comments from the government of the Islamic Republic of Afghanistan on the CPE are attached at the end of this evaluation.

I. World Bank Group Strategies

This evaluation considers the Bank Group's assistance to Afghanistan highly relevant and responsive to client needs, particularly during the initial period of reengagement.

The initial strategy responded to the conditions prevalent when the Bank Group reengaged in November 2001 with a transitional government that inherited very weak capacity. Initial Bank Group reengagement in Afghanistan was set out in the March 2002 Transitional Support Strategy (TSS; World Bank 2002), which focused on recovery and reconstruction. Strategic priorities were "essential governance institutions and capacity, high-priority, high-impact reconstruction programs to restart the economy and social services; coordinated donor assistance under government leadership; and a better knowledge base and analytical underpinning for the work of the international community and for future Bank assistance." A second TSS (World Bank 2003), in line with the government's reconstruction strategy, was approved in February 2003 and focused on: (i) improving livelihoods; (ii) fiscal strategy, institutions, and management; (iii) governance and public administration reform; and (iv) enabling private sector development.

These priorities were based on a Preliminary Needs Assessment, conducted jointly by the Asian Development Bank (ADB), the United Nations Development Programme (UNDP), and the World Bank. The World Bank–administered multidonor Afghanistan Reconstruction Trust Fund (ARTF) is the main source of external finance for the non-security recurrent budget. Its focus has shifted over time toward investment financing and an Incentive Program to support public financial management reforms.

The focus of the two TSSs was appropriately on building core state institutions, delivery of services to build confidence in the state, rehabilitating critical infrastructure, and initiating analytical work to build the knowledge base for future development assistance. The Bank has worked consistently on these core state functions and delivery of social services, recognizing that these are long-term endeavors.

Bank Group strategy under the 2006 and 2009 Interim Strategy Notes (ISNs) was slow to evolve beyond the initial foundations for development to a longer-term strategy for sustainable growth. Projects and programs under the 2006 and 2009 ISNs largely continued from those initiated after the Needs Assessment under the TSSs. They were still relevant, but could have benefited from further adaptation to evolving opportunities and needs. Activities programmed under the ISNs were insufficient to ensure achievement of the strategic objectives of the ISN pillars, which affected the relevance and efficacy of Bank Group programs.

An ISN, like a TSS, enables the processing of all operations under Bank Operational Policy 8.0 – *Rapid Response to Crises and Emergencies*. And, unlike a full-fledged CAS, it is not required to have a results framework. The 2006 and 2009 ISNs organized the Bank Group's strategy for Afghanistan around three pillars: (i) building the capacity of the state and its accountability to its citizens; (ii) promoting growth of the rural economy and improving rural livelihoods; and (iii) supporting growth of the formal private sector, including through infrastructure development. The Bank was to deliver the bulk of Bank Group support, with the International Finance Corporation (IFC) and Multilateral Investment Guarantee Agency (MIGA) intervening largely under pillar 3.

The strategies laid out in the ISNs were informed by core analytical work such as the Country Economic Memorandum (World Bank 2004a) and the Public Finance Management Review (World Bank 2005a). In some cases, strategic choices were influenced by an agreed division of labor with other partners, such as ADB's assumption of the lead role in infrastructure. In other cases, the Bank changed its strategy. An initial choice to focus on higher education and skills development, for example, was deferred to focus initially on primary school education in response to client and donor demand. In agriculture a judgment about client ownership and capacity led to avoidance of this sector for many years, although more recently a change in leadership has opened new opportunities.

Approaches varied by sector and, in hindsight, practitioners in the various sectors could have learned more from one another. In some sectors, institutional and resource constraints were addressed by mobilizing the private sector (in information and communications technology and the financial sector, for example) and the nonprofit sector (in health and the National Solidarity Program), with a focus on strengthening government capacity for regulation and oversight rather than service delivery, and on impact evaluation and third-party monitoring to track performance. The sectors with weaker outcomes (education, agriculture, power, water) did not have such robust systems for results monitoring.

While there was acceptable progress toward most of its major relevant objectives, given the challenges that Afghanistan faces, the program was unable to fully achieve the objectives under each of the three pillars.

The Bank Group strategy for FY12–14 has been put forward as another ISN, taking into account the uncertainty created by the impending 2014 transition in security arrangements. The ISN (World Bank 2012b) is accompanied by an in-depth analysis of the economics of transition to help the government develop a sustainable growth path. This work is likely to affect future donor commitments to Afghanistan and the design of the next Bank Group strategy. In the meantime, the 2012 ISN has restructured its pillars into support for: (1) building the legitimacy and capacity of institutions; (2) equitable service delivery; and (3) inclusive growth and jobs. The mining sector has received greater emphasis, since it is expected to catalyze regional growth along natural resource corridors. Other programs are largely a continuation of those initiated under previous Bank Group strategies, and they have been regrouped within the new pillars in the 2012 ISN. In the CPE, which primarily covers the period up to FY11, the programs are assessed against the pillars of the previous ISNs.

II. Results of Bank Group Support

BUILDING THE CAPACITY OF THE STATE AND ITS ACCOUNTABILITY TO ITS CITIZENS

Strategic objectives under this pillar encompassed: (i) public financial management (strengthen core systems, enhance fiscal sustainability and transparency, and increase the effectiveness and equity of subnational expenditures); (ii) public sector governance (build a reformed and sustainable civil service accountable to its citizens to provide affordable, accessible, and adequate services); (iii) health (promote rapid improvement in service delivery); and (iv) education (support the provision of services that are affordable, accessible, and of adequate quality, increasing enrollment at the primary, secondary, and vocational levels, with an improvement in gender parity).

The Bank has used extensive analytical and advisory activities (AAA), policy-based lending, and technical assistance to effectively strengthen public financial management functions in core government institutions. Afghanistan now has a relatively strong public financial management framework, impressive revenue growth, and greater assurance that funds provided through the budget are used effectively.

Accounting and financial management reporting have become more accurate and timely with the adoption of the Afghanistan Financial Management Information System. The use of the ARTF to pay salaries has ensured timely and reliable payment to staff, while facilitating quick disbursement of donor funds and accountability in their use. The ARTF also supported an Incentives Program for the government to undertake difficult reforms.

Nonetheless, achievement of the objectives of building capacity for budget formulation and execution, including improvements in fiscal management and spending efficiency at many line ministries and subnational entities, has been slow, and while a Public Procurement Law and amendments have been adopted with Bank support, many complementary actions needed for effective implementation have yet to be taken, creating substantial procurement bottlenecks.

In public administration, Bank support through extensive AAA, policy-based lending, and capacity-building investments has led to important reforms, but significant shortcomings persist. Bank support has led to adoption of a civil service law and regulations for administrative reform oversight, more transparent recruitment, reduction in the number of ministries from 34 to 26, and pay and grading reforms.

Nevertheless, public administration remains vulnerable, as there is little evidence that the new laws, procedures, and regulations are translating into improved civil service performance. Despite the inroads made with the support of the Bank to reduce leakage and increase donor trust, the government's ability to control corruption and enforce anti-corruption measures remains weak. The achievements have relied mainly on a "second civil service" of contracted staff who are paid relatively high salaries, some of whom are working for other development partners, without an agreed plan to hand over tasks to civil servants on pay scales that the government can afford.

Afghanistan has achieved remarkable gains in health service accessibility and improvements in health outcomes. Basic health services have been extended to cover all 34 provinces. From 2002 to 2009, the infant mortality rate fell by 22 percent and under-five mortality fell by 26 percent. The number of functioning health establishments and trained midwives (from accredited schools) increased fourfold from 2002 to 2010, and the proportion of facilities with skilled female health worker(s) has increased from 25 to 72 percent. Despite data constraints, there is evidence of reductions in maternal mortality rates and fertility rates and of increased contraceptive prevalence.

The Bank assisted the government with the institutional design of a national health program for rapid, effective service delivery of the Basic Package of Health Services, using Performance-based Partnership Agreements with nongovernmental organizations (NGOs) and third-party monitoring managed by the Ministry of Public Health. Bank investments of $224 million and three high-quality AAA helped consolidate the approach, which became the institutional framework for structuring donor assistance to the sector.

In education, access at the primary level has improved significantly, but challenges remain in quality and in higher education. Primary school enrollment increased from 1 million students in 2001 to 7.2 million in 2011. Enrollment of girls has grown from a negligible number to almost three million. Bank assistance included projects for primary and secondary education, higher education, and vocational skills training, but higher education and skills training have had more modest outcomes. Early investments focused more on access than quality. Bank assistance provided grants for purchase of school supplies and equipment in almost 10,000 schools and construction of over 5,000 classrooms.

School infrastructure has improved, but there are indications, including from the project's midterm review, of gaps in construction quality. In addition, over half of the schools with infrastructure grants do not comply with gender equity criteria for girls' attendance, which is hindered by, among other things, the absence of boundary walls and latrines.

The Bank has supported in-service teacher training in 23 provinces and training facilities have increased from four teacher training colleges in 2002 to 42 teacher training colleges and 137 distance learning centers in 2011. Women now constitute 31 percent of teachers. Unlike the health sector, the education sector does not have a system for monitoring performance outcomes and would benefit from greater Bank investment in strategic economic and sector work and results monitoring.

PROMOTING GROWTH OF THE RURAL ECONOMY AND IMPROVING RURAL LIVELIHOODS

Bank objectives were to: (i) expand support for successful rural programs where there are high returns in terms of legitimate economic outputs and poverty reduction and (ii) actively pursue enhanced linkages between activities and programs in rural areas, particularly between rural development programs of the Ministry of Rural Rehabilitation and Development and the Ministry of Agriculture, Irrigation, and Livestock. The 2009 ISN also intended to support the wider agriculture-rural development strategy dialogue and development of rural enterprises.

The overall impact on the core objective of promoting growth in the rural economy and improving rural livelihoods has been modest. Nonetheless, individual projects—rural roads, irrigation rehabilitation, horticulture and livestock, and the multisector National Solidarity Program (NSP)—within the pillar achieved their objectives, after delays and restructuring of some. Bank support to help generate growth in the rural economy addressed emergency needs such as rehabilitation of rural roads and irrigation canals and improved production efficiency in the horticulture and livestock subsectors—areas where no other donors had substantial programs. Of Afghanistan's approximately 40,000 kilometers of rural roads, 10,000 kilometers have been rehabilitated since 2001. Almost 60 percent of this was with Bank/ARTF support, which financed 5,900 kilometers of rural roads and provided about 8 million days of employment. Agricultural projects made little progress for two-to-three years and will have addressed about 19 percent of Afghanistan's irrigation sector and much less in horticulture and livestock by 2012.

The government views the NSP's reach of three-fourths of Afghan villages as one of its biggest achievements and wants remaining communities to benefit from the program. NSP objectives were to support its rollout across the country to empower rural communities to manage small infrastructure and development programs and to build social capital among them. Resources invested in the NSP ($1.3 billion) are almost twice those invested in other activities under pillar 2. This has enabled outreach to some 29,000 villages throughout Afghanistan and financing of over 55,000 local projects. The NSP is reported to have created opportunities for social empowerment of rural women, whose participation in community groups has become more acceptable (although uneven across the country). While early results from community mobilization are encouraging, institutional sustainability is a substantial unresolved issue that will continue to be a challenge in the transition period.

While rural poverty reduction suggests a positive effect on livelihoods, results are uneven—reflecting varying support levels—across provinces. The NSP does not aim to, and therefore cannot be expected to, be a major contributor to economic growth. Instead, the primary drivers of the rural economy are the massive donor expenditures, which provide significant short-term employment for many rural people, and the illicit opium industry (estimated at 9 percent of gross domestic product [GDP] in 2011), which provides substantial cash income to small farmers. Among other commodities, which used to be significant drivers of the rural economy, the average production of wheat (Afghanistan's core staple food), while rising, is still vulnerable to considerable drought-induced fluctuations, and exports of raisins (Afghanistan's principal export) have reached only 60 percent of the average annual levels achieved during the 1980s.

SUPPORTING GROWTH OF THE FORMAL PRIVATE SECTOR

Objectives were to: (i) continue support for infrastructure—power, infrastructure maintenance, and urban development and water supply— that remained in high demand and (ii) provide direct support to the private sector through microfinance, industrial estates development, investment guarantees, and natural resources (mining), in addition to telecommunications. IFC's support and MIGA's guarantees were primarily for pillar 3 activities.

While the outcomes of Bank Group support under this pillar have been mixed, results have been noteworthy in microfinance, communications, and mining. Bank Group performance and results have been good in three important segments: (i) microfinance, which services a large segment of private business as well as the poor and women; (ii) information and communications technology (ICT), which is beginning to have an impact on public and private sector efficiency and governance; and (iii) mining and hydrocarbons, which have the potential to become a driver of growth.

In telecommunications, Bank and IFC financing and MIGA guarantees supported private sector investments, and the Bank Group had significant inputs in the policy, legal, and regulatory framework and related institution building. Bank Group interventions have also contributed to economic empowerment of women through microfinance loans, with a positive impact on economic decisionmaking and savings (69 percent of clients save money, compared with 34 percent before the loans). Bank Group projects that financed rehabilitation of infrastructure eventually achieved their intended outputs, although the projects have had implementation issues.

Bank Group performance and results in supporting the investment climate, power, and urban development were much weaker. While security remains an underlying constraint to private sector investments, so does the policy and governance environment. Under these circumstances, it has been difficult to develop a relevant and focused program to strengthen the investment climate. In the power sector, staffing-transition issues weakened project supervision and a successful initial dialogue with the government and donors. In the urban sector, where the client expected the Bank to play a leading role, Bank projects have had mixed results. While under some projects, infrastructure has been built, several urban projects were affected by design and implementation problems, which led to costly delays and weak outcomes. Although there is now a recognition of the need for upgrading existing informal settlements, a common thread has been lack of progress in addressing key issues such as clarifying property rights (especially land rights), creating institutions, and building capacity and skills.

III. Drivers of Success and Weakness

Internal drivers of success included the quality of AAA (in some sectors), customization of design to the country context, and staff capacity. Sound analytical work, in the form of up-front analysis and judicious use of nonlending technical assistance (NLTA), appears to have positively influenced outcomes in public financial management, health, ICT, microfinance, and IFC's Business Advisory Services for horticulture and other business development. The lack of strategic analytical work in some sectors (such as agriculture and urban) hampered the development of Bank assistance and effective donor coordination. The Bank has been aware of political economy constraints, such as in the context of the drug economy and corruption (and more recently in work on the economics of transition). Nonetheless, in view of the political economy and uncertainties, the Bank Group could usefully engage in scenario planning with other partners to prepare for, rather than react to, changes in country conditions.

The Bank's AAA work is greatly appreciated by the government and donor partners, and the balance between analytical studies and technical assistance enhanced AAA impact. But analytic work suffered from systemic weaknesses in planning and managing AAA, especially during the initial years, resulting in some loss of institutional memory.

The mining sector, which is likely to have a transformative impact on the economy, stands out as an area where the primary contribution of the Bank was made through its knowledge work. The Bank's assistance is helping the government leverage mining sector investments toward broader regional growth. Keeping in mind the country's governance challenges and competing financing needs, sector work needs to be complemented with a revenue management plan that protects allocations for development and social expenditures.

Contracting out health and microfinance service delivery and community mobilization to NGOs enabled the health sector, microfinance, and the NSP to achieve outcomes rapidly, and maintaining these institutional arrangements is critical to their success.

Policy dialogue in the health, communications, and microfinance sectors was facilitated by a realistic assessment of the capacity of the public sector and of the potential of the private and voluntary sectors, as well as acceptance of the comparative advantage of each (with the government in the role of enabler and regulator rather than service provider). Many NGOs had been operating in Afghanistan before and during the Taliban era, and capitalizing on their field presence enabled the Bank Group to accelerate support for the government's strategic priorities.

The effectiveness of these programs was enhanced when they were accompanied by clear results frameworks and explicit arrangements for monitoring and evaluation. However, the results vary: some programs primarily monitor outputs, while others include third-party monitoring of outcomes. Their ability to make course corrections to strengthen program implementation is affected accordingly.

The worsening security situation since 2007 has further limited the Bank Group's ability to undertake field supervision. The establishment of clear results frameworks for credible monitoring of all programs supported by the Bank Group is even more urgent.

With the help of incentives for staff posted in conflict countries, the Afghanistan program has been largely successful in mobilizing staff for the country office, which allowed more intensive support to the client in those sectors. IFC also based a country officer located on World Bank premises in Kabul in 2008.

In core areas such as public financial management, the need for constant support made field presence an imperative. Programs in other sectors—health, ICT, and mining—were effectively designed and managed by task team leaders based elsewhere, but with staff continuity and frequent country visits.

While staff decentralization was important during implementation, for program design and re-design, sector knowledge and in-depth experience has proved to be even more important than decentralization. Nevertheless, unavailability of country-based staff (urban, power) or frequent staff turnover with uneven expertise and experience over time (civil service reform, agriculture, education, NSP) has affected several programs over the past few years. Security constraints limit the overall size of the country office, and the Bank Group program will have to rely on a judicious mix of staff posted in country, in neighboring countries, and at headquarters.

External drivers of success included strong country ownership, client capacity, and alignment of objectives and approach with partner organizations. Selectivity under the TSSs was driven by priorities clearly articulated by the interim government. Most successful programs have their origins in that period. The subsequent Afghanistan National Development Strategy (ANDS) was more ambitious, with 22 National Priority Programs, which made selectivity more difficult. The government is now attempting to consolidate these into a smaller number of priorities.

Client capacity constraints were overcome initially by deploying additional personnel, funded by the United Nations Development Programme, and subsequently through the ARTF's recurring cost window. Capacity for core functions in apex organizations, especially in the Ministries of Finance and Economy, has enabled improvements in financial management and procurement. Capacity-building has been easier where service-delivery functions were outsourced for public health and the NSP, while the ministry retained responsibility for oversight. This is not feasible in all sectors, but its potential has not been fully utilized even in sectors such as agriculture, where it may be feasible. International experts gradually gave way to Afghan staff as client capacity increased, though in many ministries capacity depends on a "second civil service" of contracted staff paid at a much higher rate than in other countries of the region, owing to skill shortages, insecurity, and competing demands for Afghan staff from other partner organizations. These staffers are employed both by government ministries (using donor funding to top-up normal salaries) and by partner organizations, and most capacity has been built among the contracted staff of donor-funded projects. The Bank supported a Ministry of Finance survey of consultants and key ministries in 2010–11 to draw attention to the significance of this form of dependency. Loss of this second civil service, either because of deteriorating security or because of a decline in aid over the upcoming transition, could substantially undermine government capacity.

Alignment of donor objectives, as in the ARTF, is also a strong determinant of success. ARTF resources are allocated only to programs where there is agreement on objectives and program design, such as with the Incentives Program (under the recurrent cost window), the NSP, Basic Health, and the Education Quality Improvement Program. Pooling of resources increases leverage and accountability, and the ARTF has been very successful in mobilizing and utilizing resources effectively. It also allows the scaling up of programs piloted with Bank resources through support for on-budget programs, increasing borrower ownership. But it comes with demand for better documentation and supervision to justify financing decisions and rising expectations of greater voice on the part of the government and financing partners.

Similarly, the MIGA-managed Afghanistan Investment Guarantee Facility (operational in FY05–11), which was designed to take the "first loss," was a useful tool to expand MIGA guarantee coverage beyond what it could manage on its own balance sheet, but its uptake remained modest.

IV. Lessons for Fragile and Conflict-Affected Situations

Although Afghanistan's history and challenges are somewhat unusual, given the enormous impact of international actors since 1979, the experience of the past 10 years offers a few key lessons relevant to other fragile and conflict-affected situations:

- In countries with weak capacity, civil society and private sector partnerships can play an important role in augmenting capacity and delivering services.

- Use of Bank resources to pilot investment projects can facilitate resource mobilization to scale up tested, ongoing operations through multidonor trust funds.

- The use of multidonor trust funds to finance an incentives program can be effective in aligning government priorities with those of development partners to support critical state-building reforms.

- Gender mainstreaming is feasible even in FCS contexts with cultural constraints if addressed systematically. Substantial results in terms of service delivery and increasing economic and social opportunities for women can be achieved when ownership of gender issues is an integral part of the country program.

- The performance of different sector programs suggests that an early focus on results and monitoring, including third-party verification, is necessary and feasible even in FCS contexts with travel restrictions and security constraints, and adds considerable value.

- Continuity, experience, and quality of staff are necessary conditions for program effectiveness; location in-country is desirable, particularly during implementation. But for program design or redesign, in-country presence is not a substitute for experience, as long as staff continuity can be maintained.

- In FCS contexts, the Bank Group needs to lay the foundations for a longer-term strategy early during the recovery phase. The use of emergency procedures should not obscure the need for long-term strategic planning or for complying with Bank requirements that would, in any case, need to be addressed during project preparation or implementation.

- Bank Group AAA can play a critical role in filling knowledge gaps in FCS contexts that often lack a good knowledge base. Preserving institutional knowledge on key sector issues and the underlying drivers of political economy to make them available to future members of the country team is vital. This is particularly important in FCS countries, where staff turnover is higher than in other countries.

V. Recommendations

While considerable progress has been achieved in many areas, significant challenges remain in others. Risks to sustainability of development gains remain high. The Management Action Record lists the relevant findings, which lead to the following recommendations warranting attention.

- **Engage the government on the need for a comprehensive, long-term human resources strategy for the civilian sectors at different levels of government, and provide assistance, in collaboration with other partners, to develop such a strategy.** Development of a strategy would entail: helping the government undertake systematic analysis of the Afghan labor market and civilian human resource needs for the next decade; strengthening coordination among development partners to ensure greater coherence in provision of higher education and skills training; development and implementation of a plan to produce adequate numbers of skilled graduates through local and foreign universities and training institutions to meet the essential needs of the public and private sector; and assistance to the government to develop affordable human resources systems to recruit and retain trained staff.

- **Focus on strategic-level analytical work geared toward long-term development strategies in sectors that are of high priority for the government.** Given the Bank Group's comparative advantage in providing knowledge services, use a mix of strategic economic and sector work and NLTA/Advisory Services to respond to country needs in priority areas, even where the Bank Group decides against immediate financial commitments.

- **Engage the government in developing local government institutions to enhance the sustainability of national programs and, in the interim, help the government develop a viable system for service delivery at subnational levels.** Development of such a system would entail: collaborating with multilateral development partners and bilateral agencies supporting local government structures and service delivery at subnational levels and drawing on the Incentives Program to develop and support a joint strategy for local governance with the Ministry of Finance; Ministry of Rural Rehabilitation and Development; Ministry of Agriculture, Irrigation, and Livestock,; the Independent Directorate of Local Governance; and relevant line departments that would give each of them a stake in the outcome.

- **Advise and support the government in transforming the NSP into a more sustainable financial and institutional model to consolidate its gains.** This would involve: scaling down the size of the second grant under NSP III to a level where the benefits can be shared more widely and equitably; and linking the Community Development Councils to higher tier(s) of subnational governance with regular intergovernmental fiscal transfers for public investments and service delivery that can be sustained by the government.

- **Focus Bank Group efforts on strengthening the regulatory environment for private sector investment** through: greater use of analytical work, technical assistance, and Advisory Services to assist the government in establishing property rights, commercial dispute-resolution mechanisms, and institutions with capacity to enforce regulations and assistance to the government and private sector stakeholders in building coalitions to support the regulatory environment for private-sector-led growth.

- As part of their commitment to expand support in fragile and conflict-affected situations, IFC and MIGA could usefully increase business development efforts targeted to new clients, including investors from the region and the diaspora, to scale up support to the private sector.

Management Action Record

IEG Findings	IEG Recommendations	
	For the World Bank:	
Planning for the civilian sectors is seriously lagging behind that for the military and there is a risk of creating an imbalance among Afghan institutions. The international community has played a vital role in assisting the government's effort to plan the manpower and technical needs for an eventual transition to Afghan-led, Afghan-managed security services. The government urgently needs a comprehensive human resources strategy to strengthen civilian institutions in parallel.	Engage the government on the need for a comprehensive, long-term human resources strategy for the civilian sectors at different levels of government, and provide assistance, in collaboration with other partners, to develop such a strategy. Development of a strategy would entail: • Helping the government undertake systematic analysis of the Afghan labor market and civilian human resource needs for the next decade. • Strengthening coordination among development partners to ensure greater coherence in the provision of higher education and skills training. • Development and implementation of a plan to produce adequate numbers of skilled graduates from local and foreign universities and training institutions to meet the essential needs of the public and private sectors. • Development of affordable human resources systems for the government to recruit and retain trained staff.	
The Bank has not undertaken strategic analytical work in several areas that are of high priority for the government (especially agriculture and urban), and which are essential to sustain the country's development process. Gaps also exist in the justice sector and jobs, which are core areas of the Bank Group's framework from the *World Development Report 2011* (World Bank 2011e).	Focus on strategic-level analytical work geared toward long-term development strategies in sectors that are of high priority for the government: • Given the Bank Group's comparative advantage in providing knowledge services, use strategic economic and sector work and nonlending technical assistance/Advisory Services to respond to country needs in priority areas, even where the Bank Group decides against immediate financial commitments.	

Agree – This effort is ongoing but is a medium-term goal.	IEG correctly identifies the need for Afghanistan to develop a long-term, comprehensive human resource strategy, and many of the factors that could be included in this. But this will take time and needs to be developed and led by the government. As a start to this process, the Bank is currently: • Helping the government build administrative reform through the Capacity for Results Project. • Helping the government develop needed skills through its Second Higher Education Project and its Afghanistan Skills Development Project. Both projects are helping equip graduates for the needs of the labor market. We realize there is still a long way to go and are working with the government and other stakeholders to respond to the challenge through both investment and analytic work. Nevertheless, development of a comprehensive human resource strategy needs to be owned and led by the government, and capacity and demand for human resource skills is best built over a medium-time period and is highly dependent on the security environment.
Partially Agree – Further deepening our analytic work is appropriate, but selectivity based on security considerations, client readiness and demand, and Bank presence and expertise, is equally important.	The overall point on the importance of maintaining a strong analytic presence across a variety of sectors is valid. The Bank has a leadership role in helping Afghanistan formulate long-term development strategies. We have done so in many areas; for example, most recently through analytic work on poverty, transition economics, and resource corridors. Nevertheless, selectivity, based on security and political economy considerations, is also important. Security considerations mean we have to prioritize use of our staff as well as take into consideration our ability to obtain information and feedback. The Bank also needs to calibrate its analytic support to both client demand and the degree of receptivity of the client. Further, in most cases, the Bank achieves the strongest results with a mix of operational and analytic support. In the areas mentioned by IEG—agriculture, urban, and justice—the World Bank has projects, and knowledge development and transfer can be achieved through technical assistance components, as well as selective analytic work. On jobs, while we are providing significant job support through, for example, our urban, rural roads, and education projects, we agree on the value of looking holistically across sectors and projects to identify constraints and opportunities.

IEG Findings	IEG Recommendations	
The absence of effective subnational government structures is a risk to the sustainability of national programs.	**Engage the government in developing local government institutions to enhance the sustainability of national programs and, in the interim, help the government develop a viable system for service delivery at subnational levels.** Development of such a system would entail: • Collaborating with multilateral development partners and bilateral agencies supporting local government structures and service delivery at subnational levels. • Drawing on the Incentives Program to develop and support a joint strategy for local governance with the Ministries of Finance; Rural Rehabilitation and Development; Agriculture, Irrigation, and Livestock; IDLG (Independent Directorate of Local Governance; and relevant line departments that would give each of them a stake in the outcome.	
The continued dependence of the National Solidarity Program (NSP) on large grants cannot be sustained, because the borrower and donors are unlikely to finance the provisioning of a second grant at the current scale to all rural communities. Providing uneven entitlements to rural communities in Afghanistan is highly risky. While the recognition of Community Development Councils (CDCs) as the lowest tier of local government is under consideration, in the absence of linkages to other subnational levels of governance, the goal of "locking in local governance" at the village level through the NSP cannot be achieved.	**Advise and support the government in transforming the NSP into a more sustainable financial and institutional model to consolidate its gains.** This would involve: • Scaling down the size of the second grant under NSP III to a level where the benefits can be shared more widely and equitably. • Linking the CDCs to higher tier(s) of subnational governance with regular intergovernmental fiscal transfers for public investments and services that can be sustained by the government.	

Acceptance by Management	Management Response
Partially Agree – We concur on the importance of clarifying roles and responsibilities at subnational levels, but also that it is important to recognize the political economy and not get ahead of government readiness. Security considerations also act as a constraint.	We recognize the critical importance of getting subnational governance right for service delivery. Certainly, within each of our operations of support to national programs, building in sustainability, including through more effective local governments, is critical. We currently have an analytic program in place for FY13 to help the government define viable models of subnational governance and intergovernmental fiscal relations. This program will be carried out in collaboration with UNDP, AusAid, and DFID and is supported by IDLG. The Bank-managed ARTF Incentive Program is working in tandem with investment operations to support improvements in subnational finance, and in particular toward greater participation of provinces in budget formulation and development of expenditure norms to allow for fairer allocation of budget across provinces. Nevertheless, the Bank cannot get ahead of the government in developing local government institutions. The Bank and other partners can provide input to the government, but decisionmaking and implementation is an inherently political process. Security considerations will also impact the pace of development and implementation of the subnational framework. Thus this remains a challenging goal for the medium term.
Partially Agree – This effort is important and ongoing, but it is too soon to comment on specific recommendations.	The issue of the NSP's long-term sustainability is of concern to us. And we are working with the Ministry of Rural Rehabilitation and Development and other government agencies— for example, IDLG, Independent Election Commission, the Ministry of Finance, and agriculture and rural development cluster ministries (Ministry of Agriculture, Irrigation, and Livestock and Ministry of Rural Rehabilitation and Development)—to identify the best way forward. An institutional option study for the NSP will be carried out in fall 2012. This would help guide the government's approach to strengthening NSP's institutional sustainability. The size and scope of grants under the NSP can only be determined in consultation with the government and donors. The level of funding needs to be substantial enough to support a growing role for them and to fight poverty at the local level. We will also soon launch analytic work on how to ensure the sustainability of CDCs. This work is supported by both MRRD and IDLG. Linking of CDCs with subnational governments is needed, but is a complex endeavor with considerable political, legal/constitutional, and financial implications.

IEG Findings	IEG Recommendations	
The absence of well-defined property rights, credible mechanisms for resolving commercial disputes, institutions with capacity to enforce regulations, and skills in the public and private sector are impediments to private-sector–led growth. Private sector investment by IFC has declined in recent years. Several MIGA guarantees had poor business outcomes, leading to a slowdown in MIGA's engagement in Afghanistan.	**Focus Bank Group efforts on strengthening the regulatory environment for private investment through:** • Greater use of analytical work, technical assistance, and Advisory Services to assist the government in establishing property rights, commercial dispute resolution mechanisms, and institutions with capacity to enforce regulations. • Assistance to the government and private sector stakeholders in building coalitions to support the regulatory environment for private sector–led growth.	
	For IFC and MIGA:	
IFC's investments and MIGA guarantees have been lumpy with an increase in investment volume but no new clients in recent years.	**As part of their commitment to expand support in fragile and conflict-affected situations, IFC and MIGA could usefully increase business development efforts targeted to new clients, including investors from the region and the diaspora, to scale up support to the private sector.**	

Acceptance by Management	Management Response
Agree – This effort is ongoing (but is a medium-term goal).	The principle of assisting the government in strengthening the private sector environment is sound. Nevertheless, it should be recognized that issues of security, governance, and infrastructure are just as, if not more, important in determining the rate of private investment as the regulatory environment.
	The Bank Group Investment Climate Advisory Team is providing technical assistance, complemented by the recently approved justice project, which includes a focus on commercial justice.
	The Bank is also providing support to various regulatory areas, including mining, telecommunications, energy, and banking.
	With respect to MIGA: In fact, the majority of MIGA's business by volume had successful business outcomes (for example, in MTN Afghanistan) – just two or three very small investments have had poor business outcomes. In any case, MIGA's slowdown in engaging in Afghanistan has been due to the closure of the Afghanistan Investment Guarantee Facility and the deteriorating investment environment, and not because of the business outcomes of previously insured projects.
Agree	IFC's annual investments have declined in recent years due to the prevailing domestic environment. However, despite the difficulties, IFC has been able to grow its overall portfolio significantly during the review period. Afghanistan is a priority IDA country for IFC, and the Corporation will use its business development teams (especially those on the ground) to continue to explore investment opportunities in the country. Priority sectors for developing a pipeline in partnership with both local and foreign/regional investors include infrastructure, agribusiness, health and education, financial markets and manufacturing and services. IFC will also continue to help strengthen the capacity of the private sector as well as the enabling environment and regulatory framework for private sector development through its Advisory arm.
	MIGA continues to make considerable efforts to work with investors into Afghanistan, and is in fact looking at creating a Conflict-Affected and Fragile Economies Facility to help do just this. However, MIGA can only support investors looking to invest, and the investment environment in Afghanistan remains very weak. The latest data from DEC shows FDI in 2010 was US$80 million versus US$270 million in 2005.

Chairperson's Summary: Sub-Committee, Committee on Development Effectiveness

On August 29, 2012, the Sub-Committee of the Committee on Development Effectiveness (CODE) considered an Independent Evaluation Group (IEG) report entitled *Afghanistan Country Program Evaluation, 2002-2011: Evaluation of the World Bank Group Program.*

Summary

The Sub-Committee welcomed IEG's findings and recommendations and commended the World Bank Group for the extraordinary work and impressive results achieved in Afghanistan. Members appreciated IEG's recognition of the World Bank Group's important role in informing discussions with government and donors through its highly relevant strategy in Afghanistan, achieving substantial progress toward its objectives under extremely difficult circumstances. They were also satisfied that most of IEG's recommendations were included in the FY12–14 Interim Strategy Note (ISN). Members stressed the valuable lessons from the evaluation for other fragile and conflict-affected states (FCS). While recognizing the convergence between IEG and management in most of the recommendations, members asked IEG if it could adapt its methodology for evaluating country programs to reflect the difficulties and complexities of working in FCS and to avoid misinterpretation of results. Members learned that IEG has been applying the methodology agreed with Operations Policy and Country Services so far, but it will consider this issue as part of the forthcoming FCS evaluation. Management acknowledged that progress in Afghanistan will largely depend on the government's capacity to sustain both change and momentum. Members asked about government ownership and capacity building, further seeking IEG and management's views on the government's comments on the evaluation. They also highlighted the Bank's increasing importance as the 2014 transition approaches, when sustainability of its interventions will be critical.

Members agreed with IEG's assessment that the Afghanistan Reconstruction Trust Fund (ARTF) has been crucial in mobilizing much-needed resources from donors and has contributed to building confidence with the government and in public expenditure management. They acknowledged the success of donor coordination through the ARTF and encouraged IEG to share results of the program evaluation and lessons learned among donors that have conducted evaluations of the ARTF and other donor actors in Afghanistan. In this regard, some members inquired about the concurrence with IEG's findings. While members supported providing Bank expertise in certain areas without in-country presence due to security and other considerations, they cautioned that it should not substitute for the work that needs to be done on the ground.

Members stressed the importance of sustainable institutional reform on governance issues and agreed with management that caution is needed to obtain government support in areas where the Bank would be able to have influence. Members also emphasized the importance of supporting local institutional development to ensure sustainable public services and resource flows. Members inquired about management's approach to achieve sustainability of gains, the risks of civil service reform, youth employment prospects, and development in the agricultural sector. Members praised the World Bank Group's achievements in mainstreaming gender issues but noted that more could be done to improve gender equality in future interventions.

The Committee noted with appreciation IEG's recognition of the satisfactory outcomes achieved by the International Finance Corporation (IFC) and agreed with management that, moving forward, IFC should provide support to strengthen Afghanistan's investment climate. They agreed with IFC's proposed focus on infrastructure, agribusiness, health, education, financial markets, and manufacturing.

Anna Brandt, Chairperson

Chapter 1
The Country Context

Afghanistan is a landlocked South Asian country, sharing borders with Pakistan and China in the east, Iran in the west, and Turkmenistan, Uzbekistan, and Tajikistan in the north. Afghanistan was born as a state in the mid-eighteenth century and was molded into its present territorial boundaries during a century of wars and diplomacy involving geopolitical rivalry between the British; Russian; and, to some extent, Persian empires. It eventually became a buffer state between the British and Russian empires.

Basic state institutions gradually began to emerge after the end of the second Anglo-Afghan War in 1880. After several decades of isolationism, and aborted reform under King Amanullah (1919–29), its geopolitical role became significant during the Cold War. Despite slow modernization during a period of relative peace and stability under King Zahir Shah (1933–73), Afghanistan remained very poor, with weak social indicators. Instability increased in the 1970s with the deposition of the king by his cousin, leading to a Communist coup and takeover in 1978 (World Bank 2012). The country became a key Cold War battleground after the Soviet Union sent its army to support Communist rule in 1979, leading to a long and destructive war. The Soviet Union withdrew its troops in 1989 under the pressure of anticommunist Mujahedin fighters. After several years of civil war, the Taliban, a hard-line Islamic movement that grew out of the Afghan refugee camps in Pakistan, came to power in 1996.

Following the September 11, 2001, terrorist attacks in the United States, military action by the United States, allied forces, and the anti-Taliban Northern Alliance overthrew the Taliban in retaliation for sheltering Osama Bin Laden, creating a unique policy opportunity for Afghanistan to embark on a development process with heavy support from the international community. Initial optimism has given way to harsher realities and the recognition that the development process is a long road, although the country has made indisputable gains over the past decade.

The United Nations–sponsored Bonn Conference in 2001 established a process for political and economic reconstruction. Following the collapse of the Taliban regime, Afghanistan's constitution was amended, designating the country as an Islamic republic with democratic elections for a National Assembly (Parliament) and the presidency. In 2002, the *Loya Jirga* (grand council[1]) chose Hamid Karzai as interim president. The period 2002–04 was one of relative peace, resembling most other post-conflict situations. The interim government launched a series of national programs selected by the government with support from a multidonor Needs Assessment (ADB, UNDP, and World Bank 2002). By 2004, the government had developed a strategic framework, "Securing Afghanistan's Future: Accomplishments and the Strategic Path Forward" (Islamic Republic of Afghanistan and others 2004), in collaboration with multilateral agencies. That strategy provided a road map for future development investments. Hamid Karzai went on to become the first democratically elected president of Afghanistan and the National Assembly was inaugurated in 2005.

| Figure 1.1 | Military Casualties in Afghanistan |

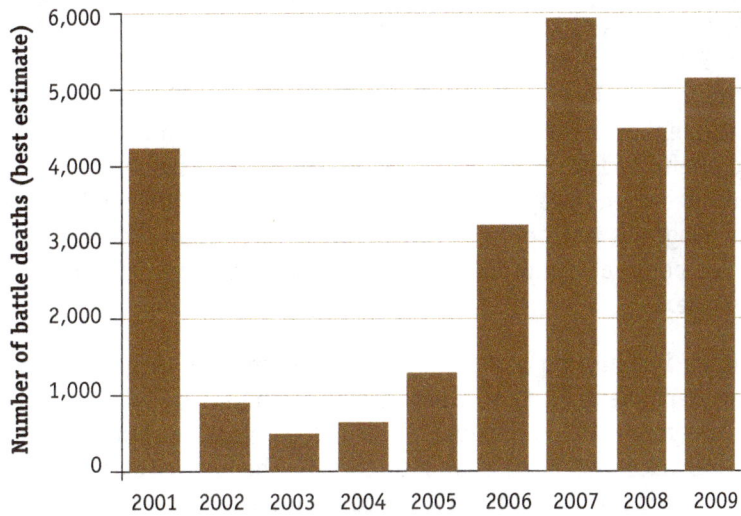

Source: Afghanistan Conflict Monitor.

The period 2005-06 was an inflection point in Afghanistan's recovery from the previous decades. On the security front, the Taliban, which appeared to be defeated in 2004, was able to regroup in cross-border sanctuaries, and conflict intensified after 2005,[2] particularly in the south and east of the country, leading to a significant spike in military casualties (figure 1.1). The attention of the United States, Afghanistan's largest international partner, had been diverted to Iraq. In 2009, Afghanistan again became its primary foreign policy focus.

Afghanistan has undergone a very tangible deterioration in security since 2006, including a spike in civilian casualties after 2006 (table 1.1), although not all these were caused by the insurgents. This has affected the Bank Group's work through increased risks to staff, restrictions on movement, further constraints on supervision, and additional measures to deal with safety. Neither the government nor its development partners were able to anticipate the inflection point or its consequences on Afghanistan's development.

There was considerable turnover in the Afghan government, because several reform-oriented leaders of the interim government chose to abstain from, or did

Table 1.1	Afghan Casualties by Year				
	2007	2008	2009	2010	2011
Civilians killed	1,523	2,118	2,412	2,777	3,021
Civilians injured	-	-	3,566	4,343	4,057

Source: Congressional Research Service (Chesser 2012).
Note: - = information not available.

not survive, the political transition to the new government. Considerable donor resources and several years were spent preparing a new development strategy, the Afghanistan National Development Strategy (ANDS), which was endorsed by the World Bank and International Monetary Fund as the country's Poverty Reduction Strategy Paper (PRSP) in 2008 (Islamic Republic of Afghanistan 2008), although the Joint Staff Advisory Note (IMF and IDA 2008) suggests that the endorsement was lukewarm. Nonetheless, the preparation of the interim PRSP, and then the full PRSP, was seen as a major milestone that, in practice, distracted attention away from implementation and delayed initiation of additional programs to meet the growing needs of Afghan citizens. Meanwhile, the need for political compromises increased governance risks in a worsening security context.

Despite gains in building a stable central government, Afghanistan remains fragile and dependent on the international community. President Karzai won a second five-year term as president in the 2009 election, but the results were disputed and accepted somewhat reluctantly. The constitution also provides for elected provincial, district, and village councils. While provincial councils held elections in 2005 and 2009, they are still seeking to find effective roles in securing provincial development, and district and village councils have not yet been elected or established. The government receives military assistance from the United States and others—notably through the International Security Assistance Force of NATO—both to maintain security and to build the capacity of the Afghan National Army. The government also receives considerable support from donors in the form of direct budget support for administrative expenditures and financing for on-budget programs, in addition to off-budget development assistance by bilateral agencies, without which the fiscal situation would be unsustainable.

Afghanistan has made important achievements in recent years, but the fragile security backdrop is a drag on the economy. The government has taken steps to lay the foundation for economic stability and growth, despite a very difficult security situation and the challenges associated with building political and economic institutions. Economic activity has been robust, with real gross domestic product (GDP) growth averaging more than 10 percent annually over the past five years. Revenue collection increased to 11 percent of GDP in 2010/11 from 8 percent in 2008/09. However, current revenue covers only about two-thirds of central government operating expenditures and less than 20 percent of total public spending. Inflation has been rising, and confidence in the banking sector has been low since the collapse of Kabul Bank in September 2010. Security spending rose by 1.3 percent of GDP, while non-security spending dropped by 0.7 percent of GDP from 2009/10 to 2010/11, as recruitment for the Afghan National Army grew by over 30 percent. The operating budget deficit, excluding grants, remained broadly stable at 4 percent of GDP, but development spending fell by 1.7 percent of GDP, and budget execution rates remain low, due to capacity constraints, difficulties in public financial management, and a worsening security situation (IMF 2011).

Continuing Conflict and Insecurity

Security conditions pose a formidable challenge to Afghanistan's development and external partner support. The Afghanistan country program operates under particularly difficult circumstances. Afghanistan is a fragile and conflict-affected state (FCS), but differs from most other FCSs in two significant ways. First, World Bank Group engagement in an FCS usually occurs during the post-conflict phase. In contrast, Afghanistan's post-conflict conditions, manifested during 2002–05, have since deteriorated markedly, with increasing attacks on civilians. Second, unlike in the majority of FCSs, in Afghanistan the international development community itself is a target of attacks (by the Taliban). The serious effect of conflict on development support is underscored by the assassination of many government officials in recent years, as well as by the attacks on U.N. facilities in 2009 and 2011. The omnipresence of insecurity and the attendant restrictions on mobility as well as the insularity of the international development community have increased steadily in the past several years, affecting working conditions for staff and hampering the delivery and effectiveness of external support.

For many of Afghanistan's external partners, geopolitical and security goals overlap development goals. For key bilateral partners, the allocation of development support is driven at least partly by geopolitical and security goals. Among other consequences, their overall development support to Afghanistan, even excluding military expenditures, has far exceeded that to other FCSs, and has frequently been channeled through Provincial Reconstruction Teams in provinces where the partners in question are involved in counter-insurgency, leading to uneven development investment across the country (World Bank 2010). In contrast, while security considerations also affect the Bank Group, those considerations have much less influence on its priorities in support of development. The government appreciates the fact that the Bank Group, like several other multilateral institutions, takes a countrywide view.

Poverty in Afghanistan

Despite the economic progress of the past few years, Afghanistan is extremely poor and highly dependent on foreign aid. The country lags behind others in South Asia on major social indicators, and living standards are among the lowest in the world: roughly 36 percent of the population lives below the poverty line (9 million Afghans are unable to meet their basic needs), and another 10–15 percent is at risk of falling into poverty. Regional and seasonal differences in incomes are important aspects of poverty in Afghanistan, which has diverse terrain, climate, and agricultural potential. The three provinces in high, mountainous areas—Bamyan, Daikundi, and Badakshan—are often inaccessible due to heavy snow accumulation in winter and have poverty rates that are much higher (45 percent) than the national average. Poverty rates are higher in the south and east and lowest in the southwest, but they are highly variable across seasons. Seasonal surveys revealed that the poverty rate ranged from 42 percent in the lean spring period to 21 percent in the summer of 2007. Forty percent of Afghan households are unable to earn any income during the winter months, rural households being most exposed to seasonality (World Bank 2010). Poverty data are not disaggregated by ethnic group, but the Kuchi (nomadic pastoralists) are reported to have the highest incidence of poverty (54 percent).

Much of the Afghan population continues to be deprived of housing, clean water, electricity, medical care, and jobs. Life expectancy is 44.6 years (UNDP 2010), compared with an average of 59 years for low-income countries overall. Only about 30 percent of Afghans have access to electricity,[3] 27 percent have access to safe drinking water, and 5 percent to adequate sanitation (World Bank 2011b). Access to education is similar for children of poor and non-poor households, but there are stark differences between the two groups in access to health care (World Bank 2010). In education, 34.9 percent of children are enrolled and regularly attend primary school; 37.6 percent of the young adult population (ages 15 to 24) is able to read and write (World Bank 2011a). Afghanistan's unemployment rate is estimated to be around 40 percent, but there is little hard data on unemployment (Economist Intelligence Unit 2008).

Patterns of exclusion and vulnerability in Afghanistan have a strong gender dimension: women have limited access to and command over productive resources. The female literacy rate is 22 percent compared with 51 percent for men, and the enrollment rate for girls is 31 percent compared with 43 percent for boys. Improvement in educational outcomes is stronger for men than women, suggesting a risk of widening gender gaps.

Role of Development Partners

The World Bank Group's financing (from the International Development Corporation [IDA], International Finance Corporation [IFC], and the Multilateral Investment Guarantee Agency [MIGA]) for development assistance to Afghanistan is modest. Although it is ranked third in total commitment amounts, the data maintained by the Ministry of Finance illustrate how Bank Group financing is dwarfed by nonmilitary development assistance provided by the United States (table 1.2) and is less than 4 percent of total nonmilitary aid to Afghanistan. Military expenditure by the international community is several times higher than development assistance.[4]

Support from principal development partners reveals overlapping priorities, but coordination remains challenging in several sectors. For several bilateral agencies, security expenditures have been the highest priority, followed by the energy sector (table 1.3). Among the sectors, agriculture and rural development have received the largest financial support from the World Bank, the European Commission, and the United Kingdom, and is the second-highest priority for Canada and Japan. However, as pointed out by representatives of the government and several development partners, most of the World Bank–administered funds (including the Afghanistan Reconstruction Trust Fund, ARTF) for agriculture

Table 1.2	Development Assistance to Afghanistan, 2002–11			
Funding source/ funding agency	Committed (US$ millions)	Share (as percentage of top 10 donors)	Rank by commitment amount	Share (percentage of total)
Asian Development Bank	1,447	4	4	
United Nations	461	1	10	
World Bank	1,565	5	3	
Canada	748	2	9	
European Union/ European Commission	1,380	4	5	
Germany	1,282	4	6	
India	830	3	7	
Japan	2,207	7	2	
United Kingdom	791	2	8	
United States	22,438	68	1	
Subtotal	33,148			77
Others	10,114			23
Total: All donors	43,261			100

Source: Development Assistance Database, Ministry of Finance, Afghanistan.

Note: The ministry database may not be complete and should be treated as indicative of relative volumes.

and rural development were allocated to the National Solidarity Program (NSP) and not for broader agricultural development, for which donor efforts are not well coordinated. The Asian Development Bank (ADB) is the lead agency in several infrastructure sectors. The urban sector has received relatively less support, except from the government of India.

As administrator of the ARTF, the World Bank is able to leverage substantial funds and facilitate coordination among development partners. Overall responsibility for coordination of development assistance was transferred in 2006 from the World Bank to the United Nations Assistance Mission to Afghanistan (UNAMA), whose strength lies in the political sphere rather than in economic and social development. However, multidonor trust funds managed by multilateral agencies provide an opportunity for coordination in the domains they finance. The World Bank administers the ARTF, which is the largest source of on-budget financing for the government. While it initially functioned primarily as the main source of external finance for the non-security recurrent budget and capital costs, its rationale has shifted over time toward investment financing and an Incentives Program. Prior agreement on the policy actions supported

Table 1.3	Assistance Priorities of Major Development Partners (as committed)										
Sector/subsector	ADB	World Bank	U.N.	Canada	EC / EU	Germany	India	Japan	U.K.	U.S.	Number of donors
Security				1	3	1		1	3	1	6
Governance and rule of law											
Governance, public administration reform, & human rights			4	4				4		4	5	5
Justice and rule of law											
Religious affairs	5				4				5		3
Infrastructure and natural resources											
Energy	2	4			5	2	2			2	6
Transport	1	7								4	3
Urban development	4					4	1				3
Mining		6									1
ICT											
Water			5								1
Education and culture											
Education		5	2			6	3			8	5
Culture, media, and youth											
Health and nutrition		2	1	3	2			5	4	6	7
Agriculture and rural development	3	1		2	1	5		2	1	3	8
Social protection											
Social protection			3								1
Refugees, returnees, and internally displaced persons									3		2
Economic governance											
Private sector development and trade		3		5		3			2	7	5
Unclassified								5			1

Source: Development Assistance Database, Ministry of Finance, Afghanistan.

Note: Top five sectors ranked by amount of assistance, with 1 as the highest.

by the Incentives Program (discussed in chapter 3) allows the Bank to ensure coordination among the parties contributing to the ARTF on key public financial management reforms. The ARTF's ability to combine preferences of contributing partners with shared strategic priorities facilitates coordination support for investment projects. The United Nations Development Programme (UNDP) is the administrator of the Law and Order Trust Fund for Afghanistan, which supports the security sector and governance. Similarly, the ADB is the administrator of the Afghanistan Infrastructure Trust Fund.

Role of Non-State Actors in Afghanistan

Civil society organizations play an important role in humanitarian assistance and service delivery. International and Afghan civil society organizations initially established a presence in refugee camps outside the country and, after the withdrawal of Soviet troops, within Afghanistan. Under Taliban rule they were the only entities providing humanitarian assistance in many regions, under extremely difficult conditions.

Civil society organizations have far greater freedom of movement than the external development-partner community—they are even able to operate in many conflict zones. Ease of access to donor funds both for their own programs and for service delivery under donor-supported projects has enabled them to grow substantially over the past decade. The Bank Group has successfully integrated partnerships built on the presence and experience of civil society organizations to supplement government capacity and deliver large-scale programs across the country in several sectors.

Transition to the Decade of Transformation

While transition planning has begun, significant challenges remain. Transition planning began in 2010 with the Kabul Process for the transfer of responsibility for security and development of Afghanistan to the government by the end of 2014. The incremental transfer of security responsibilities to Afghan National Security Forces started in mid-2011, with the aim of placing the country's security fully under Afghan control by the end of 2014 (World Bank 2011a). The May 2012 NATO summit in Chicago was convened to ensure long-term international assistance to Afghanistan's security forces.

The transition in security arrangements will also coincide with a significant political and economic transition. The second, nonrenewable term of President Karzai also ends in 2014. Afghanistan has not yet experienced succession of leadership, and this could pose additional challenges. The economy has grown at the rapid pace of 9 percent annually, driven largely by military expenditures, which exceed civilian aid to Afghanistan. Real GDP per capita increased by 75 percent from 2002 to 2009. The transfer of security responsibilities to the government and the related decline in military expenditures, together with a possible reduction in donor assistance, is expected to slow growth. While security is high on the agenda, ensuring the sustainability of the civilian administration and sustaining development investments are equally critical and are heavily dependent on the political will and commitment of Afghanistan's development partners.

The government has made effective use of international conferences to discuss and mobilize international support for its strategic and security priorities. The international community provided $57 billion in development assistance to Afghanistan during 2002–11. At the Bonn Conference in November 2011 and the Tokyo Conference in August 2012, the government and the international community discussed appropriate levels of sustained support for Afghanistan during what is being billed as the "decade of transformation" after 2014.

Evaluation Methods and Limitations

Evaluation of the Afghanistan country program was particularly challenging because security conditions constrain country missions and physical mobility inside and outside Kabul. These limitations are a permanent feature for the country team and were also encountered by the evaluation team. In view of country constraints, the evaluation team supplemented usual Country Program Evaluation (CPE) sources with the following measures to generate additional evaluative evidence: (i) a review of the entire portfolio of the Bank's analytical and advisory activities (AAA) and IFC's Advisory Services; (ii) a review of the program's impact on gender; (iii) a study of enhanced pay arrangements for civil servants; (iv) a beneficiary survey using radio/mobile phones; (v) feedback from social media, including a Facebook survey; and (vi) focus group discussions with facilitating partners of Bank programs. Findings from these sources were triangulated with feedback from the numerous meetings with representatives of government agencies and partner organizations and findings from the literature review. The evaluation was also constrained by difficulty in accessing relevant documents in a timely manner.

Given the country context and the continued insecurity, this evaluation has placed greater emphasis on learning from the Afghanistan experience than on accountability. For that reason, the report has not been organized solely around the pillars and their ratings. Nonetheless, for consistency with other CPEs—including those done in other FCS countries—the standard methodology for all CPEs (see appendix B) has been included in this evaluation, and the ratings reported in appendix A.

It should be noted that the ratings of the Bank Group's assistance program are based on an assessment of the extent to which the intended objectives stated in Bank Group strategy documents were relevant and achieved; it is not a rating of Afghanistan's overall development progress, nor a rating of Bank Group performance. The metrics against which each CPE is assessed are derived not from a uniform set of targets, but from the statement of objectives in Bank Group strategy documents. Management has queried whether the benchmarks for FCS should be the same as for CPEs in other countries. Answering this question is beyond the scope of this evaluation, but the relevance of separate benchmarks can be examined further in IEG's upcoming FCS evaluation.

The next chapter of this report discusses Bank Group strategy over the past 10 years and gives an overview of cross-cutting issues, including the financial assistance program, portfolio performance, AAA, and the ARTF, which is the primary vehicle for donor coordination administered by the World Bank. Chapters 3–5 of the CPE discuss detailed results for each of the three pillars laid out in the Interim Strategy Notes (ISNs). This is followed by a separate chapter on the overall results, achievements, and challenges of Bank Group support to Afghanistan over the past 10 years. A final chapter highlights key lessons and makes recommendations to strengthen future Bank Group assistance to Afghanistan.

Notes

1. The Loya Jirga (literally grand council) is a forum unique to Afghanistan in which, traditionally, tribal elders—Pashtuns, Tajiks, Hazaras and Uzbeks—have come together to settle affairs of the nation or rally behind a cause. Historically it has been used to settle inter-tribal disputes, discuss social reforms, and approve a new constitution. About 1,500 delegates from all over Afghanistan took part in the 2002 Loya Jirga in Kabul.

2. After declining from more than 4,000 in 2001 to less than 1,000 per year, battle deaths in Afghanistan started rising again in 2005 to almost 6,000 in 2007, and have stayed in the 4-5,000 range ever since ("Afghanistan Conflict Monitor"). For more information about the Afghanistan Conflict Monitor, see http://www .conflictmonitors.org/countries/afghanistan/daily-briefing/.

3. The Afghan Ministry of Energy and Water, 2010.

4. Current military spending in Afghanistan by the United States alone is estimated to be around $10 billion per month.

References

ADB (Asian Development Bank), UNDP (United Nations Development Program), and World Bank. 2002. *Afghanistan: Preliminary Needs Assessment for Recovery andReconstruction*. New York, NY: UNDP.

Chesser, Susan G. 2012. Afghanistan Casualties: Military Forces and Civilians. Washington, DC: Congressional Research Service. Available at: http://www.fas .org/sgp/crs/natsec/R41084.pdf.

IMF (International Monetary Fund). 2011. "Islamic Republic of Afghanistan: 2011 Article IV Consultation and Request for a Three-Year Arrangement Under the Extended Credit Facility—StaffReport." IMF Country Report No. 11/330. Washington, DC: IMF.

IMF (International Monetary Fund) and IDA (International Development Association). 2008. "IslamicRepublic of Afghanistan: Poverty Reduction Strategy Paper—Joint Staff AdvisoryNote." IMF Country Report No. 08/193. IMF, Washington, DC.

Islamic Republic of Afghanistan. 2008. *Afghanistan National Development Strategy 1387–1398 (2008–2014): A Strategy for Security, Governance, Economic Growth & Poverty Reduction.* Kabul.

Islamic Republic of Afghanistan, ADB (Asian Development Bank), United Nations Assistance Mission to Afghanistan, UNDP (United Nations Development Program), and the World Bank Group. 2004. "Securing Afghanistan's Future: Accomplishmentsand the Strategic Path Forward." A Government/ International Agency Report, March 17, 2004. Prepared for International Conference, March 31, 2004. Availableat: http://www.cmi.no/afghanistan/?id=5&Government-of-Afghanistan.

UNDP (United Nations Development Program). 2010. *Human Development Report 2010— The Real Wealth of Nations: Pathways to Human Development.* New York: UNDP.

World Bank. 2002. "Afghanistan—Transitional Support Strategy." Report No. 23822 AF. Washington, DC: World Bank.

———. 2010. "Poverty Status in Afghanistan." Washington, DC: World Bank.

———. 2011a. "Afghanistan—World Bank Country Brief." Washington, DC: World Bank.

———. 2011b. "Non-Communicable Diseases (NCDs) in Afghanistan." Policy Brief, Washington, DC: World Bank.

———. 2012. *Afghanistan in Transition: Looking Beyond 2014.* Washington, DC: WorldBank.

Chapter 2
World Bank Group Strategy and Program

World Bank Group Strategy

This evaluation covers the period from the Bank Group's reengagement in Afghanistan in FY02 through end-FY11. During this period, the country relied extensively on the support of the international development community, and the World Bank Group has provided both emergency assistance and development financing to support development of Afghan institutions and mitigate poverty. Bank assistance during FY02–11 was guided by two Transitional Support Strategies (World Bank 2002, 2003) and two ISNs (World Bank 2007, 2009). These strategy documents lay out the direction of the Bank Group's program of lending, grant, and guarantee operations and the AAA of IDA, IFC, and MIGA. They also discuss the ARTF, a considerable portion of which is spent on cofinancing or scaling up of Bank-financed projects.

Initial Bank Group reengagement in Afghanistan was set out in the March 2002 Transitional Support Strategy (TSS), which focused on recovery and reconstruction. Strategic priorities were "essential governance institutions and capacity, high-priority, high-impact reconstruction programs to restart the economy and social services; coordinated donor assistance under government leadership; and a better knowledge base and analytical underpinning for the work of the international community and for future Bank assistance."

A second Transitional Support Strategy in line with the government's reconstruction strategy was approved in February 2003 and was to cover a period of 18–24 months, during which time the government would start working on a PRSP and the Bank would initiate preparation of a Country Assistance Strategy (CAS). The second TSS focused on (i) improving livelihoods; (ii) fiscal strategy, institutions, and management; (iii) governance and public administration reform; and (iv) enabling private sector development. Investment priorities were based on the Preliminary Needs Assessment, jointly conducted with the ADB and UNDP, and crucial analytical work was undertaken to fill knowledge gaps and underpin future Bank Group strategy.

Subsequent ISNs reframed Bank Group support into higher-level strategic development objectives. Although no full-fledged CAS has yet been prepared for the Bank Group's Afghanistan program, the ISNs discussed in 2006 and 2009, respectively,[1] organized the Bank Group's strategy for Afghanistan around three "pillars," with support for gender issues mainstreamed across them. The bulk of the assistance was to be delivered by IDA, with a more modest role for IFC and MIGA in the third pillar.[2] The three pillars are:

- Building the capacity of the state and its accountability to its citizens
- Promoting growth of the rural economy and improving rural livelihoods
- Supporting growth of the formal private sector, including through infrastructure development.

The Bank Group's strategy is aligned with the country's own development strategies. The initial strategy responds to the conditions prevalent when the

Bank Group reengaged in Afghanistan in November 2001, with a transitional government that inherited very weak capacity. International agencies collaborated with the government to develop a joint strategy, "Securing Afghanistan's Future: Accomplishments and the Strategic Path Forward" (see Islamic Republic of Afghanistan and others 2004), which established the government's priorities, building on the national programs already initiated by the interim government. The Afghanistan Compact between the international community and the government, adopted at the January 2006 London Conference, affirmed commitment to "cooperate in creating conditions allowing the people of Afghanistan to live in peace and security under the rule of law, with a strong government which protects human rights and supports economic and social development in the country." The Compact signaled the intention of relying more on the country's own institutions for development cooperation.

The preparation of the ANDS enhanced ownership by the new government but consumed most of its tenure. Despite the urgency of implementation, rather than formalizing the 2004 strategy as the government's PRSP, the donor community supported the government in a lengthy and expensive process to prepare an Interim PRSP (I-PRSP) and then a full PRSP by 2008. The ANDS identified 22 National Priority Programs under three overarching goals: (i) security; (ii) governance, rule of law, and human rights; and (iii) economic and social development. The time-consuming and all-embracing ANDS has been difficult to operationalize, since the sequencing and costs of the 22 National Priority Programs were not specified. Although all Bank Group programs align with two of the strategic goals of the ANDS, the programs represent such a comprehensive list that prioritizing key areas for strategic support, building on the Bank Group's comparative advantage, has been a bigger challenge than alignment with the government's strategy.

Assessment of Overall Strategy

The central tenet of the *2011 World Development Report* (World Bank 2011, p. 2) is that "strengthening legitimate institutions and governance to provide citizen security, justice, and jobs is crucial to break cycles of violence." Even though these were not, and could not be expected to constitute, explicit objectives of the Bank Group's strategy, the experience of Afghanistan provides relevant lessons for the Bank Group's future approach to FCS situations.

Bank Group strategy, reflected in the TSSs, was appropriate to the initial period of reengagement. The core of the Bank's strategy is derived from the Needs Assessments undertaken in FY02–03 (ADB, UNDP and World Bank 2002). The focus under the two TSSs was appropriately on building core state institutions, delivery of services to restore confidence in the state, rehabilitating critical infrastructure, and building the knowledge base for future development assistance. Priority was given to development of public financial management (PFM) systems with strong fiduciary controls; outreach to rural communities through a community development program (the NSP) to promote a sense of inclusion among rural communities; rehabilitation of rural roads and irrigation systems to support rural development and short-term employment; and restoring public health and education services.

These choices were consistent with the urgent needs of Afghan reconstruction and with the objectives of the *World Development Report 2012* (World Bank 2012b) of strengthening legitimate institutions and governance and creating short-term jobs for citizens. In some cases, the Bank changed its strategy: an initial preference to focus on higher education and skills development was modified to include primary and secondary education in response to client and donor demand, and in agriculture a judgment about client ownership and capacity led to avoidance of this sector.

The Bank's subsequent approach to strategy formulation laid out in two ISNs structured the Bank's assistance into three pillars, but the substantive design of the Bank's assistance did not change to reflect the evolving context. In part, this was a consequence of the need to maintain continuity of ongoing programs initiated under the TSSs. The 2003 ISN was a two-year plan. However, the next strategy, expected to be a CAS, was not discussed until 2006, and that too has an ISN. Had the Bank built on the government's 2004 strategy, prepared with extensive support from the Bank and UNDP, a CAS might have been feasible, but by 2006 the insurgency had grown substantially. In 2009, the Bank opted for another ISN, which continued with the same pillars and operations envisaged under the 2006 ISN. Although the 2009 ISN recognized growing governance and security challenges, it did not scale back the ambitious objectives laid out in the previous one. Both ISNs reflect a continuation of approaches initiated under the TSSs, with some small-scale initiatives to fill gaps, but without an overall road map of the foundations for future growth.

Strategic choices were also influenced by the division of labor with other development partners, such as ADB's lead role on infrastructure, but in a number of sectors—such as agriculture, urban development, and private sector development—where multiple development partners were involved, coordination worked in parallel and coordinated support to those sectors remains challenging. Donor coordination, which shifted to UNAMA in 2006, has not been able to ensure adequate coverage of key development priorities. While in some sectors—such as public financial management, health, and mining—the Bank undertook strategic analytical work, in other key sectors of high importance to the government—such as agriculture and urban development sectors—the Bank missed the opportunity to lay out a strategic road map that may have enabled a coherent approach for donor support. In two other sectors where the Bank was engaged—education and civil service reform—the lack of effective donor coordination for a human resources strategy led to disjointed efforts in higher education, skills development, and civil service capacity building.

With the benefit of hindsight, the strategic goals of the 2006 and 2009 ISNs appear overly ambitious and, given the challenges that Afghanistan faces, fell short of full achievement under each of the three pillars. Although the

2009 ISN recognized growing governance and security challenges, the 2009 ISN continued with the same pillars and objectives envisaged under the 2006 ISN and opted not to scale back the ambitious objectives laid out in the previous document. Under the two ISNs, the state's capacity has improved, yet governance challenges persist and indicate that accountability to citizens is still weak. Outreach to rural communities has been strengthened, but the impact on rural livelihoods has been limited. To fuel rural growth, progress is needed beyond broad-based rehabilitation, into strategic on-farm investments. Significant achievements in communication and microfinance have been made, but the business environment continues to grapple with major security, infrastructure, and financial sector constraints.

The program instruments were insufficient to fully achieve the strategic objectives of the pillars. Under pillar one, the Bank program did not include any activities or programs to strengthen accountability to citizens and, in the absence of a coherent approach to subnational governments, the Bank has not been effective in achieving its goal of integrating community and subnational government planning and accountability mechanisms into the overall PFM framework. Under pillar two, substantial investments have gone to short-term job creation and much less to strategic investments that promote rural growth and sustainable livelihoods. Under pillar three, the mining sector has the potential to play a transformative role in the geographic corridors likely to be impacted by proximity to the mines, if complementary investments are made to broaden its benefits. However, security and governance constraints continue to dampen the rest of private sector investment. The Bank has been a regular participant in the Regional Economic Cooperation Conference on Afghanistan, which meets twice a year, but has not fully leveraged its convening power to prioritize regional integration, to attract regional investment, and to create economic interdependence as a means of enhancing regional security.

In hindsight, an assessment of Bank performance reveals that there was inadequate learning regarding institutional design and performance monitoring across sectors. In some sectors, weak client capacity was addressed by mobilizing the private sector (in information and communications technology and the financial sector) and the nonprofit sector (health and the NSP), with a focus on strengthening government capacity for regulation and oversight rather than service delivery. In other sectors (health and microfinance), early emphasis on results measurement and use of third-party entities to assess performance provided a good feedback loop to address implementation issues. The sectors with weaker outcomes (education, agriculture, power, water) did not have such robust systems for results monitoring.

The World Bank Group's Operational Program

From FY02 to FY11 the Bank Group committed $2.4 billion in IDA credits and grants and some $100 million in net commitments by IFC, [3] issued $78 million in MIGA guarantees, [4] and administered larger sums of funding from other donors through trust funds (over $4 billion). This has been complemented by an extensive program of AAA by the World Bank and Advisory Services by IFC. During the period reviewed, 20 percent of the Bank's administrative budget was spent on project preparation, 38 percent on supervision, and 33 percent on AAA.

Bank Group investment in AAA was appropriately frontloaded and sequenced. Investment in building a knowledge base was frontloaded, with much greater expenditure on AAA (46 percent of country budget[5]) during FY02–06 than in FY07–11 (25 percent). As a result, the ISNs were better informed by core analytical work undertaken during TSS implementation. And the composition of AAA evolved from more economic and sector work (ESW) during the earlier years toward more technical assistance (appendix E). Resources for technical assistance increased from 36 percent to 44 percent of the country budget and the number of technical assistance activities was much larger, since such activities cost much less than ESW. However, in some sectors the knowledge base remains weak, as discussed in the section on AAA below.

Portfolio Performance

The Bank Group's cumulative lending and grant portfolio in Afghanistan (including funds administered by the Bank Group) consisted of 104 operations with associated commitments of $6.6 billion from FY02 to FY11. Of these, some $4.2 billion have come through the ARTF, and the remainder consisted of IDA grants and credits, IFC investments (with commitments of $100.3 million), and MIGA guarantees (five projects with gross exposure of $78.2 million). [6] The IFC and MIGA operations fall primarily under the third pillar, supporting the growth of the formal private sector, while Bank support extends to all three pillars.

While Bank Group resources were allocated roughly equally across the three pillars, over half of ARTF resources were allocated to state building (pillar 1), and a fourth to the rural sector (pillar 2). Taken together, half of the combined Bank Group and ARTF resources supported state building, a third supported the rural sectors, and one-sixth was invested in private sector growth, including infrastructure. ARTF support to the government for recurring and capital costs—the original purpose of establishing the ARTF—amounted to $2.3 billion. The flagship community-based rural development program (NSP) received $909 million from the ARTF in addition to the $398 million in IDA grants during FY02–11, amounting to 20 percent of Bank Group/ARTF resources.

Early projects have performed well, but implementation risks have increased in the Bank's active portfolio. IFC's investments have been lumpy and its committed portfolio grew from $58 million in 2008 to $93 million in 2011, largely due to a $30 million additional investment in a telecommunications project. MIGA guarantees tailed off after 2008 until its significant support in FY12 to the same telecommunications project. The performance of IFC and MIGA reflects, in part, the difficult environment for foreign direct investment, which declined significantly after 2007. IEG assessments of the 22 completed Bank operations in Afghanistan indicate that these had better development outcome ratings (86 percent moderately satisfactory or better) than the average for South Asia (76 percent) and the Bank as a whole (76 percent). (See appendix J, tables J.12 and J.14). Almost half of the completed projects (41 percent) were found to be fully satisfactory; the rest were moderately satisfactory. The unsatisfactory projects were in the education sector, civil service capacity building, and avian flu. The Bank's active portfolio has a higher proportion of problem projects. As of end-FY11, IFC has an active portfolio with six companies; 88 percent of this investment is in one telecommunications company. MIGA's primary exposure is also in the telecommunications sector. Three of the five MIGA guarantees supported under the Small Investment Program were cancelled due to poor business outcomes.

The riskiness of the Bank's portfolio under implementation increased substantially after 2007 and is now twice as high as the South Asia average (appendix J, table J.16). In FY11, 39 percent of projects in Afghanistan were at risk compared with 20 percent for South Asia, while the percentage of commitments at risk is 26 percent for Afghanistan and 14 percent for South Asia, indicating that likely outcome ratings may decline. The percentage of projects at risk in Afghanistan is now more in line with the average for FCS (42 percent at risk), and commitments at risk in Afghanistan are lower than the average for FCS (49 percent at risk). Given the challenging conditions in Afghanistan, and the increasing riskiness of the country context, these outcomes are noteworthy.

AAA Review

The World Bank invested considerable resources in AAA and IFC undertook Advisory Services in key sectors. In all, the Bank Group invested more than a third of the total operational budget (including trust funds) for Afghanistan in 107 AAA products during FY02–11. The heavy emphasis placed on AAA was appropriate considering the need to (i) rebuild the Bank's knowledge base for Afghanistan after a prolonged hiatus in country relations, (ii) provide technical assistance to the new government in policy and program design and to help build institutional capacity, and (iii) provide analytical underpinnings for donor assistance to Afghanistan.

The Bank Group's knowledge contributions were assessed by reviewing all the AAA tasks undertaken by the Bank and Advisory Services by IFC using a cluster approach.[7] Given their quantity and diversity, as well as the links among them, it was most efficient to review them as clusters. In consultation with the country unit, the 107 products were grouped ex-post into 17 sector or thematic groups. Although these products had not been designed as programmatic AAA, many of them were obviously interrelated or follow-up tasks building on previous analytical work. The AAA review assessed adequacy of the results (likely to be) achieved by the cluster, and appropriateness of the Bank performance in designing and implementing the tasks in the cluster. Adopting a quasi-programmatic approach to the analysis of knowledge products and services led to a better understanding of the synergies among them, as well as more realistic assessment of the impacts of each of these knowledge clusters on the country program.

The quality of the Bank Group's knowledge services drew uniformly high praise from both government counterparts and other donors active in Afghanistan. The Bank's work assessing the economic implications of the coming transition was mentioned by many interlocutors as a good example of what the Bank is uniquely qualified to contribute toward challenges faced by the Afghan government and the donor community, much like the previous strategic contributions to donor conferences during the early years of reengagement. Other cross-cutting AAA, such as the analyses of poverty, gender, and the environment have also had significant impacts on the policy dialogue with the client and development partners and have been lauded by client and development partner representatives.

The Bank Group's knowledge products contribute to better performance of its other assistance, but they are also valued as strategic contributions that the Bank is uniquely qualified to undertake in cross-cutting areas and as strategic sector analyses. At the operational level, lending operations underpinned by strong AAA have outperformed those lacking such inputs. In several sectors, the lack of strategic ESW has prevented the development of a longer-term strategic program. Clients and development partner representatives urged the Bank Group to undertake more AAA, even where it is not in the lead (such as in the agriculture, power, and urban sectors).

The sectoral and thematic composition of the AAA was broadly appropriate, but the results achieved vary considerably among different clusters. The most notable contribution of AAA was toward design of the Bank's own lending program. At the operational level, lending operations underpinned by strong AAA and impact evaluations have outperformed those lacking such inputs.

The AAA also had significant impacts on government policies and programs in several areas—PFM, health, information and communications technology (ICT), microfinance, and business advisory services. The mining sector, which is likely to have a transformative impact on the country's economy, stands out as an area where the primary contribution of the Bank was through its knowledge work. The results in public administration, private sector development, and the financial sector were mixed. AAA efforts aimed at strengthening PFM were more effective than Bank efforts at helping to curb corruption and build sustainable capacity among the Afghan civil service to manage the core functions of the government. In other sectors, the lack of strategic ESW has prevented the development of a longer-term program.

In terms of Bank performance, there was evidence of good technical quality and, for the most part, relevance and timeliness was also appropriate, with some notable gaps. Client consultations suggest that in several areas (such as the education, agriculture, and urban sectors), the Bank missed opportunities for helping the government with strategic AAA that could have helped prioritize investment programs consistent with available financial and human resources.

The Bank was less successful in achieving client and stakeholder involvement during design and implementation of some of the AAA tasks (such as PFM, public administration and governance, private sector development, and infrastructure). Feedback from some development community representatives in the field also noted the need for improved dissemination of the Bank's AAA.

Efficient management of the AAA resources was another area of concern. Efficiency suffered from systemic weaknesses in planning and managing Bank AAA in the Bank's nonlending portfolio. Especially during the initial years, quality control processes and documentation of outputs and results received insufficient attention. But urgency does not justify lack of accountability, which seems to arise, in part, from systemic weaknesses in Bank management of AAA, but also because of inadequate oversight within Afghanistan. Several AAA tasks were either not completed or not recorded and were not retrievable. Management oversight and accountability for IFC's Business Advisory Services, which rely on a structured results-based instrument for planning, monitoring, and oversight, was much better.

Given constraints on resources and the Bank's implementation capacity in Afghanistan, selectivity in development support is desirable. In the Afghan context, given the paucity of country knowledge as well as limited Bank Group resources in relation to overall aid flows, the assistance strategy could have leveraged its technical depth and invested more in analytical work in selected areas. The Bank could thus have usefully complemented its financial support in some areas with strategic analytical work in other areas where financial support may come from other partners or from future Bank operations.

Afghanistan Reconstruction Trust Fund

The ARTF, a trust fund established in 2002, is administered by the World Bank and funded by 32 donors. As of December 2011, donors had pledged $4.8 billion for the ARTF. The ARTF is now the largest single source of external on-budget financing for the Afghan government. The ARTF is a financing mechanism that coordinates assistance from key donors so that the government can make predictable, timely, and accurate on-budget payments for approved recurrent and investment costs. The investment window supports projects and programs aligned with the government's priorities and, in turn, with those of the Bank's ISNs. The ARTF has financed about two-thirds of the program administered by the Bank.

Administration of the ARTF has been an integral part of the Bank's work in Afghanistan and has allowed the Bank to play a key role in convening and influencing donor/government dialogue. The ARTF has developed from a narrow trust fund focus into a significant and effective platform for dialogue, donor coherence, and coordination with the government. While other mechanisms for donor coordination also exist in Afghanistan, the government and development partners alike appreciate the development focus of the ARTF.

The ARTF has evolved significantly over time, expanding support to the investment window and modifying the recurrent window in response to the changing context and country needs (box 2.1). At its inception in 2002, the

---

Box 2.1 Afghanistan Reconstruction Trust Fund

The Incentive Program was introduced as an innovation in FY09 under the recurrent cost window to leverage recurrent cost financing into an effective instrument for policy dialogue and reform. The Incentive Program was introduced when the government's own revenue was increasing and the relevance and appetite for unconditional budget support among donors was diminishing. Unlike Bank-financed development policy grants, the Incentive Program provides a vehicle for Bank staff to coordinate their policy dialogue with other development partners to encourage and support the government to undertake key reforms. The program supports improved public financial management by requiring compliance with fiduciary standards, adjusting them to the realities of the country, and training public officials in implementing them. ARTF conditionality for the recurrent cost window also offers incentives for government to address difficult reforms.

The ARTF has a number of positive features:

- Governance of the ARTF has improved; The Ministry of Finance is now a member of the Management Committee that approves project allocations; other members, in addition to the Bank, include the ADB, the Islamic Development Bank, and the United Nations.

- The government has achieved agreed targets, which under the last Incentive Program included enhancing domestic revenue generation, improving public sector governance, and enabling private sector development. The proportion of incentive-based ARTF funding is expected to increase over time.

- Donors finance the ARTF in part because it gives them more leverage to influence reforms under the Incentive Program than they would have on their own.

- The ARTF has proved an efficient, quick-disbursing mechanism thanks to the recurrent cost window and the NSP.

- Donors have more confidence in the Bank's fiduciary controls than if they were providing budget support directly to the government.

- ARTF is often used to scale up activities that have been piloted with the Bank's own IDA grants or credits.

- To accommodate the priorities of donors, preferencing is allowed for up to 50 percent of ARTF contributions; however, the rolling, three-year financing strategy takes priority in guiding allocations, and might eventually replace preferencing.

- The ARTF has hired a monitoring agent to undertake field verification of NSP health and rural roads outputs through 1,500 site visits in the first year. This will offset the inability of the Bank team to undertake field monitoring.

The ARTF has been subject to two comprehensive, external evaluations and an independent audit by the Office of the Special Inspector General for Afghanistan Reconstruction; the reviews have all been generally positive.

Sources: IEG discussions with stakeholders; ARTF Web site http://www.worldbank.org/artf: Scanteam 2005, 2008; World Bank 2012b.

---

fund was set up to support the government's operating budget through a recurring cost window to ensure continuity and predictability in an emergency situation. Over time, the priority of the ARTF shifted away from recurrent financing, toward development financing, and an increasing share of ARTF's resources is being devoted to investments (from 4.5 percent in 2002 to an average of 51 percent over the last three year period, 2009–11). The shift in focus has resulted in predictable financing for the government's development priorities, reduced transaction costs of a fragmented donor community, and helped deliver significant results on the ground.

A key feature of the ARTF has been the complete alignment with and integration into the Bank's program as well as the ANDS. The fee income is part of the broader resource pool and provides the country program with an overarching work program, which has ensured complete integration of ARTF projects into the Bank's engagement with Afghanistan. ARTF projects are now prepared, implemented, and supervised in the same manner as any IDA project.[8]

ARTF resources supplement the Bank's own country program, thus enhancing the Bank's ability to contribute to Afghanistan's development. Most projects are cofinanced by IDA and share preparation and supervision costs. Cofinanced projects have tended to be prepared and piloted with IDA financing (and in some instances with funds from the Japanese Social Development Fund) and proposed for ARTF financing after implementation arrangements have been put in place, reducing the start-up costs and risks to the ARTF. ARTF funds have supported the scaling up of such national programs. The ARTF administration fee used to be 1.5 percent of donor commitments and has recently been increased to 2 percent to cope with the high cost of the country program and the significant additional security arrangements needed in Afghanistan.

The financing strategy has been evolving to increase predictability and longer-term planning. Over time, the ARTF has evolved from year-to-year financing to a three-year financing strategy, which allows the ARTF to engage in thorough consultations with the government and development partners on priorities over a longer period. This strengthens transparency and predictability for core investment programs and the recurrent budget and also ensures that the Bank is able to manage its own capacity to implement the program by aligning ARTF financing with the Bank's own strategy cycle under the ISN. The three-year financing strategy has also encouraged some donors, such as Norway, to move to a three-year financing framework.

Earmarking of funds through a system of preferencing by donors remains a somewhat contentious issue. The ARTF permits donors to express a preference for applying up to 50 percent of their contributions toward support for individual programs, but it does not permit geographic preferencing. In recent years, some donors have been increasing the share of preferenced funds for certain programs, due, at least in part, to direction from their legislatures and concerns over corruption and weak government capacity. However, other development partners have expressed confidence in the ARTF by eliminating preferencing. The United Kingdom and Norway, who represent 23 percent of current ARTF financing, have entirely eliminated preferencing. Overall, 40 percent of ARTF funds are currently preferenced.

Donor contributions to the ARTF are expected to grow significantly. Financing channeled through the ARTF accounted for 63 percent of total resources[9] committed under Bank Group–financed or –administered operations in Afghanistan as of January 2012. Of the remainder, 35 percent is accounted for by IDA credits and grants, and 2 percent by IFC operations. With the commitment made at the 2011 Bonn Conference to increase the volume of external development support administered on budget to 50 percent from the current 27 percent, contributions to the ARTF may grow even more. The FY12–14 ISN estimates an ARTF allocation of $2.4 billion, subject to donor contributions. This is more than five times the size of the IDA allocation ($430 million) for Afghanistan. Not surprisingly, development partners are seeking greater voice in the governance of the ARTF.

Some governance changes were introduced following recommendations from previous ARTF evaluations. The first was to develop a three-year framework and strategy, allocating funds between recurrent and investment costs, all based on priorities from the ANDS. This has helped ARTF to be more strategic, based on donors' estimates of available funds, since 2010. A Strategy Working Group, consisting of key donors and the Ministry of Finance, has been set up to advise the Steering Committee on the strategy. Second, an Incentive Program was instituted in FY09 to support government-led reforms. Since then, an increasing proportion of recurrent cost window funding has been incentive-based (from 14 percent in 2009–10 to 29 percent in 2012–13).

Giving the Ministry of Finance (MOF) a seat at the table as an integral member of the ARTF Strategy Working Group has enhanced country ownership. The MOF appreciates being part of the decision-making process for allocation of ARTF resources, but would prefer greater voice in the selection of programs to be financed by the ARTF to ensure stronger alignment with government priorities.

The introduction of third-party monitoring in FY12 allows much better understanding of ARTF outreach. There have been some reports of inferior construction of assets, which is of concern to some donors, especially because security constraints in many districts make it impossible to assess progress directly (Ecorys 2012). The ARTF has addressed this by hiring a monitoring agent, International Relief and Development, to conduct on-site visits, with geo-referencing to verify field construction. The first phase, undertaken in FY12, covered the education, NSP, and rural roads programs, using mobile phones and geo-referencing to verify outputs. While these three programs are only a subset of the overall portfolio, and the monitoring is essentially able to capture physical results rather than outcomes, it is a major step forward. The ARTF administrator is planning to include irrigation in the next phase as well as to pilot community-based monitoring.

The Kabul Bank crisis placed the ARTF at risk when development partners held back disbursement until the case was resolved. Several partners believed the Bank had not used its leverage sufficiently with the government and criticized the Bank for not being an "honest broker" between the donor partners and the government. The Bank had suspended payments from the Recurring Cost Window but was concerned that delaying disbursements could have repercussions on the policy dialogue and Incentives Program and cause irreparable harm to the projects financed by the investment window of the ARTF, due to the government's cash-balance situation. At times during these discussions, the partnership established between the Bank and some of its ARTF partners came under considerable stress. Fortunately, the crisis was resolved in November 2011 and disbursements were quickly renewed, enabling many donors to disburse funds rapidly before the close of their fiscal year.

Previous evaluations were positive about access to information for the ARTF, but some donors have expressed concern about the adequacy and timeliness of information needed for decisionmaking. Information sharing and transparency were described by an early evaluation as "best practice" (Scanteam 2005), with extensive information on the Web, despite the small size of the Bank team managing the ARTF. During IEG's consultations, however, several donors mentioned the inadequacy of, and last minute delivery of, documentation to financing partners before strategy and decision meetings, constraining their ability to consult with their headquarters and make more meaningful contributions at these meetings. More timely availability of essential documentation would enable more substantive involvement by donors who would like to be more engaged in the ARTF.

The 2012 ISN

Continuing insecurity and political risks, combined with the uncertainties associated with the 2014 transition, resulted in a decision by Bank Group management to prepare another ISN for the next phase of support. An ISN provides management with greater ability to respond rapidly to emerging crises. The challenge for the Bank Group will be to focus on the foundations for long-term strategic development, while maintaining flexibility should the need arise for rapid adaptation.

In terms of strategic realignment, the new ISN discussed in 2012 is more realistic in matching program interventions with the objectives of its pillars. The Bank Group strategy for FY12–14 has been put forward as another ISN because of the uncertainty surrounding the 2014 transition (World Bank 2012a). The pillars in the new ISN have been restructured more appropriately as (i) building the legitimacy and capacity of institutions, (ii) equitable service delivery, and (ii) inclusive growth and jobs.

For the most part, the underlying programs maintain continuity with previous Bank Group strategies, but they have been regrouped under these pillars, recognizing the governance role of the NSP under the first pillar as more important than its role in rural growth. Health and education have moved from the governance pillar to the second pillar, along with rural and urban service delivery. The mining sector receives greater emphasis, because it is expected to catalyze regional growth along natural resource corridors.

However, in other critical areas there continue to be gaps in the Bank's strategy. In two key areas where the borrower seeks Bank support—agricultural development and urban development—the Bank has not yet developed a comprehensive strategic approach. For much of the review period, the World Bank Group did not have a well-developed strategy to assist the government in the justice sector or in human resources development, both of which are crucial to sustaining public administration and private sector growth and where alternate strategies have not been put forward by other donors. A new project has recently been launched to strengthen civil service capacity over the next few years, and a justice sector project is now under preparation.

Notes

1. An ISN (like a TSS) enables the processing of all operations under Operational Policy 8.0: Rapid Response to Crises and Emergencies and, unlike a full-fledged CAS, is not required to have a results framework.

2. Elsewhere, IFC and MIGA operations in Afghanistan have thus far found little foothold.

3. The original commitment amount for IFC was $105 million.

4. The existing MIGA guarantee of $75 million was replaced in FY12 with new and expanded coverage to MTN Dubai Ltd, increasing total MIGA coverage for the project by another $80.4 million to $150 million. The project name was also changed to MTN Afghanistan.

5. This includes Bank budget and Bank-executed trust funds.

6. An additional $3.5 million in first-loss coverage was insured by the MIGA-managed Afghanistan Investment Guarantee Facility (a trust fund that was established in FY05 and financed by the ADB, DFID, and Afghanistan, using the proceeds of a $5 million IDA credit). The facility closed in FY11.

7. For more detailed on the AAA methodology see appendix E.

8. Harmonization of procedures for recipient-executed trust funds with those for IBRD/IDA operations was formally adopted by the Bank in FY07.

9. As of January 2012, the World Bank had approved $437 million in IDA credits, and $1,915.7 million in IDA grants, compared with the commitment of $4,195 million from ARTF resources for closed and active operations in the Afghanistan portfolio.

References

ADB (Asian Development Bank), UNDP (United Nations Development Program), and World Bank. 2002. *Afghanistan: Preliminary Needs Assessment for Recovery and Reconstruction.* New York, NY: UNDP.

Ecorys. 2012. *Evaluation of Norwegian Development Cooperation with Afghanistan 2001–2011.* Prepared for the Norwegian Agency for Development Cooperation Evaluation Department. Oslo: Norad.

Islamic Republic of Afghanistan, ADB (Asian Development Bank), United Nations Assistance Mission to Afghanistan, UNDP (United Nations Development Program), and the World Bank Group. 2004. "Securing Afghanistan's Future: Accomplishments and the Strategic Path Forward." A Government/ International Agency Report, March 17, 2004. Prepared for International Conference, March 31, 2004. Available at: http://www.cmi.no/afghanistan/?id=5&Government-of-Afghanistan.

Scanteam. 2005. *Assessment, Afghanistan Reconstruction Trust Fund: External Evaluation Final Report.* Oslo: Scanteam.

World Bank. 2002. "Afghanistan—Transitional Support Strategy." Report No. 23822 AF. Washington, DC: World Bank.

———. 2003. "Afghanistan—Transitional Support Strategy:." Report No. 25440 AF. Washington, DC: World Bank.

———. 2007. "Land Acquisition in Afghanistan: A Report." Washington, DC: World Bank.

———. 2009. *Interim Strategy Note for the Islamic Republic of Afghanistan for the Period FY09–FY11.* Report No. 47939-AF. Washington, DC: World Bank.

———. 2011. *World Development Report 2011: Conflict, Security and Development.* Washington DC: The World Bank.

———. 2012a. *Interim Strategy Note for the Islamic Republic of Afghanistan for the Period FY12–FY14.* Report No. 66862-AF. Washington, DC: World Bank.

———. 2012b. *World Development Report 2012: Gender Equality and Development.* Washington, DC: World Bank.

Chapter 3

Building the Capacity of the State and Its Accountability to Its Citizens

Context

From the outset, the Bank recognized rebuilding essential governance institutions and capacity as an urgent but long-term objective. When the Afghanistan Interim Administration took power in 2001, ministries lacked basic materials and equipment. There were chronic skill deficits in areas such as procurement, expenditure programming, budget preparation, accounting, financial control, and audit, as well as human resources, project, and program management. Most women, who made up 43 percent of government employees before the Taliban (ADB, UNDP, and World Bank 2002, p. 15), had been dismissed, and many senior personnel had either emigrated or taken on alternative, part-time employment.

The Afghan civil service, divided into Tashkeels (staff allotments) for each ministry, had common pay scales, terms, and conditions that signaled unity and fairness. However, public service provision was extremely limited (Evans and others 2004, vol. 2, pp. 6–7, 15). While the previous Taliban government had maintained military control over most of the country, they made little effort to build a civilian administration that could provide public services. Structures for raising customs and other taxes were rudimentary. Few children benefited from primary education, and infant mortality was high.

Starting from these initial conditions, the Bank's 2002 TSS had the highly relevant objective of "rebuilding or strengthening essential governance institutions and capacity, particularly in areas important for facilitating the overall reconstruction, economic recovery and aid process (World Bank 2002: 12)." The 2003 TSS reframed this as "the continued development of a well functioning state that is accountable to its citizenry and able to ensure the delivery of services in an equitable, efficient and effective manner (World Bank 2003: 19)."

The 2006 ISN broadened this objective, which is aligned with the government's 2004 Investment Plan. It specified that it would include developing both human and financial capacity, with the latter including reforms in customs and taxation, and contingent on the emergence of a vibrant and legitimate private sector. It signaled the importance of combating corruption and of providing tangible benefits to citizens through essential services.

The 2009 ISN reframed the same objective as pillar 1, which is aligned with the government's 2008–13 ANDS. The ISN added additional priorities for mainstreaming governance and anticorruption into the activities supported by the Bank, including engaging with the newly elected government on a governance and anticorruption agenda, engaging on governance issues through the ARTF and NSP, and engaging with the Independent Directorate of Local Governance on a transparent fiscal framework, with enhanced monitoring by Community Development Councils (CDCs).

On this strategic foundation, the Bank supported government efforts in four key areas: putting in place the basics of a functioning public financial management and procurement system that could mobilize resources for reconstruction in an effective and transparent manner; building capacity to recruit and retain the essential skills needed to manage an effective and accountable public service, including law and justice, national statistics, and mechanisms to combat corruption; building basic systems for health and social protection; and expanding and improving the quality of public education. The Bank's work in these four areas is analyzed below.

Public Financial Management

WORLD BANK GROUP OBJECTIVES

The objectives were to strengthen core systems, heighten fiscal sustainability, and improve transparency and accountability. A key goal was better management and accountability of on-budget expenditures. There was also a desire to extend core reforms beyond apex institutions in Kabul and actively support the dialogue between government and donors in order to come to a consensus on subnational governance, capacity building, and local service delivery. The Bank intended to support the MOF and line ministries in using the budget process to make expenditures at the subnational level more effective and equitable by improving provincial allocations on a sectoral basis and integrating community and subnational government planning and accountability mechanisms into the overall public financial management framework. The results are summarized in table 3.1.

RESULTS

Afghanistan has a relatively strong PFM framework, but significant challenges remain. The framework is better than would be expected for a country of its per capita income that started virtually from scratch 10 years ago. It has achieved impressive revenue performance (up from 3 percent of GDP in 2002/03 to 11 percent in 2011/12) and greater assurance that funds provided through the budget are used effectively. Accounting and financial management reporting have become more accurate and timely. The use of the ARTF to pay salaries has ensured timely and reliable payment to staff, while facilitating quick disbursement of donor funds to scale up implementation of national programs.

More recently, the Incentives Program supported by the ARTF has provided further impetus to PFM reforms. Despite the progress, significant challenges remain. Budget formulation and execution are hampered by weak project planning by line ministries and unpredictability of donor financing. Off-budget expenditures remain significant, even though all Bank-managed operations are on budget. However, the decisions by bilateral partners to keep funds off-budget are not necessarily due to the status of PFM; such decisions are also affected by political or other considerations.

There have been some improvements in fiscal management and spending efficiency at line ministries. Ministries help formulate the budget through

Table 3.1	Summary Results of Pillar 1—Public Financial Management
Results associated with Bank Group goals	**Bank Group contribution to results**
Bank Group Objective: Strengthen core systems, heighten fiscal sustainability, improve transparency, and use the budget process to make expenditures at subnational level more effective and equitable.	
A relatively strong PFM framework, impressive revenue growth, and greater assurance that funds provided through budget (including most Bank-administered resources) are used effectively. Less-than-expected progress in several key areas: • Budget formulation and transparency (making headway but still weak) • Procurement (lack of qualified contractors; lack of financial infrastructure; weak capacity of implementing agencies) • External audit (replacement act for the Control and Audit Office law has been drafted but not been approved) • Extending core reforms to line ministries and subnational units • Many steps still to be taken in the PFM road map to further reduce fiduciary risk.	Extensive AAA, four Development Policy Operations, and three capacity building investments helped to: • Draft new laws and regulations • Provide Implementation support on domestic revenue mobilization, expenditure control, treasury and cash management, and financial reporting • Monitor achievements through Public Expenditure and Financial Accountability (PEFA) assessments, Public Expenditure Reviews, and other high-quality AAA. The Bank's management of the ARTF gave it leverage to provide significant non-IDA funding through the budget, while ensuring fiduciary rigor. ARTF support improved PFM by demanding compliance with fiduciary standards and training public officials in implementing them. The ARTF Incentive Program also offered incentives for the government to address difficult reforms.

their inputs to the MOF, and all processes in budget execution depend on their contracting services, requesting payments directly into the Afghanistan Financial Management Information System, and reconciling expenditure to authorizations. But substantial capacity weaknesses in project preparation and implementation remain to be addressed. Subnational units of the MOF (called *Moutoufiats*) have online, real time use of the Afghanistan Financial Management Information System, but the capacity of most other subnational units for PFM is weak.

A National Audit Law has been drafted that clarifies the role of the Control and Audit Office as an independent review function with no oversight or responsibility for internal audit, which opens the way for the application of Article 61 of the Public Finance and Expenditure Management Law. The draft also provides for independence both in mandate and in reporting for the CAO, but it is still awaiting approval by the Parliament. And while a Public Procurement Law and amendments have been adopted, many complementary actions needed for effective implementation are still lacking, such as expanding the low level of qualified contractors, access to banking, guarantees, insurance, and ability to furnish bid and performance guarantees. Capacity in most line ministries for processing procurement is weak, and there are interruptions and delays in contract implementation, in part due to security issues (World Bank 2010).

The strategic relevance and technical quality of the Bank's PFM operations are commendable, especially considering the difficult country context. In the early years, the emphasis was appropriately on expenditure control and the establishment of basic mechanisms for cash protection and management, including single treasury account, payroll, and simple accounting. As discussed above, these PFM achievements will need to be consolidated over the next few years to strengthen budget planning and execution capability. Key results achieved and those still to be achieved are given in table 3.2. (Also see table 3.5, Status of Performance Benchmarks.)

World Bank Group Contributions

Bank support came from PFM components totaling about $239 million in four Development Policy Operations and seven Investment Operations funded by

Table 3.2	Public Financial Management Results and Shortcomings
Results achieved	**Still to be achieved**
• Eighteen PEFA process indicators improved from 2005 to 2007. • Open Budget Index Score improved from 8 percent to 21 percent from 2008 to 2010. • Afghanistan Financial Management Information System now connects to all 54 line ministries and agencies and all 34 provinces. • Good progress on reduction of fiduciary risk associated with ARTF-funded expenditures and ARTF asset monitoring by monitoring agent since 2011. • PFM benchmarks under the Incentives Program have been achieved. • Ministries hold appropriations and authorize expenditures, while cash is centrally controlled. • Central government financial statements are published each month within 25 days of month's end, and audited annual appropriations statements (Qatia) are submitted to Parliament within six months of fiscal year end. • A debt management system supports quarterly debt reporting, and debt-to-GDP ratio has been reduced from 12 percent to 6 percent, meeting enhanced HIPC benchmark. • A database is maintained for 669,000 registered government employees, which is the basis for setting up payroll applications in 70 locations in Kabul and 9 provincial *Moutoufiats*. • Payroll management has improved through direct deposits of salary payments to the bank accounts of 450,000 government employees through the verified payment program as of December 2011, with plans to increase to 520,000 by 2014. • MOF's Internal Audit Department has set up a Fraud Investigation Unit, with a qualified auditor and training program, and an Information Technology Audit Section. • Procurement Policy Unit created and functioning; Public Procurement Law and the Public Financial and Expenditure Management Law have been approved, along with key amendments. • Subnational units are extensions of the line ministries, and of the MOF in the case of *Moutoufiats*, which have online, real time use of the Afghanistan Financial Management Information System.	• Three out of four PEFA outcome indicators (PI-1-4) are given the lowest rating, indicating that with the exception of good performance on revenue, improved processes are not translating into better overall expenditure management results, in part because of the use of contingencies in the operating budget due to provisions for security and the Incentives Program. • PFM needs to grow beyond the initial, correct emphasis on cash management, payroll, and record keeping, to affect medium-term expenditure programming, budget preparation, and other upstream aspects of PFM, a process that may take 20–30 years to be fully realized. • Weak project planning by line ministries, unpredictable donor resources, and very weak subnational PFM capacity contributed to a development budget execution rate for 2009/10 of 40 percent, down from 54 percent in 2006/7. • Many steps still to be taken in the PFM road map to further reduce fiduciary risk. • No progress on increasing proportion of non-wage recurrent expenditures. • Many complementary actions needed for adequate implementation of the legal and regulatory framework have not been taken: the financial regulations have been drafted but are yet to be approved; procurement capacity in most line ministries is weak. • The draft National Audit Law meets international standards but it has not been approved by Parliament.[a] • Although the Budget and Finance Commission reviews the budget, the accounts of fiscal operations, and external audits, and the budget is ratified by the House, the role of the Parliament in the budgeting process and financial oversight remains weak in practice.

a. It is on the calendar for discussion in SY1391.

IDA and the ARTF (see appendix J, table J.18), and $1.1 million in AAA. The package of parallel investment operations and AAA provided the government with essential content and operational support to use the development policy resources productively. This support from the Bank, along with parallel efforts from the U.K. Department for International Development (DFID), UNDP, the U.S. Agency for International Development (USAID), Japan, and the ADB, among others, sought to help establish a functioning PFM and procurement system led by the MOF in areas where there was sufficient political willingness to move forward, such as a legal framework (Public Finance and Expenditure Management Law, Public Procurement Law, and Pension Law and key amendments); basic budget, treasury, and revenue mechanisms, including increased budget allocation for health and education, improved access to key financial information, a basic computerized treasury system for processing payments and producing reports, a verified payments system for payroll, a basic institutional structure (such as a reorganized Budget Department, Fiscal Policy Unit, Cash Management Unit, unified chart of accounts, Central Bank payment system, Control and Audit Office, Central Procurement Facility), and a cadre of staff, led by a "second civil service" of contracted, technical, and professional staff to operate this structure in the MOF, line ministries, and the subnational administration.

Twenty-nine percent of Bank support (and 52 percent of IDA support) provided for achieving these results came from four Development Policy Operations (Programmatic Support for Institution Building I, II, and III and Strengthening Institutions). The remainder came from a combination of Investment Operations (Emergency Public Administration Project, Strengthening Financial Capacity, and Public Financial Management Reform), technical assistance, and ESW on public expenditure management, procurement, and fiduciary safeguards that provided the government with essential content and operational support to use the development policy resources productively.

The ESW included a 2005 flagship report (World Bank 2005) that set the baseline and provided analysis of major PFM issues that informed Bank support, and the Public Expenditure and Financial Accountability (PEFA) Assessments (World Bank 2005, vol. 2, and 2008c) that provide a measure of progress against international benchmarks. Some ESW was less useful, such as the "gap analysis" work (World Bank 2007) that provided 23 pages of recommendations covering virtually the entire accounting, financial reporting, and auditing spectrum, without any guidance on prioritization, and without regard for capacity realities. While some of the recommendations have since been implemented (such as adoption of Institute for International Public Sector Accounting Standards cash standards and International Standards of Supreme Audit Institutions audit standards, and improvements in internal audit), the report would have been more helpful if it had identified which key gaps were likely to be especially important, taking into account the Afghan context, including issues of weak educational institutions to support an accounting profession and security issues, and how these gaps could be filled in a realistic and cost-effective fashion and within an appropriate time frame.

The ARTF supported improved PFM by upholding fiduciary standards, adjusting them to the realities of the country, and offering incentives for the government to address difficult reforms. The transformation of the recurrent cost window into an Incentives Program that is growing in proportion to unconditional budget support annually is an innovation worthy of note.

The approach to skills development was multifaceted, including the injection of highly skilled Afghan consultants from around the world, on-the-job mentoring of local staff, and training courses through the Afghanistan Civil Service Institute and other sources. However, the Bank and its development partners have not been able to address weak project planning of government-funded investments, extensive off-budget expenditures, capacity constraints in line ministries and subnational authorities, lack of parliamentary approval for external audit that is independent of the executive, and lack of prosecutorial support from the attorney general, leading to serious remaining weaknesses in the accountability framework that have worsened corruption.[1]

The Bank has worked with the government to take some initial steps to address potential mining revenues, such as Extractive Industries Transparency Initiative candidature, and a proposed 2013 Development Policy Loan trigger. Heightened policy dialogue is needed on providing additional protection to mining revenues, before these revenues start to expand and become targets for rent-seeking.

Public Sector Governance

WORLD BANK GROUP OBJECTIVES

As with public financial management and procurement, state capacity and accountability issues are addressed in most Bank projects. Health and education projects support a combination of contracting-out service delivery and building administrative capacity, as analyzed later in this chapter. Projects to improve rural livelihoods, such as the NSP, work to empower communities to direct local development of much-needed infrastructure and to put in place systems to ensure timely payments, improve project quality, and strengthen overall management capacity. Projects promoting the growth of a competitive private sector help to establish legislative and regulatory frameworks, environmental and social planning, and rigorous bidding processes for exploiting natural resources, as analyzed in chapter 5.

This section analyzes projects that helped to build and improve core administrative and judicial institutions and capacities at the national and subnational levels (table 3.3). The Bank's objective was to build a reformed and sustainable civil service accountable to its citizens to provide services that are affordable, accessible, and adequate.

RESULTS

Bank support, along with parallel efforts by the International Monetary Fund (IMF), UNDP, USAID, and DFID, among others, has led to adoption of new laws and regulations, more transparent recruitment, reduction in the number of ministries, and pay and grading reforms. A basic size and structure for the civil service has been set, defining the numbers of staff needed across ministries and agencies; setting an affordable pay scale for civil servants, including pensions; and beginning the process of making the civil service rules based.

Nevertheless, high-level, off-budget corruption is perceived as getting worse, despite PFM reforms intended to reduce the degree of leakage from the core budget. There is little evidence that the new laws, procedures, and regulations are translating into improved civil service performance. What achievements there are have relied mainly on a second civil service of contracted staff who are paid relatively high salaries, without an agreed plan to hand over tasks to civil servants on normal pay scales. Some key results achieved and those still to be achieved are given in table 3.4.

WORLD BANK GROUP CONTRIBUTION

The Bank supported the sector with $214 million from a mix of development policy and investment operations (see appendix J, table J.19) and $3 million in AAA. The objectives and technical quality of the Bank's support were relevant to the government and Bank strategies, and aligned with the Bank's analytical work, as well as with work supported by other development partners.

Bank support was aimed at development of a regulatory framework for the civil service (including new policies, laws, and regulations); new structures (Independent Administration Reform and Civil Service Commission [IARCSC]) to manage human resources and civil service reforms; and pay and grading reform with new average pay scales two-to-three times the previous ones in return for merit- and results-based human resources management.

The Bank also supported short-term incentive programs to attract a "second civil service" of skilled Afghans and to compensate them for the opportunity cost of leaving jobs overseas.[2] This scheme also aimed to compete with pay

Table 3.3 Summary Results of Pillar 1—Public Sector Governance	
Results associated with Bank Group Goals	**Bank Group contribution to results**
Bank Group Objective: Building a reformed and sustainable civil service accountable to its citizens to provide services that are affordable, accessible, and adequate.	
Some progress with statistics, pay and grading, merit-based recruitment, pensions, and other human resources processes, but many challenges remain: • The actual quality of "reformed" processes and related training provided is mixed. • Most of the gains rely on a "second civil service" of professionals outside the civil service paid on a significantly higher scale. • Little headway on legal and judicial reform and on combating corruption.	Extensive AAA, four Development Policy Operations, eight capacity-building investments, including funding for very attractive contracts for Afghan consultants in key senior positions helped to: • Draft new policies, laws, and regulations. • Regraded 25 ministries and 325,000 civil service positions. • Strive for civil service appointments to be made on merit basis. • Construct courthouses and other basic judicial infrastructure.

Table 3.4	Key Results and Shortcomings in Public Administration and Governance

Results achieved	Still to be achieved
• Civil service law adopted with accompanying regulations providing job security for most civil servants and institutional mechanisms for administrative reform oversight. • Basic human resources monitoring, recruitment based on open advertisement of new positions, and number of ministries reduced from 34 to 26. • Twenty-five ministries and agencies completed pay and grading process, with 325,000 positions regraded. • Merit-based recruitment and other performance-enhancing human resources procedures introduced. • Pension regulations adopted by the cabinet. • Favorable opinion ratings on public administration and government performance.[a] • High-quality statistical surveys, such as the Afghanistan Mortality Survey 2010, carried out by the Afghan Public Health Institute, the Ministry of Public Health, and the Central Statistics Organization. • The size and growth of the civilian civil service is reasonable (up from 327,000 in 2004 to approximately 355,000 in 2011[b]), though when security forces are included, the total increases to around 700,000. • Design standards for and construction of courthouses, law libraries, legal aid offices, and pay and grading reforms for prosecutors. • Afghanistan has become a candidate country for the Extractive Industries Transparency Initiative. • The High Office of Oversight and Anticorruption maintains a register of assets of high-ranking officials, conducts investigations of allegations of corruption, and carries out public awareness campaigns.	• Most of the gains rely on a second civil service of well-paid professionals paid under contract at rates far in excess of those in other countries of the region, with only the early beginnings of a credible plan for sustainability; see appendix I. • Insufficient coordination between Ministry of Finance and Independent Administration Reform and Civil Service Commission (IARCSC). • Need to monitor adherence to a rigorous recruitment and performance appraisal process; some units have migrated all staff to higher pay scales. • Bank needs to follow up on government implementation of agreed anti-corruption measures to address worsening public perception of corruption (which increased from 42 percent in 2006 to 56 percent in 2011).[c] • Monitoring of government actions to recover loss of $825 million misappropriated by politically well-connected borrowers from Kabul Bank, which administered salaries for Afghanistan's soldiers, police, and civil servants. • Lack of support from the Attorney General's Office held back legal and judicial reforms. • Strong resistance to reforms in some line ministries and agencies where factional networks vie for remunerative posts. • Systemic weaknesses and unclear service delivery responsibilities at the subnational level.

a. Asia Foundation 2011. These results have a statistical sampling error of +-4.1 percent at 95 percent confidence level.

b. *Afghanistan in Transition —Looking Beyond 2014* (World Bank 2012a). Depending on the population estimate you use, the ratio of civil servants to population in Afghanistan is about 1.3 (based on a population of 26 million) compared to Pakistan's 1.97, Sri Lanka's 3.04, Bangladesh's 0.62 , Nepal's 1.23, and India's 1.25 (World Bank estimates).

c. This setback is also measured in Transparency International's Corruption Perception Index. In 2005, Afghanistan ranked 117 out of 159 countries covered; by 2010 its rank was 176 out of 178 countries.

levels offered in Afghanistan by international agencies and nongovernmental organizations (NGOs) for staff with similar skills. These staff are employed both by government ministries (using donor funding to top-up normal salaries) and by partner organizations. Most capacity has been built among the contracted staff of donor-funded projects, rather than in the core civil service (World Bank 2012a). The Bank also supported improvements in national statistics and in the state justice system through construction of courthouses and other basic judicial infrastructure.

The Bank's AAA gave a useful picture of the legacy of basically sound administrative practices, reasonably well understood if not always adhered to, and the need to build on this legacy rather than trying to replace it with something different (Evans and others 2004, vol. 2). The Bank has provided good high-level analysis of civil service challenges (for example, World Bank 2008, 2009b, 2009c), which contributed to the establishing of the Presidential Commission on National Technical Assistance. However, more attention should have been paid to the development of a more granular human resources strategy covering:

- How to build on the legacy commitment of Afghan civil servants to public service
- How and when Afghanistan will transfer civilian responsibilities from foreign to Afghan contract staff and civil servants
- The appropriate proportion of Afghan contract staff to civil servants moving forward, and how large a civil service is required
- What all this will cost and how it will be paid for
- How to ensure the production of adequate levels of graduates with essential skills by local and foreign universities.

The Capacity Building for Results Project is beginning to support ministries in developing clear plans for human resource development, and also supports government in developing human resource strategies for cross-cutting areas such as financial management, procurement, and human resources management, but implementation is just beginning.

The Bank also undertook some early analytical work on subnational governance that suggested a two-pronged approach: the state should deliver some basic support to deconcentrated units, and there should be some cautious increases in delegation, including incentives triggered by simple measures of administrative effort, fewer delays in staff appointments and payroll, and physical reconstruction of provincial and district facilities (Evans and others 2004, vol. 1).

This approach was correctly premised on the fact that according to its constitution and history, Afghanistan is a unitary state, with appointed governors and a limited subnational presence of line ministries. However, the results have been uneven. The constitution provides for elected provincial, district, and village councils. Provincial councils were elected in 2005 and 2009 but with limited, unclear functions (Lister and Nixon 2006), and they are still seeking effective roles in securing provincial development, while district and village councils have not yet been established. Bank support focused instead on subnational public administration. Payroll systems have improved, as discussed in the previous section, but other PFM standards for deconcentrated units at the subnational level are very weak. Some bilateral donors are assisting the provinces where they are working to strengthen local government facilities, but these efforts are not consistent and only cover a handful of provinces. In many areas, programs supported by project funding or Provincial Reconstruction Teams have more resources, and some even have a more established presence at the local level than do formal units of local government.

The cabinet endorsed a 2010 commitment to make Afghanistan a candidate country for the Extractive Industries Transparency Initiative (EITI). This obligates the country—within two years—to publish all payments of taxes, royalties, and fees from its extractive sector, and requires extractive companies operating in Afghanistan to publish what they have paid to the government. However, many steps still need to be taken in the PFM road map to further reduce fiduciary risk on these and other government revenues to acceptable levels, as pointed out in the previous section.

Other post-conflict countries have faced repeated cycles of violence due to conflict over natural resources (Collier 2009). To address this risk, the Bank should advise the government to consider models from other countries[3] for providing special protection to natural resources revenues, with a view to putting in place mechanisms before significant increases in revenue occur and rent-seeking practices have been established. The government also needs to communicate more clearly and compellingly its natural resource policies to the Afghan people.

Some Bank projects expected too much in too short a time. For example, the Civil Service Reform Project had to be restructured to align better with the implementation capacity of the IARCSC, which had a change of leadership in the early days of the project. The challenges of that project were likely heightened on the Bank side by the high turnover of task team leaders (four over a four-year period).

Another type of challenge is seen in the Bank's Judicial Reform Project, which focused on the centralized state justice system. The project supported improvements in areas with client ownership, such as design standards for and construction of courthouses, law libraries, and legal aid offices and pay and grading reforms for prosecutors, but judicial reforms were held back by lack of support from the Attorney General's Office. The Bank tried to address some of these challenges in an ARTF-funded operation approved in December 2011: Capacity Building for Results. This operation has a number of design features intended to address the shortcomings of past support, including joint management by the MOF and IARCSC, high-level controls to prevent rent-seeking through recruitment practices, a results-based approach to access funding and assess ministry performance, and predictable levels of funding over a five-year period.

The reliance on the "second civil service" for gains in public administration and governance leads to multiple challenges. Training and institutional development often take a backseat to doing the tasks themselves. There is salary competition for individuals who move out of the civil service, and then from project to project, with the resulting difficulty in filling key civil service positions.

There is a risk of sustainability if security deteriorates or donor funding decreases, and the risk that the extreme pay differentials will become politically and socially untenable. (See Islamic Republic of Afghanistan 2010 and appendix I.) There is the added risk that as foreign forces leave, fiscal and political economy constraints may make it impossible for the regime to sustain the administrative improvements that have been achieved. The dominance of security forces in the public payroll and operational budget poses the additional risk of a power imbalance between the military and civilian sectors.

An overall assessment of the Bank's support for public administration and governance needs to take into account the difficult security environment and the challenge that the Bank's resources are dwarfed by those of much larger players. Given these challenges, the Bank has helped to put in place elements of a functioning civil service, which has had some success in providing citizens with essential services. However, there are significant shortcomings. Bank operations have not been able to deliver all that was promised, and the quality of enacted reforms is uneven. While formal laws, regulations, and processes for the functioning of the civil service have been put in place, actual changes in behavior have been slow to take hold. Most of the results achieved are dependent on consultants and Afghan civil servants on enhanced pay arrangements financed by donors, which is not sustainable.

Overall Assessment for Public Financial Management and Public Sector Governance

Table 3.5 summarizes the achievements of performance benchmarks in the PFM and PSG sectors.

Table 3.5	Status of Performance Benchmarks	
Source	**Benchmark**	**Status**
Public financial management[a]		
2003 TSS	Accurate and timely payment of government payrolls.	Achieved.
2003 TSS	Effective management and reduction of fiduciary risk associated with ARTF-funded expenditures; development component procedures smoothly functioning, with effective appraisal of proposals.	Good progress, but still many steps to be taken in the PFM road map to further reduce fiduciary risk to acceptable levels so that donors can increase budget assistance.
2003 TSS	Non-wage recurrent expenditures growing (especially outside of Kabul), with monitoring of use and asset management plans where appropriate (ARTF).	No progress on increasing non-wage recurrent expenditure.[b] Asset monitoring by monitoring agent ongoing since 2011.
2006 ISN	Procurement Policy Unit created and functioning, and finalization of procurement regulations in compliance with the new Public Procurement Law.	Considerable progress, with most ministries now preparing procurement plans, but serious weaknesses remain in spending ministries and agencies and in limited ability of the market to furnish bid and performance guarantees.
2006 ISN	Implementation of core development budget (actual expenditures as percentage of original budget), 65 percent.	No progress.
2006 ISN	Public access is granted to budget documents, monthly financial reports, annual financial statements, external audit reports, and contract awards and bids.	Some progress. Enacted budget, in-year reports and a mid-year review published. An audit report published, but quality compromised by the lack of an adequate Audit Law.

Table 3.5	Status of Performance Benchmarks (continued)	
Source	**Benchmark**	**Status**
2009 ISN	Progress in rolling out public financial management systems and capacity to line ministries and subnational jurisdictions.	Afghanistan Financial Management Information System fully functional, but public financial management capacities beyond MOF generally very weak.[d]
2006 & 2009 ISNs	Further increase in government revenues as a percentage of GDP.	Achieved: 11 percent of GDP in 2010/11 exceeds IMF target, and regional average.
2009 ISN	Increased donor resources being channeled through government budget systems.	Slow progress (total donor funds on budget have slowly increased to 27 percent).
2009 ISN	Progress in incorporating provincial budget planning into the medium-term budgetary framework.	No significant progress.
Public administration and governance[c]		
2003 TSS	Organizational improvements (such as streamlining number of ministries).	Number of ministries reduced, but quality of other organizational improvements uneven.
2003 TSS	Improvements in the skills level of the civil service.	Some progress. Pay and grading process under way; skills deficiencies remain, particularly in line ministries and subnational authorities.
2006 ISN	IARCSC able to process 1,000 merit-based appointments each year in grades 1 and 2, and able to supervise appointments in grades 3 and below.	Achieved, but quality of appointments is uneven.
2006 ISN	Functions and structures defined for six ministries.	Some progress.
2006 ISN	Anticorruption strategy adopted by government and regulations on civil servants conduct passed.	Achieved, but survey data indicate a perception that corruption has worsened.

a. See also tables 3.1 and 3.2.

b. O&M in 2005/6 budget was 21 percent (IMF 2007, Art IV). In 2008/9 budget O&M was 12 percent; in 2010/11 budget O&M was 17 percent (IMF 2011, Art IV). All budgets include budgeted security costs.

c. See also tables 3.3 and 3.4.

d. Source. World Bank (2010c).

HEALTH

World Bank Group Objectives

In the health sector, the primary objective was to promote rapid improvement in basic service delivery. Never robust, Afghanistan's health status and system were in critical condition in early 2002. Life expectancy was estimated at 47 years for males and 45 years for females. Only about 5 percent of births were attended by health workers with any form of modern health training, which, in the context of Afghanistan's very in high total fertility (between seven and nine births per married woman), made it probable that on the order of 1 in 12 women died in childbirth. The infant mortality rate and under-five mortality rate were estimated at 165/1000 and 257/1000 respectively, very high relative to neighboring Pakistan (90/1000) and Iran (26/1000) at the time.

In 2001, the bulk of the population had limited or no access to health services. Although early work on assessing health resources suggested that as many as 11,000 providers were still in the country, there were far too few female providers at all levels, and few providers or administrators in government positions. Those that had not left the country were working in private practice or with NGOs, which were providing about 80 percent of the health services available at the time the Taliban fell.

Results

Afghanistan has achieved remarkable gains in health service accessibility and improvements in health outcomes (table 3.6). Data from the Ministry of Public Health (MOPH) indicate that the number of functioning health facilities increased from about 496 in 2002 to more than 2,000 in 2011. The number of trained midwives (from accredited schools) increased from about 467 in 2003 to more than 1,950 by 2010, and the proportion of facilities with a skilled female health worker increased from 25 percent to 72 percent in the same period.

These accomplishments address Afghanistan's significant gender issues, both directly, by providing services of particular relevance to women, and indirectly, by creating a significant number of jobs as community health workers as well as more highly trained community midwives. This has led to an increase in the number of outpatient visits from 0.23 in 2004 to 1.20 in 2011, and increases in birth attendance by skilled providers from about 14 percent in 2003 to 34 percent in 2010 (Figure 3.1).

Today, basic health services have been extended to cover all 34 provinces and there have been remarkable gains in health outcomes. From 2002 to 2010, the infant mortality rate fell from 165 to 103 (38 percent) and under-five mortality fell from 257 to 149 (42 percent), and the total fertility rate decreased from 7.2 to 6.3. Meanwhile, the maternal mortality ratio is estimated by an interagency

Table 3.6	Summary Results of Pillar 1— Health
Results associated with Bank Group goals	**Bank Group contribution to results**
Bank Group Objective: Promote rapid improvement in service delivery in the health sector.	
• Strong strategic vision and policy framework established in 2002/3 helped Ministry of Public Health (MOPH) ensure delivery of a basic package of health services • Capacity to manage contracting out to NGOs complemented with relatively robust monitoring of trends in service access, quality, and utilization by an independent monitoring entity. Strong MOPH role in donor coordination, with three major development partners following complementary approach to service delivery and system development, now facilitated through ARTF financing. • Functioning public health care facilities increased from 496 in 2002 to over 2,000 in 2011; coverage of basic health services reached all 34 provinces. From 2002 to 2010, the infant mortality rate fell by 38 percent, under-five mortality fell by 42 percent, and the maternal mortality ratio declined significantly from an uncertain baseline to about 460/100,000.	• Strategically focused policy dialogue in early stages focused on how to implement a vision strongly owned by the government and maintained throughout period. • Flexible and responsive approach to building capacity within MOPH for management of NGOs providing service delivery through a "learning by doing" approach in two supporting investment projects; three complementary AAA products document early gains and identify future policy issues; donor inputs coordinated by complementary IDA and ARTF support. • Bank encouraged and supported independent, third-party monitoring of service delivery outputs and outcomes. • IFC investments in a private hospital in FY09 contributed to reaching nearly 8,000 patients in Afghanistan.

Figure 3.1

Results from Surveys on Trends in Delivery Care from a Medically Skilled Provider, Afghanistan, 2003–10

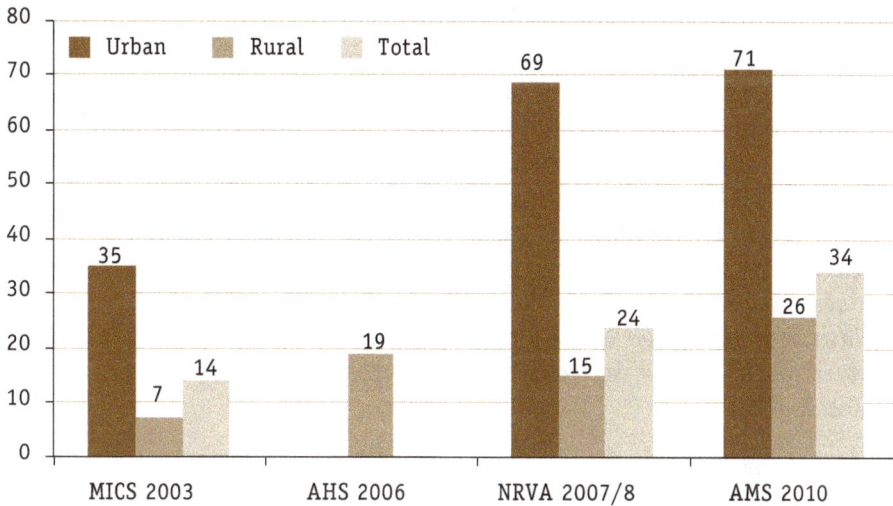

Source: Afghanistan Mortality Survey 2010 (p 80).

Note: AMS 2010 is based on the last live birth in the five-year period prior to the survey; the Bank's National Risk and Vulnerability Assessment 2007/8 (Icon Institute 2009) and the Multiple Indicator Cluster Survey 2003 (UNICEF 2003) are based on the last live birth in the two years prior to the survey; Afghanistan Health Survey 2006 is based on the last live births to currently married women in the two years prior to the survey (JHU and IIHMR 2008).

report to have declined significantly from an uncertain baseline to about 460/100,000.[4]

Improvements in health services are affirmed by independent evidence from IEG's beneficiary survey.[5] The 2012 survey, conducted in two provinces, found that almost 60 percent of respondents reported improvement in access to health services, with results somewhat better for Nangarhar Province in the east than for Herat in the west. The results from a Facebook survey[6] conducted by IEG were even higher: 73 percent of those polled in Dari or Pashtu reported the existence of a health facility within an hour's walk of their village. Reports from other sources also attest to significant improvements in health sector performance. The Asia Foundation's 2011 survey (Asia Foundation 2011) across the 34 provinces of Afghanistan shows that the accessibility of health care services is viewed positively by 68 percent of respondents.[7] This is consistent with the fact that the proportion of respondents giving a positive assessment of the availability of clinics, hospitals, and medicines in 2011 is the highest recorded in any year.

At the same time, it is evident to observers in the MOPH and elsewhere that Afghanistan will continue to face challenges in the health sector for some time. Infant and under-five mortality rates in Afghanistan are still higher than the average for low-income children elsewhere, and much remains to be done to improve the quality and responsiveness of the services that are available. The Agency Coordinating Body for Afghan Relief recently reported, based on 48 focus groups held between July 2011 and September 2011 (ACBAR, 2011), that:

> Progress has been patchy and inadequate. Afghanistan still has one of the worst health indicators in the world, with 50 women dying daily during pregnancy or childbirth and one child in five dying before their fifth birthday. Of the approximately 14,000 primary and secondary schools, nearly half have no building—leaving children to study in vulnerable open spaces, often without any text books. Conflict, insecurity, and weak state capacity have clearly been a challenge. But all too often, the *focus has been on increasing the quantity of services and their coverage, with too little attention given to the quality of those services, the ability of the population to use the services, or their sustainability.* [emphasis added (ACBAR 2011: 1)]

A recent study of national health accounts in Afghanistan also suggests that health financing will be a major future challenge (Islamic Republic of Afghanistan 2011). Total health expenditures in Afghanistan were about $1.1 billion in 2008/2009, almost 10 percent of the country's GDP. Of total health expenditure, government sources of funding accounted for 6 percent; donor sources, 18 percent; and private sources, 76 percent. Out-of-pocket spending on health was $31 per person out of a total per capita expenditure of $42. While implementation of the Basic Package of Health Services (BPHS) has greatly improved access to and utilization of simple, primary levels of care, high levels of private spending for secondary and tertiary care suggest considerable future challenges in improving sector efficiency and equity.

The relevance and efficacy of the Bank's work in the health sector stems from its three-pronged approach to assist the government— *policy dialogue* coordinated with other donors and technical agencies to develop a sector strategy, *specific investments* through IDA aimed at immediate improvement of the delivery of health services, and *analytical work* to guide strategic planning and evidence-based decision making. Starting from a Joint Needs Assessment mission in 2002, led by the Bank and the World Health Organization (WHO), the MOPH gave priority to delivery of a BPHS for provision of cost-effective services to control communicable diseases and improve and extend reproductive health, child health, and nutrition-related services. WHO played a key role in helping the MOPH flesh out the details of the service standards for the BPHS.

World Bank Group Contributions

The Bank also assisted the government in developing the institutional design of a national health program for rapid, effective service delivery, particularly through effective analytic work during the Preliminary Needs Assessment. In this design, MOPH retained responsibility for managing the BPHS and for contracting out service delivery to NGOs (box 3.1). The program included

Three Elements of Success in the Health Sector

The impressive results achieved in the health sector must be attributed to the government's investment program and support from several donors, in addition to the Bank's investments. Three elements of the early decisions made appear to be significant factors underlying the relative success in health sector achievements:

- There was early agreement with the MOF and the MOPH that development partners would work to assist the MOPH to align donor support with the BPHS, which created a common approach to improving access across provinces. Developed through intensive collaboration among donors, technical assistance, and with strong leadership from the MOPH, the BPHS set out very clear guidance on what interventions would be supplied for each of the basic elements of the health system, including specification of roles, requisite inputs, and specifications for how performance of specific interventions would be monitored. This established a common set of service delivery standards that was used by all development partners and providers. In the process of agreeing to the BPHS, the government and donors made significant efforts to rapidly scale up training and deployment of community health workers and female health providers and strengthen the basic functions of the MOPH at the national, provincial, and district levels.

- The government and development partners agreed, in a highly innovative and, at the time, quite controversial decision, to contract out the delivery of a BPHS to NGOs. Each of the three major development partners active in the sector developed different approaches to the contracting out process. The European Union (EU) and USAID managed the contracts themselves or through the offices of contracted technical assistance agencies, and the Bank worked to ensure that the MOPH would learn how to manage the Performance Partnership Agreements, which were lump sum contracts employed by NGOs to provide the BPHS.

- Particularly significant in view of the need to hold NGOs accountable for delivering the BPHS, the Bank provided support to results management (through the development of capacity to provide independent monitoring of service delivery quantity and quality) through a contract, which was competitively bid, with the Johns Hopkins University working in collaboration with the Indian Institute of Health Management Research. The JHU and IIHMR team in turn developed a Balanced Scorecard, which employed intensive observation and questionnaires of a random sample of health facilities at the district level to routinely assess six dimensions of service delivery quantity and quality. This helped the government improve significantly the availability and use of information on service delivery results in decision making. There is little question that the Bank's early focus on getting the government's policy framework focused on effectively balancing NGO commitment and the development of strong stewardship functions, particularly the capacity of the MOPH to hold NGOs accountable for results in service delivery, contributed to evident gains in the health sector.

strengthening the policy and leadership roles of the MOPH and its capacity to manage the contracting process and regulate service delivery through robust monitoring and evaluation of the performance of contracted service providers. The approach was also endorsed by the MOF and became the institutional framework for structuring donor assistance to the sector.

As evidence of the broad success of the initial approach to supporting the BPHS, the Bank sought to deepen and broaden its policy advice through strategically valuable analytic work in the latter half of the evaluation period. A major review of the health program (Belay 2010) consolidated lessons learned through the contracting approach for delivery of the BPHS. The review included a comprehensive assessment of health workforce planning issues, as well as documentation of the extent and implications of the very high levels of out-of-pocket health expenditure. In addition, the Bank conducted the first national-level assessment of nutrition issues in Afghanistan, which included policy recommendations for direct service provision (through adjustments in the design of the BPHS, which are now under way) and encouraged the development a multisectoral response to nutritional issues (Levitt and others 2011).

Noting the significant impact of the prolonged conflict and insecurity on the population, the Bank prepared a constructive policy brief on mental health issues and possible avenues for addressing them in 2011 (World Bank 2011). Each of these studies was carefully disseminated through short, accessible, policy-focused summaries that were published and distributed in Dari as well as English. The three high-quality AAA products have strengthened the learning process approach and enabled broader knowledge sharing from the Afghan experience.

The Bank complemented its policy advice with an investment program of $224.0 million.[8] The FY03 Emergency Health Sector Reconstruction and Development Project ($59.6 million IDA grant, plus two additional financing grants of $30 million and $20 million) served as the vehicle for putting key elements of the national health policy into place, using Performance-based Partnership Agreements for the MOPH to manage NGO contracts. Over 5 percent of project costs were earmarked for the baseline and follow-up surveys and project assessments. The Strengthening Health Activities for the Rural Poor (SHARP) Project, approved in FY09 with IDA ($79 million) and ARTF ($34 million) funding, along with $17.7 million from the Japan Social Development Fund (JSDF), continues support to the BPHS and the contracting-out process, including the MOPH's stewardship capacity, monitoring and evaluation, and additional research for impact evaluation of the results-based financing model. The project has ensured program continuity through Performance-based Partnership Agreements in the eight provinces supported by the BPHS, along with direct service delivery by the MOPH using contracted-in staff in three provinces. USAID is now channeling its support to NGO contracts through the MOPH, and the EU anticipates moving to the same structure in the near future. The Bank also made important, smaller-scale investments in building capacity to respond to potential avian flu issues and to address HIV/AIDS (contracting NGOs to provide harm-reduction services). This is an appropriate approach given that the relatively small scale of HIV/AIDS in Afghanistan is driven primarily by injecting drug use.

EDUCATION

In 2001 the Afghan education system had limited capacity to supply basic school inputs such as buildings, teachers, materials, and textbooks. The school curriculum was limited and focused heavily on religious content taught to boys. Girls were excluded from the system. Teachers received no formal training and were not paid on time. Female teachers had been forbidden from teaching. Approximately 21,000 teachers served the school-age population, and most of these were under-educated. In 2002, there were only four functioning teacher training colleges in the country, with the capacity to produce 400 teachers each year.

The largest challenges to higher education were access and education quality. Under Communist and Taliban rule, higher education was largely sidelined. This had deleterious effects on the quality of faculty as well as university infrastructure. Most qualified faculty left the country. There were no investments in equipment and infrastructure, so universities deteriorated from their height in 1978, when Kabul had some good universities. There were no private universities in 2002, and all university education was centralized.

World Bank Group Objectives

The objectives were to increase enrollment at the primary, secondary, and vocational levels, with an improvement in gender parity. In 2001, the education system had extremely limited capacity, with fewer than a million boys and no girls in school. The government and donors identified education, particularly primary education, as a priority. Household demand for education grew immediately after the fall of the Taliban. The most acute challenges were lack of education infrastructure; a shortage of teachers, especially female teachers; education quality; and higher education.

Bank Group objectives over the past decade have been broadly aligned with the country strategy in the sector. Bank Group activities can be divided into two distinct periods: The early reengagement period in 2002–05 and the period after 2006 when stronger leadership in the Ministry of Education introduced a National Education Strategy and the Ministry of Higher Education introduced its own strategy. In February 2002, IDA, along with the Afghan Interim Authority and several other development partners, participated in a Joint Comprehensive Needs Assessment. An estimated $130 million was committed to finance the education sector for the first two years. Different development partners were quick to engage in the primary education subsector. After 2002, it was decided that recurrent costs would be financed by the ARTF.

Results

Three projects supported the education sector: Education Quality Improvement Program (EQUIP I and II), Strengthening Higher Education Project (SHEP), and the Afghan Skills Development Project with increased school access but mixed results in other areas (table 3.7).

Primary school enrollment has increased, with significant improvements in school infrastructure. Early investments focused more on access to schooling than on school quality. Primary school enrollment increased from

1 million students in 2001 to 7.2 million in 2011, resulting in a gross primary enrollment rate of 97 percent (net primary enrollment rate of 50 percent) and a gross secondary enrollment rate of 46 percent by 2010.[9] School infrastructure has significantly improved, and the ministry estimates that nearly half of primary schools now have a boundary wall, a separate latrine for girls, and drinking water, although the 2011 midterm review found that nearly three-fourths of schools were lacking boundary walls. The ratio of female to male primary school enrollment increased from 46 percent in 2002 to 69 percent by 2010 (appendix J, table J.7).

Substantial effort is now going into teacher training. In 23 provinces the Bank has supported in-service teacher training, while USAID supported this training in the remaining 11 provinces. Going forward, the Education Quality Improvement Program (EQUIP) is taking over this training role in all 34 provinces. The government has worked to increase the number of training colleges. From four functioning teacher training colleges in 2002, there are now 42 such colleges and 137 distance learning centers that connect teachers,[10] and the number of women participating in the teaching profession is on the increase. The Ministry of Education estimates that 31 percent of the 180,000 teachers enrolled in training colleges are female.

Investment in developing measurement and evaluative systems has been insufficient to monitor changes in educational outcomes. The evidence base for assessing improvements in educational outcomes, such as improvements in literacy and numeracy, is highly constrained. Data on retention rates and the amount of instructional time children receive in a year (ideally 700–900 hours), proxies for changes in educational outcome, are not encouraging. Retention rates are quite poor, suggesting that almost a fifth of children drop out before

Table 3.7	Summary Results of Pillar 1—Education
Results associated with Bank Group goals	**Bank Group contribution to results**
Bank Group Objective: Increase enrollment at the primary, secondary and vocational levels, with an improvement in gender parity.	
• Primary school enrollment increased from 1 million students in 2001 to 7.2 million in 2011 (net enrollment rate 50 percent). • Females comprise nearly 40 percent of primary school enrollment. • Some progress in enrollment in secondary, vocational, and higher education. • The Ministry of Education and Ministry of Higher Education developed national strategies, though the higher education law has not yet been approved by the Parliament. • There have been substantial investments in training teachers and generating more university faculty. • In vocational training, a National Qualifications Framework is under negotiation, and institutions for training have been established.	• Three projects supported the education sector: Education Quality Improvement Program (EQUIP I and II), Strengthening Higher Education Project (SHEP), and the Afghan Skills Development Project. • EQUIP is aligned with the National Education Sector strategy and has provided technical support toward achieving student enrollment and teacher training objectives. • SHEP was slow to start, but in the later period it provided assistance for improving university management and governance as well as resources for training faculty with partner universities abroad. • The Bank has worked to coordinate the National Qualifications Framework and provide vocational training through the Afghan Skills Development Project.

grade six, and limited data suggest that the target of 700 hours per year is not met in many schools (see discussion in Ecorys 2012).

Progress in higher education has been mixed. The Strengthening Higher Education Project (SHEP) had a slow start but the project duration has been extended and, in the later period, it has provided assistance for improving university management and governance as well as resources for training faculty with partner universities abroad. Currently 160,000 students are enrolled in university, a number that is expected to double in upcoming years since Afghanistan has a youth bulge, with more than half of its population below the age of 25. Funding of university education in the public sector remains centralized, though universities do have some autonomy over curriculums and what they teach.

There are now 24 functioning universities, and private universities are also operating. More faculty members are going abroad for degrees, but quality, of both faculty and of the education that students receive remains problematic. One current challenge is how to absorb youth into the labor market and how to provide them with useful and productive skills, whether through higher education or technical and vocational training. A total of 2,700 students have been enrolled under the Technical and Vocational Training Project, a very small number for a national program, and the project has suffered implementation problems.

World Bank Group Contribution

Although the Bank Group's assistance to the education sector has been aligned with the country strategy and national strategies, the Bank lacked a strong strategic vision in the initial years of reengagement, in part because other donors, such as the United Nations Children's Fund (UNICEF), were expected to play a more significant role. The initial Needs Assessment in the education sector did not present a set of clear policy options and did not help the government identify priorities for future policy for which there was sustained ownership. Nor did it help align the efforts of the many donors who were keen to participate in the sector to align around a clear vision of the future educational system. An early commitment to support the development of a strategic policy framework for the sector, incorporated in the first EQUIP (EQUIP I), was not completed. The Bank's analytic work in the sector was inadequate; more investment in strategic AAA could have helped early on in developing a strategic vision.

The government did not find the Bank's initial emergency operation particularly responsive to the need for fast, visible progress. The Bank initially committed to providing assistance to the higher education subsector and to supporting female participation and enrollment through nonformal education mechanisms and early childhood development activities. These were to be supported by an Emergency Rehabilitation and Development Project. After project approval, the Ministries of Finance and Education decided that investments in nonformal education and early childhood programs were not immediate priorities. The

Bank responded to client demand and the emergency project was restructured, with a new focus on assistance to improve school quality (in parallel with investments to improve access) through community mobilization for general education, particularly for girls, and developing a medium-term policy framework and improving the government's capacity.

Bank projects supported all three education subsectors: EQUIP I and II covered primary and secondary education, and SHEP covered tertiary education. Both projects are central to the implementation of the government's national educational policies. Bank AAA also contributed directly to the preparation of the Afghanistan Skills Development Project, a technical and vocational training project that was approved in 2007. All of these projects sought to develop sustainable, country-owned, and country-managed projects, but the results have been mixed.

Community mobilization under the EQUIP program has enhanced local ownership, but inadequate supervision affected quality. EQUIP has played a significant role in helping the government increase student enrollment and provided technical support for teacher training, but the design of EQUIP placed little emphasis on results or on monitoring and evaluation. Social mobilization activities have been conducted in 11,000 communities and resulted in locally owned school improvement plans, and more than 9,900 schools have received Quality Enhancement Grants. With support from EQUIP, there have also been substantial gains in school infrastructure. Ministry data indicate that more than 3,400 classrooms were built under EQUIP I, and a further 1,800 are being built under EQUIP II (Ecorys 2012, pp. 48–50).

Despite these gains, there are indications—including from the Bank's midterm review of the EQUIP program—of gaps in construction quality that are attributable, at least in part, to limited capacity and leakage in the use of funds, issues exacerbated by difficulties in supervision of school construction and performance caused by increasing security risks.[11] An independent monitoring agent, recruited for the ARTF in 2011, is conducting field verification of physical facilities, but supervision of education services remains challenging, and verification of school facilities is just one aspect of a functioning education program. Donors, too, have expressed concern about the quality of monitoring and reporting in EQUIP (see, for example, Ecorys 2012).

Despite the gender-sensitive design of the EQUIP program, significant challenges remain in closing the gender gap in education. The program encourages girls' education by prioritizing girls' schools, recruitment and training of female teachers, and female representation in the School Management Committees *(shura)*. However, results are mixed (Jackson 2011). Overall, enrollment rates have improved. EQUIP I and II have enabled enrollment of 701,043 boys and 469,130 girls. School *shuras* have been established in 11,000 communities and almost 10,000 schools received Quality Enhancement Grants for purchase of school supplies and equipment, and over 5,000 classrooms were built.

However, over 30 percent of schools completed through infrastructure grants do not comply with the gender-equity criteria necessary for girls' attendance. An inspection carried out for the 2011 midterm review found that 50 percent of the schools were missing latrines and over three-quarters were without boundary walls. These elements are significant barriers to female education in Afghanistan. Dropouts are also a serious concern, particularly for girls as they graduate from primary education; this is not covered adequately by EQUIP's monitoring system. Conditional cash transfers have been used effectively to increase enrollment rates for girls by about 10 percent in Pakistan and Turkey and by over 30 percent for girls transitioning from primary to secondary education in Cambodia (World Bank 2012b). Such incentives could overcome both cultural and economic constraints to girls' education, but are not yet part of the Afghanistan program. Insecurity and the absence of female teachers are reported to be the main factors inhibiting female education (AIHRC 2010).

Security constraints have been aggravated by rising insurgency in the past few years, especially in some parts of the country, and these have acted as a significant deterrent for girls' education. The impact of the 2014 transition on girls' education in particular, and gender equality in general, is among the biggest worries of the Afghan government and its international partners.

While EQUIP succeeded in gaining country ownership of projects and activities, this was not fully the case in higher education or technical and vocational training, which had a slow start and have had more modest outcomes. The higher education law has not yet been approved by the Parliament, and a National Qualifications Framework for vocational training is still under negotiation. SHEP started slowly due to a design flaw that assumed universities could operate in a decentralized manner, when in fact they are highly centralized and not allowed to collect their own income. Subsequently, SHEP addressed the design flaw by providing block grants to 12 universities and improving university management, as well as providing resources for training faculty at universities abroad. Although the initial design of the project was flawed, over time the Bank has aligned itself better with the government's national priorities and supported the Ministry of Higher Education in developing a strategy.

The Afghan Skills Development Project achieved modest outcomes during FY08–11. The project has been successful in providing support to six institutions for technical and vocational training and in establishing the National Institution of Management Administration, a new institution designed to train junior management personal, junior accountants, and ICT technicians. It successfully graduated 1,510 students in 2011, and 1,058 of these graduates were given diplomas by the University of Jyvskala of Finland. In informal technical and vocational training, the project financed the training of 7,500 poor women, marginalized farmers, and youth.

While the project was analytically sound, responding to three economic concerns—youth unemployment, reduced employment prospects for Afghan citizens, and the country's success in getting children re-enrolled in school—

it suffered from the challenges of coordinating across 11 ministries. In addition, the program has suffered implementation problems largely due to staff turnover and shortcomings in government leadership. In 2010, several government staffers working on the project left, and the project did not have any disbursements during FY10. Inconsistencies in donor support for skills development also hamper the development of a coherent approach. Some support in-country skills training, others send students abroad for training. One complaint heard in the field was that the availability of Bank staff has varied. While the Bank was perceived to be more responsive in the past, clients feel that it has become increasingly difficult to access the Bank's team.

Overall Assessment for Health and Education

Table 3.8 summarizes the achievements of performance benchmarks in the health and education sectors.

Table 3.8	Status of Performance Benchmarks	
Source	Benchmark	Status
Health		
2003 TSS	Number of children immunized	Good progress: By 2006, full immunization (BCG, OPV3, DPT3, and measles) increased from 15 percent to 27 percent (rural); by 2010, immunization for measles had increased to 62 percent.
2003 TSS	Number of people with access to/reached by basic public health services	Good progress: By 2006, contraceptive prevalence increased from 5 percent to 15 percent, skilled antenatal care from 4.6 percent to 32.3 percent; skilled birth attendance from 6.0 percent to 18.9 percent
2006 ISN	70 percent DPT coverage among children 12–23 months of age; 90 percent of rural population with access to BPHS	Good progress: 85 percent coverage in 2008 (HMIS data) compared to 2006 data.[a] DPT1 (60 percent), DPT2 (48 percent), DPT3 (35 percent). By 2008/09, 82 percent of the population had access to primary healthcare
2006 ISN	Average quality of care in publicly financed health facilities as measured by balanced scorecard reaches 60 percent	Achieved: The national median score for the average performance across the 26 indicators in BSC increased from 50.4 percent in 2004 to 71.7 percent in 2008
2009 ISN	Progress in achieving universal access to the BPHS with increased gender parity in access to services	Good progress: Outpatient visits per capita increased from 1.20 in 2010 to 1.27 in 2011.
Education		
2003 TSS	Number of children in school, disaggregated by gender	Good progress: 4.3 million children enrolled in school by 2003, of which 34 percent were female
2006 ISN	10 percent net enrollment increase (yearly) in primary education and an increase in the enrollment of girls from 40 percent net to 50 percent	Good progress in enrollment, especially in primary education. Under EQUIP I and II, 701,043 boys and 469,130 girls enrolled.[b]
2009 ISN	Further increase in enrollment at the primary, secondary and vocational levels, with an improvement in gender parity	7.2 million in school by 2011, of which over 40 percent are girls. Slow progress in vocational levels with 2,700 students enrolled and 1,510 graduated from NIMA.

Note: DPT = diphtheria, pertussis, and tetanus; BCG = Bacillus Calmetter-Guérin; OPV = oral polio vaccine.

a. Earlier data are from Afghanistan Household Survey conducted by Johns Hopkins University in 2006.

b. EQUIP data are from Mid-Term Review of July 2011.

Risks to Development Outcomes

Public Financial Management: The slow progress on upstream budget preparation and procurement by line ministries and subnational entities risks undermining the progress made on accounting, financial control, and reporting, and hampers improvements in service delivery. This risk is heightened by the faster increases in core expenditures (particularly those related to security) relative to domestic revenues and the threat to fiscal and macroeconomic stability.

Public Sector Governance: The reliance on the second civil service for gains in public administration and governance leads to multiple risks, as signaled above: the risk of sustainability if security deteriorates or donor funding decreases and the risk that the extreme pay differentials will become politically and socially untenable. There is also the risk that as foreign forces leave, the regime may find it necessary to roll back the administrative improvements that have been achieved, in order to make greater use of public resources to make the nontransparent transfers to elite supporters needed to sustain a ruling coalition. The dominance of security forces on the public payroll and operational budget poses the additional risk of a power imbalance between the military and civilian sectors.

Health: While there is broad agreement among government officials and development partners on the relative success in the health sector due to the outsourcing of public health services to NGOs, there are risks to sustaining these results over the next decade. The continuity and quality of NGO services is dependent on the responsiveness and transparency of the contracting process, which has come under increasing stress since the integration of the program within MOPH. This is due to a lack of consistency in the length and scope of contracts; changes in the nature of contracts from "cost-plus-quality contracts" to "least-cost contracting"; and lack of ownership of the contracting-out approach, particularly among provincial health authorities.

The other key element of the program—third-party monitoring for results measurement—has suffered delays in implementation of the service delivery/balanced scorecard because of security issues and technical debates among the service provider, the Bank, and the MOPH. Early resolution of these issues to maintain a third-party verification system is essential for the preparation of a new sectorwide health program.

While there is growing demand for secondary and tertiary hospital services, it is important that work on secondary and tertiary levels of care not come at the cost of basic primary care.

Maintaining the momentum established on reproductive and women's health, which has been the main factor in improving health outcomes, is critical. However, retention of newly trained midwives in rural areas is low, with many recent graduates preferring to work in Kabul or other urban areas. Sustaining early gains in the health sector will not be possible without continued support for training and placement of female health workers.

Education: There is evident government ownership and widespread demand for education, but several risks remain. The country risk arising out of insecurity is substantial, particularly for female education, but high government ownership and beneficiary demand may suffice to offset this risk. The main risk to this subsector arises from the sustainability of the recurrent budget to fund teacher salaries.

Coordination across multiple institutions and ownership is a continued risk for higher education and technical and vocational training. The efforts to develop a National Qualifications Framework and address the fragmentation of coordinating partners in the Afghan Skills Development Project are steps in the right direction toward sustainability. There are now more frequent meetings across ministries on vocational training, but there is lack of real ownership among the ministries. This is a risk going forward. Without continued Bank support to coordinate the project, the vocational training program may not be sustainable. Similarly, while SHEP has made improvements in engaging the Ministry of Higher Education, this remains one of the weaker ministries, requiring more intensive supervision by Bank staff.

The sector has also suffered from frequent staff turnover in the Bank's team. Over the past 10 years the project has had five task team leaders. Individuals in the ministry feel that it has lacked a sense of continuity throughout the period, adding to sustainability risks. While in-country postings of two years are not unusual in FCS, there appears to be a need to consider alternate methods of ensuring continuity, either through support from staff in neighboring countries or by continued support from staff that are no longer based in the country office.

Notes

1. The same broad conclusions were reached by the IMF, which found "treasury, budgeting, and tax administration are fully functional. . . . (but) Low execution rates reflect capacity constraints, unrealistic multiyear budget and spending patterns with significant front-loading of spending, and poor procurement planning and contract management." IMF 2011, pp. 5, 15.

2. The top pay grade of the Bank-supported Management Capacity Program is $7,500 per month, which is over 11 times the top pay grade under the government's enhanced pay and grading scheme for civil servants.

3. For example, Nam Theun 2 Poverty Reduction Fund (Lao PDR), Oil and Natural Gas Sovereign Fund (Timor-Leste), Stabilization Fund (Mongolia).

4. Recent data are mostly from World Development Indicators which has figures validated by inter-agency estimates. The Afghanistan Mortality Survey (AMS), November, 2011 reports slightly lower figures but some scholars question the

internal consistency and therefore face validity of the AMS survey findings, particularly those pertaining to southern provinces (see, for instance, Hill, 2012). The maternal mortality ratio is from Trends in Maternal Mortality 1990-2010: WHO, UNICEF, UNFPA and The World Bank estimates (2012).

5. The beneficiary survey was conducted in January-February 2012 using radio advertisements to solicit responses from Nangarhar Province in the east and Herat Province in the west. Those responding with an SMS were surveyed in Dari and Pashtu by calling back their mobile phones. The survey received 298 respondents from Nangarhar and 366 from Herat.

6. The Facebook survey was conducted in February-March 2011.

7. The government's performance is rated most positively in the Asia Foundation survey with regard to the provision of basic services such as education (85 percent), healthcare (68 percent), and security (62 percent). Furthermore, in 2011, fewer respondents identified electricity, roads, and healthcare as major local problems than in almost any previous year, suggesting that progress is being made in these areas too.

8. The Health Sector Emergency Reconstruction and Development Project and two supplements ($110 million), the Strengthening Health Activity Project ($79 million IDA and $17 million from ARTF), the Afghanistan HIV/AIDS Prevention Project ($10 million), and support for an HIV/AIDS Prevention Project ($10 million) and for Avian Flu ($8 million)

9. World Development Indicators.

10. "Teacher training report," Ministry of Finance.

11. In 2009 the World Bank and Ministry of Education supported a study of security risks at the school level, which was conducted by CARE International. The study, based on analyses of databases maintained by the ministry and UNICEF, and more than 1,000 interviews of stakeholders at various levels, found that more than 670 attacks were carried out in 2008, including arson and murder of teachers and students, most frequently, arson of school buildings or inventory. About 20 percent of local education personnel interviewed stated that they had been threatened. Of all attacked schools, girls' schools account for 40 percent, while mixed schools (32 percent) and boys' schools (28 percent) made up the rest. NGO-supported schools seem to be less targeted than government-supported schools. The study concludes that "education stands the strongest chance of being optimally protected if the analysis, decision-making and implementation power of schools security is decentralized to the provincial, district and community levels" (Glad 2009).

References

ACBAR (Agency Coordinating Body for Afghan Relief). 2011. "Health and Education in Afghanistan: An Empty Gift." ACBAR, Kabul.

ADB (Asian Development Bank), UNDP (United Nations Development Program), and World Bank. 2002. *Afghanistan: Preliminary Needs Assessment for Recovery and Reconstruction*. New York, NY: UNDP.

AIHRC (Afghanistan Independent Human Rights Commission). 2010. *Afghanistan Independent Human Rights Commission Annual Report (1 January to 31 December 2009)*. Available at: http://www.unhcr.org/refworld/docid/4bb31a012.html.

Asia Foundation. 2011. *Afghanistan in 2011—A Survey of the Afghan People*. Kabul: Asia Foundation.

Belay, Tekabe A., ed. 2010. *Building on Early Gains in Afghanistan's Health, Nutrition and Population Sector*. Directions in Development Series. Washington, DC: World Bank.

Collier, Paul. 2009. *War, Guns and Votes*. New York: NY: HarperCollins.

Ecorys. 2012. *Evaluation of Norwegian Development Cooperation with Afghanistan 2001–2011*. Prepared for the Norwegian Agency for Development Cooperation Evaluation Department. Oslo: Norad.

Evans, Anne, Nick Manning, and Anne Tully, with Yasin Osmani and Andrew Wilder. 2004. *Subnational Administration: Assessment and Recommendations for Action*. Washington, DC: World Bank.

Glad, Marit. 2009. *Knowledge on Fire: Attacks on Education in Afghanistan: Risks and Measures for Successful Mitigation*. A study conducted by CARE on behalf of the World Bank and Ministry of Education of Afghanistan. September 2009. Available at: http://www.care.org/newsroom/articles/2009/11/Knowledge_on_Fire_Report.pdf.

Hill, Kenneth. 2012. Gains in Afghan Health. Too Good to be True? Washington, DC: Center for Global Development Brownbag, June 4, 2012. Available at: http://www.cgdev.org/doc/blog/Gains_in_Afghan_Health_CGD_Talk_pdf.pdf.

ICON-INSTITUTE. 2009. *National Risk and Vulnerability Assessment 2007/08: A Profile of Afghanistan, Main Report*. Cologne: ICON-INSTITUTE. IEG (Independent Evaluation Group, World Bank Group). 2007. *Development Results in Middle-Income Countries: An Evaluation of the World Bank's Support*. Washington, DC: World Bank.

Islamic Republic of Afghanistan. 2010. "Report on Analysis of Donor-funded Remuneration for Individuals Working in the Government."

———. 2011. "National Health Accounts Afghanistan 2008-2009: Preliminary Findings." Ministry of Public Health with USAID, Kabul.

Jackson, Ashley. 2011. *High Stakes: Girls Education in Afghanistan*. A joint agency research paper carried out with the Afghan Civil Society Forum, Afghan Development Association, Afghan Peace and Democracy Act, Afghan Women's Network, Afghan Women Services and Education Organization, All Afghan Women's Union, CARE Cooperation Center for Afghanistan, Coordination of Afghan Relief, Coordination of Humanitarian Assistance, Education Training Center for Poor Women and Girls of Afghanistan, Legal and Cultural Services for Afghan Women and Children, Oxfam,

Sanayee Development Organization, Shuhada, and the Swedish Committeefor Afghanistan. Oxford, U.K.: Oxfam International. Available at: http://www.oxfam.org/en/policy/high-stakes-girls-education-afghanistan.

JHU (Johns Hopkins University, Bloomberg School of Public Health) and IIHMR (Indian Institute of Health Management Research). 2008. *Afghanistan Health Survey 2006: Estimates of Priority Health Indicators.* Kabul: Ministry of Public Health.

Levitt, Emily, Kees Kostermans, Luc Laviolette, and Nkosinath Mbuya. 2011. *Malnutrition in Afghanistan.* Directions in Development Series. Washington, DC: World Bank.

Lister, Sarah, and Hamish Nixon. 2006. Provincial Governance Structures in Afghanistan: From Confusion to Vision? AREU Briefing Paper. Kabul: Afghanistan Research and Evaluation Unit.

United Nations Children's Fund (UNICEF), Central Statistics Office (Afghanistan). Afghanistan Multiple Indicator Cluster Survey. 2003. New York, United States: United Nations Children's Fund (UNICEF). Available at: http://www.childinfo.org/files/AfghanistanResults.pdf.

World Bank. 2002. "Afghanistan—Transitional Support Strategy." Report No. 23822 AF. Washington, DC: World Bank.

———. 2003. "Afghanistan—Transitional Support Strategy:." Report No. 25440 AF. Washington, DC: World Bank.

———. 2005. *Afghanistan: Managing Public Finances for Development.* Report No. 34582-AF. Washington, DC: World Bank.

———. 2007. "Afghanistan: Public Sector Accounting and Auditing: A Comparison to International Standards." Report No. 41041-AF. Financial Management Unit, South Asia Region, Washington, DC: World Bank.

———. 2008. *Afghanistan—Building an Effective State: Priorities for Public Administration Reform.* Kabul: AINA Media Culture Center.

———. 2010. *Public Expenditure Review 2010: Second Generation of Public Expenditure Reforms.* Washington, DC: World Bank.

———. 2011. "Non-Communicable Diseases (NCDs) in Afghanistan." Policy Brief, Washington, DC: World Bank.

———. 2012a. *Afghanistan in Transition: Looking Beyond 2014.* Washington, DC: World Bank.

———. 2012b. *World Development Report 2012: Gender Equality and Development.* Washington, DC: World Bank.

Chapter 4

Promoting Growth of the Rural Economy
and Improving Rural Livelihoods

Context

The agriculture sector (including livestock but excluding opium poppy production) accounts for about 30 percent of GDP and employs about 65 percent of the national labor force. If the estimated value of illegal opium poppy production (which replaced cotton on many farms in 2000) is included, the agriculture sector accounts for at least 35 percent of the economy. An overview of the issues associated with the opium poppy production in Afghanistan is presented in box 4.1. The agriculture sector also provides livelihoods for about 75 percent of the population, and hence per capita rural incomes and welfare are much lower than in urban areas.

Rural incomes vary substantially between regions due to the differences in growth resulting from the wide range of topographic, climate, water resource, and soil conditions across Afghanistan. Growth and reduced variability in agricultural production and rural development have been high priorities in the government's development strategies.[1] Nevertheless, the NSP has been the Bank's flagship in this cluster of activities. While the NSP's support for agriculture has been modest in the context of Afghanistan's need to stimulate growth, it has made an important contribution to social stability in rural areas.

The Bank Group's strategy for promoting rural growth and improved rural livelihoods included: (i) support for rural programs where there are high returns in terms of legitimate economic outputs and poverty reduction and (ii) linkages between rural development programs of the Ministry of Rural Rehabilitation and Development (MRRD) and the Ministry of Agriculture, renamed the Ministry of Agriculture, Irrigation, and Livestock (MAIL).

The Bank Group supported this strategy through assistance in three areas from 2002 to 2011: rehabilitation of rural roads ($352 million); the NSP ($1.35 million); agriculture/rural development, which includes rehabilitation of water delivery for irrigation systems, rejuvenation of the horticulture and livestock sectors, development of rural enterprises, and related activities to generate rural livelihoods ($389 million). The third of these includes support for developing a focused agriculture-rural development strategy, as well as water resources development in the Kabul Basin for urban and rural use.[2] The most recent ISN (World Bank 2012) also envisaged that IFC would scale up its work in the horticulture sector.

Rural Roads

In 2000, rural roads in Afghanistan were in extremely poor condition, having suffered wartime destruction and decades with almost no repair or maintenance. This was a substantial constraint to delivering social services to rural areas and to the efficient marketing of agricultural products. One of the government's national initiatives agreed at the Bonn Conference in 2001 was the National Emergency Employment Program (NEEP), a labor-intensive program to rehabilitate rural roads throughout Afghanistan.[3] NEEP was intended to rapidly

Background

Afghanistan produces more than 90 percent of the world's high-quality opium. High prices make it the most profitable crop, and strong demand has driven the estimated value of this illegal crop to about $1.4 billion, about 9 percent of GDP in 2011. Taxes of 10 percent on the opium trade imposed by the Taliban have financed their activities; not surprisingly, poppy-producing areas have the highest incidence of insecurity and conflict. As a USAID report (USAID and Checchi and Co. Consulting 2007) noted, "The comparative advantage of Afghanistan in opium production lies solely in its lawlessness." Nevertheless, poppy production has raised the incomes of many farmers, processors, and traders, and has led to lower poverty in poppy-producing provinces—23 percent compared to 36 percent for all provinces. Drug addiction in Afghanistan is also reported to be increasing.

Bank Studies

The Bank has made a substantial investment in studies of the drug industry over the past decade. The first, "Drugs and Development in Afghanistan" (Byrd and Ward 2004), concluded that "The nexus of drugs with insecurity and warlords" threatened "the entire state-building and reconstruction agenda." The paper recommended aggressive interdiction combined with an alternative livelihoods strategy. The second was a collaborative effort with the United Nations Office of Drugs and Crime, which resulted in analytical papers focused on relevant issues in FY07 (Buddenberg and Byrd 2006). There is no evidence that the papers had a significant impact on government antinarcotics policies or programs. The final study conducted in collaboration with DFID (Ward and others 2008), examined how incentives could be used to influence farmers to diversify away from opium to other high-value agricultural crops. However, evidence in this paper that farmers in major poppy-producing areas could be attracted to diversify from opium to other crops was weak.

Bank Strategy

In its appraisals of the Emergency Irrigation Project and the Horticulture and Livestock Projects the Bank asserted that the projects would generate incentives for diversification out of poppy production. This has not occurred, and this rationale for agricultural projects was dropped.

The Bank's latest ISN indicated that the Bank "will not be playing an active role on counter-narcotics," although it would help "build the institutions and open the economy that will help give the rural population other options to illicit activities."

Sources: Byrd and Ward 2004; Buddenberg and Byrd (eds) 2006; Ward and others 2008; UNODC 2011; Islamic Republic of Afghanistan and World Bank 2010; Ministry of Economy and World Bank, "Poverty Status in Afghanistan," July 2010. USAID and Checchi and Co. Consulting 2007; World Bank 2012b.

generate employment in rural areas at a subsistence wage and provide a safety net to as many people as possible in as short a time as possible. The context for this project was a degraded rural roads system and chronic deprivation in rural areas, compounded by the negative impact of severe droughts in 2000 to 2002 and again in 2004. These factors conspired to displace large populations, creating massive disruptions to rural livelihoods.

WORLD BANK GROUP OBJECTIVES

The objectives were to rehabilitate rural access roads to relieve constraints on delivering social services, improve marketing efficiency of agricultural products, and provide employment for poor rural households. For the 80 percent of the

Afghan population living in rural areas, incomes were barely at subsistence levels when the Bank's assistance programs for improving rural access, based on labor-intensive methods, were launched. These objectives were relevant to the development strategies of the government and the Bank Group.

RESULTS

The results are summarized in table 4.1. The first rural road rehabilitation program, the Labor Intensive Works Program, was started during the Bank's re-engagement in Afghanistan. The program, initiated in May 2002, focused on providing employment and rehabilitating irrigation systems and rural roads at the provincial and district levels. It was part of the Emergency Community and Public Works Empowerment Program, the initial phase of the NSP. In early 2003, the Labor Intensive Works Program separated from the larger program and eventually became Phase I of the NEEP, which focused exclusively on rural roads through the Ministry of Public Works (secondary roads) and the MRRD (tertiary roads).

Following a government and Bank review of the program in 2004/2005, the rural roads rehabilitation program was reoriented to focus less on employment generation and more on improving the quality of roads and their sustainability. Afghanistan has approximately 40,000 kilometers of rural roads, about 10,000 kilometers of which have been rehabilitated since 2001. Close to 60 percent of the rehabilitation was done with World Bank/ARTF assistance, but Provincial Reconstruction Teams funded by bilateral agencies and the U.S.-financed Commander's Emergency Response Program also provided financial support for rural road rehabilitation.

Table 4.1	Summary Results of Pillar 2—Rural Roads
Results associated with Bank Group goals	**Bank Group contribution to results**
Bank Group Objective: Further rehabilitation of rural access roads (ISN, May 5, 2009) and provide employment for poor rural households.	
• Of Afghanistan's approximately 40,000 kilometers of rural roads, 10,000 have been rehabilitated since 2001. Close to 60 percent of this work was done with Bank/ARTF assistance. • Provincial Reconstruction Teams and the Commander's Emergency Response Program, both financed by the United States, also provided financial support for rural road rehabilitation, together with the Bank/ARTF-funded NSP and a few bilateral donors. • The government states it now has the capacity to implement rural road rehabilitation programs itself due to the Bank's support for staff training.	• Three rural road rehabilitation projects (NEEP, the National Emergency Employment Program for Rural Areas, and the National Emergency Rural Access Project) were financed by the Bank and the ARTF. Together they rehabilitated close to 5,900 kilometers of rural roads and provided about 8 million days of employment. However, sustainability of rural roads remains a challenge. • The Bank and the government have differed on policy issues for rural roads, such as their width and surfacing. • A policy on the width and surfacing for rural roads could have been resolved five years ago when the government requested Bank advice on rural access policy. The Bank did not respond, and preparation of a rural access policy was stalled. It is being prepared as part of the National Emergency Rural Access Project.
Source: IEG evaluation.	

The government/Bank review revealed that employment benefits from the Labor Intensive Works Program and NEEP were not accruing to the poorest groups in the population. The roads were often located far from village settlements and construction quality was poor. These projects therefore had not functioned as intended. The National Emergency Employment Program for Rural Access Project (NEEPRA), approved in June 2002, placed greater emphasis on the quality of rehabilitation, reconstruction, and maintenance of essential rural access infrastructure, using labor-based approaches when appropriate, enhancing short-term employment opportunities for the rural poor. The National Emergency Rural Access Project (NERAP), which was approved in FY08 and followed NEEPRA, also adopted this model. These objectives were relevant to Afghanistan given the devastation of its rural infrastructure and high rural unemployment.

Substantial progress was made on achieving physical targets. The first two Bank-assisted projects to focus exclusively on rural roads (NEEP and NEEPRA) had a combined target to rehabilitate 6,500 kilometers of rural roads; they had rehabilitated 4,670 kilometers when the projects closed. The ongoing NERAP Project, with a rehabilitation target of 3,600 kilometers, had rehabilitated 1,260 kilometers of rural roads by mid-FY11. Taken together, these three projects accounted for 60 percent of all rural road rehabilitation over the decade and generated about 8 million days of employment, compared with their original combined target of 9.5 million days.

Nevertheless, the Bank made little progress on policy issues. The government/Bank review of the Labor Intensive Works Program and NEEP also drew attention to the absence of an "explicit rural development strategy" and a "cohesive rural transport or an overall transport policy" (Islamic Republic of Afghanistan and World Bank 2005, p. 5). Subsequently the government asked the Bank to assist in the preparation of a rural access policy to inform the NERAP.

Although the Bank prepared a Policy Note in 2007 (World Bank 2007d), there is no record of a government response. It took another four years (when the NERAP project was being appraised) to initiate preparation of a formal rural access policy, which is expected to be completed by the end of 2012. In the meantime, the Bank and the government differed on policy issues for rural roads, such as their appropriate width and surfacing, which are major concerns for a country with considerable geographic variation and severe winter conditions.

Bank staff has advised that an agreement was reached on rural road standards for the National Rural Access Program in mid-2011, and there was a regular dialogue with the government authorities on issues such as the relative responsibilities of the Public Works Department and MRRD, as well as a strategy for maintenance. However, the government response to the CPE reflects continued concern that the rural roads program needs to adapt to the geography and climatic conditions of the country. As it is, there continue to be differences between the Bank and the government on the match between the rural roads program and Afghanistan's rural transportation needs. The lack of a policy has also been reflected in the inadequate arrangements for maintenance of rural roads. If not addressed successfully, this issue will remain a threat to the sustainability of all rural roads.

The contribution of the rural road rehabilitation program is acceptable progress toward the target, given the difficult security circumstances. However, the substantial delay in assistance in preparation of a rural access policy, belatedly being addressed under the NERAP, and continued gaps in the strategy for maintenance of rural roads were significant shortcomings.

National Solidarity Program

NSP is widely recognized as one of the government's key National Priority Programs. The 2012 ISN calls it the flagship of the Bank's program in rural areas (World Bank 2012, p. 23). The program relies on facilitating partners, contracted by MRRD, to organize rural communities into locally elected CDCs, and to help them identify priority subprojects to be financed by a grant to each CDC.

WORLD BANK GROUP OBJECTIVES

The Bank Group's objectives during the evaluation period were to strengthen community-level governance and to improve the access of rural communities to social and productive infrastructure and services by completing, expanding, and building on the rollout of the NSP across the country. The objectives were relevant to the government's 2004 and 2008 development strategies.

RESULTS

"NSP increases connections between villages and the central government and ... improve(s) the perceptions of male villagers of . . . government representatives. . . . The program, at this interim stage, is found to improve access of villagers to drinking water and electricity, but does not appear to impact the access of villagers to infrastructure or result in any changes in overall economic activity, female socialization, or levels of community trust or the prevalence of disputes" (Beath and others 2010, p. 73).

The outputs achieved by the NSP are remarkable in both scale and geographic coverage (table 4.2). Since 2003, the NSP has reached all 34 provinces and resulted in the establishment of 27,360 CDCs, which have undertaken at least 59,629 locally identified subprojects.[4] There is little doubt that NSP grants to communities have improved local capacity to plan and manage development or rehabilitation of basic public infrastructure in rural areas. These subprojects have largely consisted of physical works for transport (26 percent), water and sanitation (24 percent), irrigation (19 percent), power (12 percent), and education facilities (10 percent).

Table 4.2	Summary Results of Pillar 2—National Solidarity Program	
Results associated with Bank Group goals	**Bank Group contribution to results**
Bank Group Objective: Strengthen community-level governance and to improve the access of rural communities to social and productive infrastructure and services.	
• Since 2003, the NSP has supported 27,360 CDCs, and financed 59,629 subprojects, 80 percent of which have been completed. • NSP grants to communities (assisted by facilitating partners) have improved local capacity to manage the planning, rehabilitation, and development of basic public infrastructure in rural areas. • NSP subprojects are primarily for transport (26 percent), water and sanitation (24 percent), irrigation (19 percent), power (12 percent), and education (10 percent). • CDCs have also contributed to building social capital and empowerment of women in rural communities, although results vary across the country.	• Four Bank-assisted NSP projects were implemented, two-thirds of the funding coming from the ARTF. • NSP's facilitating partners obtained funds from other donors to broaden their activities beyond NSP's scope. The result has been additional services to communities. • Government and Bank programs are using the CDCs as entry points for other development projects. • The sustainability of NSP will depend on the transition of CDCs into village councils (envisaged under the constitution). A proposal for this transition is currently under consideration by the government. However, the links with other tiers of local government are still being debated.
Source: IEG evaluation.	

At the outcome level, results are more modest. Results from the 2009 survey for the impact evaluation[5] showed improvements in villagers' perceptions of well-being and that villagers are more optimistic about future economic changes. However, at the time of that evaluation, there were no significant impacts yet on objective measures of economic welfare, such as levels of household income or consumption. The results from the 2011 survey were not available at the end of 2012.

Gender impacts of the NSP have been positive but have not yet translated into outcomes. The NSP has produced a small change in the beliefs of male villagers concerning the involvement of women in village governance. The men had become more open to the existence of women's councils and a larger proportion supported the participation of village women in the selection of the village headman.

There is no evidence, however, of the impact of the NSP on attitudes toward female participation in community life generally. The NSP has not affected the frequency of socialization among female villagers, although it increased slightly the tendency of women to leave their compound without a male chaperone and the probability of village women holding meetings with women from other villages or with government officials (Beath and others 2010, p. 46).

The program has resulted in increased involvement of women in income-generating activities, but there is no evidence yet of impacts on asset ownership by women, on the control of women over earned income or owned assets, or on the involvement of women in household decisions. Gender impacts also vary considerably across the country (Echavez 2012).

NSP's impact on social capital and local governance is less clear and more contested than its impact on local infrastructure development. The 2009 evaluation found that NSP did not have any impact on measures of community trust or solidarity (Beath and others 2010, p. 52) or on the outbreak of village disputes or tribal feuds. The governance effects come from the formation and functioning of CDCs and the increased connections between villages and select government and nongovernment institutions (Beath and others 2010, p. 41). The interaction between citizens and the government within the project domain has improved, but the NSP had limited impact on the legitimacy of government authority (Beath and others 2010, p. 45). And in terms of the spillover effects on other development programs and civic activities, the evidence on governance remains weak.[6]

The evidence on community-level democratic governance at the village level is unsubstantiated. Although CDC elections are expected to be held every three years, and feedback from the facilitating partners indicates some rotation does occur. Since September 2006, when the role of the German Agency for Technical Cooperation (GTZ) as oversight consultant was discontinued, neither the Bank nor MRRD have been able to monitor these elections systematically. Some studies have found that the CDCs function largely as a conduit for development funding, but that other customary social organizations—*shuras* (religious councils) and *jirga* (traditional tribal assemblies)—play a stronger role in dispute resolution (especially for local land disputes) and enhancing personal safety and security (Murtazashvili 2009).[7] An audit of the NSP by the Special Investigator General for Afghanistan Reconstruction of the NSP concludes that the data do not exist to establish improvements in local governance by the formation of CDCs (SIGAR 2011, p. 17).

IEG found positive benefits reported by two-thirds of respondents, although there was some regional variation in results. IEG's beneficiary survey, conducted in two provinces, found that 69 percent of respondents reported NSP activities in their village, with slightly higher numbers in Nangarhar than in Herat. Overall, 65 percent of respondents perceived improvements in rural infrastructure (roads, irrigation, or water supply) and 68 percent in agricultural livelihoods in the past five years. But results were lower with regard to their own financial situation (52 percent reported improvement), and there was considerable disparity across the two provinces: 68 percent from Nangarhar said they were financially better off compared with 39 percent from Herat[8] (appendix G).

The absence of viable local government organizations keeps the CDCs from establishing formal links with subnational government structures. The Afghan constitution provides for a three-tiered local government system with provincial, district, and village councils functioning under the national government within a unitary state. However, the Independent Election Commission has been unable to hold local government elections, and the provinces and districts are currently headed by governors nominated by the president. Subnational governments in some provinces have received direct assistance from Provincial Reconstruction Teams and bilateral donors, but there is wide variation among them due to lack of an agreed local government design within the government and ineffective coordination among partner organizations.

In the absence of an elected local government system, the government is considering a proposal put forward by MRRD to recognize the CDCs as interim village councils to undertake local government functions. Some CDCs have also clustered together to undertake multivillage subprojects with funding from sources outside the NSP, including the Japan International Cooperation Agency (JICA) and the Japanese Social Development Fund. In more than 300 districts, MRRD has encouraged CDC representatives to establish district *shuras* (District Development Assemblies [DDAs]) with the support of a UNDP project.[9] However, these efforts to federate the CDCs are not formally integrated within the NSP, and MRRD's proposal to recognize the district *shuras* as district councils, parallel to the village councils, has met with greater resistance from both the IDLG and the NSP's financiers.

While there appears to be some reluctance to partner with the DDAs, since their capacity has not been assessed and is reported by management to be uneven, there are *prima facie* no grounds to believe that the CDCs have uniformly strong capacity either. The challenge of transforming the CDCs and DDAs into formal village and district councils should not be underestimated. Nonetheless, from a governance perspective, the CDCs as village councils are more likely to be sustainable if they are linked to the district and/or provincial levels and their respective roles in longer-term development activities clarified.

WORLD BANK GROUP CONTRIBUTION

The Bank's most significant and relevant contribution was the initial design of the NSP, which allowed rapid outreach to rural communities across the entire country. The need for a community-based development program was identified during the Preliminary Needs Assessment and elaborated more fully in the discussion paper produced by a Joint Donor Mission in March 2002.

The Bank also provided support to MRRD to build their capacity to manage such a large-scale, nationwide program, and substantial resources from IDA and the ARTF enabled the NSP to reach every province in Afghanistan.

The NSP has relied heavily on a single grant investment ($200 per household) for village-level projects to catalyze formation of CDCs. The rapid success of the NSP can be attributed to the simplicity of its design and the ability of the MRRD to mobilize a network of facilitating partners, many of which already had a field presence in the provinces and were willing to facilitate formation of CDCs, even in conflict-affected districts.

CDCs have potential as an entry point for local development, but the NSP's monitoring system does not capture parallel activities undertaken by other agencies in the NSP target areas and may well be underestimating these effects. To consolidate the initial gains of the NSP, the government and the Bank are encouraging other programs operating in rural areas to use the CDCs as entry points for rural development activities, but related activities by the facilitating partners and other donor partners remain unrecognized by the Bank.

Feedback from a sample of facilitating partners revealed that most of them were already carrying out additional development or humanitarian activities—such as microfinance, water and sanitation, health, education, and community-based disaster risk management—with financing from other sources. Since these activities are not part of the Bank-financed program, their role in sustaining the CDCs beyond the initial grant-financed subproject is not tracked or measured by the Bank and MRRD, even though they are, in effect, a "program subsidy" to the NSP. Even the project paper for NSP III is silent on this supplemental role of the facilitating partners.[10]

UNDP supports formation of DDAs *(shura)*, composed of CDC representatives through the National Area-Based Development Program. The Bank prepared a Discussion Paper on district governance in Afghanistan (World Bank 2011b),[11] but this has not had any impact on the NSP. JICA has also financed multivillage projects through CDCs, but neither UNDP- nor JICA-supported activities have been formally integrated with Bank-financed NSP activities. Consequently, development partners have often worked at cross purposes, and the whole is less than the sum of its parts. At the very least, the Bank is missing an opportunity to compare which of these sets of programs are more effective in enhancing local-level governance and institutional sustainability.

For a program of this size—by far the largest administered by the Bank in Afghanistan—there is relatively little formal AAA. External agencies have undertaken numerous studies and evaluations (for example, see Brick 2008a, 2008b; Ecorys 2012; Murtazashvili 2009; SIGAR 2011; Torabi 2007), and a randomized impact evaluation (Beath and others 2010) has been undertaken, whose final results are expected in FY13. The impact evaluation only analyzes nationwide results and is missing the opportunity to assess the impact of two important variables—regional/cultural diversity and facilitating-partner program diversity among the regions.

The one-off intervention in the NSP program is a significant design flaw. A Policy Research Report (Mansuri and Rao 2012) based on a review of over 450 projects finds that unless designed carefully, participatory projects often fail to build cohesive and resilient organizations. "Only when projects explicitly link community-based organizations with markets, or provide skills training, do they tend to improve group cohesiveness and collective action beyond the life of the project" (Mansuri and Rao 2012: 25). The report finds that community participation programs are most effective when they are systematically linked to state institutions: "most successful programs tend to be those implemented by local governments that have some discretion and are downwardly accountable.... Local participation appears to increase, rather than diminish, the need for functional and strong institutions at the center (Mansuri and Rao 2012: 31)."

Mansuri and Rao conclude that local participation does not work when it is merely the ad hoc creation of a project. It works when it has teeth, when it builds on organic movements, when it is facilitated by a responsive center, when it is adequately and sustainably funded, and when interventions are conditioned by a culture of learning by doing. While the effect of the initial stimulus provided by a project grant is undeniable, for the benefits to be sustained the NSP needs to keep the CDCs engaged either by continuous support in other sectors or through regular fiscal transfers to local communities on a much smaller, affordable scale.

The NSP made substantial progress toward its stated objectives, but the financial sustainability of the current model is in doubt. Under NSP III, the Bank has approved a second round of project grants on the same scale ($200 per household), in addition to extending the first-round grants to villages not previously reached.

The simple design of the NSP has ensured a high disbursement rate, increasing the attractiveness of the program, increasing donor tolerance for the relatively high 28 percent spent on the facilitating partners and administrative costs, about half of which is spent on community mobilization and capacity building of CDCs.[12] It is highly unlikely that the government or donor partners will agree to continue this level of funding for nationwide coverage by a second round of NSP grants, given the realization that overall aid levels might shrink after 2014. Either the size of the second grant needs to be reconsidered or the program will result in unequal entitlements to different villages, a risky strategy in a conflict environment. Unless the NSP is formally linked to higher levels of local governance structures and CDCs receive regular intergovernmental fiscal transfers on a sustainable scale, financial sustainability cannot be assured.

Procurement and payment delays place hidden costs on program implementation. The MRRD operates through performance-based contracts with the facilitating partners, and the contracts are continuously renewed and extended as the program expands. Implementation has been hampered by procurement and payment delays. The SIGAR audit found that 14 percent of payments to facilitating partners between 2009 and 2011 were delayed (SIGAR 2011, p. 21). This is an underestimate, however, because it does not include the delays in contract signing. The majority of facilitating partners interviewed reported that procurement delays were even more problematic and, in previous years, they were instructed to start work in new areas even before receiving signed contracts. The procurement process is reported to have improved in the past year.

The Bank has contributed substantially to the government's program, ensuring access of rural communities to social and productive infrastructure and services on a large scale, and to creating CDCs, which have a potential role in local governance, but the NSP contribution to the overall objectives of pillar 2 was modest. The contribution of the NSP to rural growth will remain modest, but its potential impact on governance and accountability is more significant. The latest country strategy (ISN 2012-14) states that "NSP III will aim to lock in the local governance structures represented by CDCs" (World Bank 2012: 23). It is simply not feasible for more than the current 40,000 CDCs (29,000 existing and another 12,000 potential CDCs) to liaise directly with the central government. It is imperative that the government and its partner organizations pool efforts to develop an agreed local governance system, either building up from the village level or linking village-level CDCs to higher tiers of local government for sustainable provision of public services. Without this linkage, the aim of locking in local governance structures cannot be achieved.

Agriculture and Water Resources Development

Consistent with its importance as a source of economic growth and formal exports, the government has given agriculture prominent attention in its development strategies. A government document entitled "Securing Afghanistan's Future: Accomplishments and the Strategic Path Forward" in 2004 projected an annual growth rate between 5 and 7 percent in agricultural production over 10 years. "Agriculture," the document said, "is the mainstay of Afghanistan's economy and will remain so in the future" (Islamic Republic of Afghanistan and others 2004, p. 53). "The Afghanistan Ministry of Agriculture, Animal Husbandry and Food Master Plan" (Chemonics International, Inc. 2006) laid out a plan for some subsectors in agriculture and proposed an agricultural growth rate of 6 percent per annum, but it did not cover most of irrigated agriculture and did not cover forestry at all.

The Afghanistan ANDS for 2008–2013 (Islamic Republic of Afghanistan 2008) reaffirmed agriculture's priority status and projected growth at 5 percent per year.[13] The government saw irrigated agriculture as the main source of growth, and therefore made rehabilitation of irrigation infrastructure a high priority in all development plans. It has been estimated that in the 1970s about 3.2 million hectares were under various irrigation technologies, from traditional systems using intricate underground water delivery systems to some modern "run of the river" systems. Currently, however, only 1.8 to 1.9 million hectares are being irrigated, generally at low levels of efficiency. Of the 3.2 million hectares, only 10 percent were being irrigated in 2010 using properly engineered systems (World Bank 2010).

WORLD BANK GROUP OBJECTIVES

The objectives were to promote growth of the rural economy and improve rural livelihoods through rehabilitation of existing irrigation systems, development of important rural enterprises (horticulture and livestock), and support for an agriculture-rural development strategy, including analysis of diversification out of poppy production, as well as contributing significantly to technical assistance to enhance agricultural support services in MAIL. IFC has contributed to this pillar and will continue to do so by supporting investments and technological innovation to improve the processing and marketing of horticulture products. These objectives were relevant because of the well-known associations between agricultural development, rural livelihoods, growth, and poverty reduction in Southeast Asia (see Hazell and von Braun 2006).

The Bank's assistance to agriculture and the generation of rural livelihoods was relevant, although original project designs were inappropriate to the circumstances in Afghanistan, and the two major projects needed to be restructured (Table 4.3). The Bank Group's program for promoting rural growth during FY02–11 included investments in the rehabilitation of irrigation systems ($266 million) and rehabilitation of small-scale horticulture and livestock enterprises ($54 million) and technical assistance for water resources development. Both projects suffered implementation problems resulting in delays by two to three years.

Only one irrigation project (Emergency Irrigation Rehabilitation Project, or EIRP, approved in FY05), with a final IDA cost of $126.5 million, was completed during the review period. The other project (Emergency Horticulture and Livestock Project, approved in FY05), estimated to cost $70.7 million, is expected to close in 2012. These emergency projects focused mainly on rehabilitation of existing production systems. Smaller projects responding to the avian flu pandemic and the global food crisis were also completed.

In collaboration with a range of donors, the Bank provided some assistance to the Agricultural Development Task Force in the MAIL aimed at (i) developing MAIL's short-, medium-, and long-term strategic priorities and investments, (ii) advising MAIL on an appropriate institutional structure, and (iii) providing analytical policy advice. The Bank also provided technical assistance to the Ministry of Economy for the periodic National Risk and Vulnerability Assessments. The objective of the technical assistance for water resources development was to promote more efficient use of Afghanistan's scarce water resources for power generation, urban, agricultural, and industrial uses in the five major river basins. Of the $388 million from IDA/ARTF, 48 percent was committed in FY10–11, which meant that implementation of half of the program had barely started by the end of FY11.

RESULTS

Total GDP for agriculture in Afghanistan increased an average of 2.5 percent per year between 2002/03 and 2010/11. An important contributor to this growth was wheat production (Afghanistan's staple food), which increased 5.8 percent per year between 2002 and 2009, as a result of growth in area harvested and yield of 3.4 and 2.3 percent per year respectively. About half of Afghanistan's wheat output is grown in irrigated areas, but irrigation systems were still not functioning well and could not reduce fluctuations in yields and production due to recurrent droughts (see figures 4.1 and 4.2).

The production of other important crops also increased, but at a slower rate, and did not reach historical levels. Grapes have typically accounted for close to half of all fruit-growing areas in Afghanistan, and raisins and grapes together are usually the most important agricultural export (FAO 2004, p. 22). Between

Table 4.3	Summary Results of Pillar 2—Agriculture and Water Resources Development
Results associated with Bank Group goals	**Bank Group contribution to results**
Bank Group Objective: Promote growth of the rural economy and improve rural livelihoods through rehabilitation of existing traditional irrigation systems; develop rural enterprises; support the wider agriculture-rural development strategy dialogue; scale up IFC's support in the horticulture sector; and use Afghanistan's scarce water resources more efficiently.	
<ul><li>Production of Afghanistan's staple food (wheat) increased, albeit with considerable fluctuations, at about 6 percent per year between 2002 and 2010 due mainly to increases in area harvested. Production of other crops also increased, but at a slower rate.</li><li>The Bank-assisted irrigation project and the horticulture and livestock project did not contribute to the high national growth rate of agricultural production because their effective implementation was delayed by two-to-three years, until 2007 and 2009 respectively.</li><li>These projects will eventually contribute to improved rural livelihoods, but their impact will be limited because so far they have covered only 19 percent of areas currently under irrigation and an even smaller percentage of horticultural areas or livestock production.</li><li>The Ministry of Agriculture, Irrigation, and Livestock engaged the Bank and many development partners in a dialogue on an agriculture-rural development strategy, which included plans for strengthening the ministry's capacity to provide services to the agriculture sector.</li><li>The Bank's analysis of water resource management options in the Kabul River Basin, in collaboration with the Ministry of Energy and Water contributed to capacity building in the ministry and its ability to design additional irrigation projects and formulate water resources policy.</li></ul>	<ul><li>The completed Emergency Irrigation Rehabilitation Project financed the rehabilitation of water supplies to numerous small to medium-scale irrigation systems as well as the installation of meteorological stations. Incremental wheat yields are reported to be 25 percent since the EIRP got under way after restructuring in 2005.</li><li>The ongoing Emergency Horticulture and Livestock Project financed rehabilitation and development of vineyards and orchards and support services for horticulture and livestock producers. Early results show productivity gains for some horticultural crops, but rehabilitation and development costs have been high.</li><li>The Bank missed the opportunity to undertake a comprehensive analysis of the agriculture sector to inform the government's agriculture strategy and the design of projects to improve productivity and reduce rural poverty. In 2009 the Ministry of Agriculture, Irrigation, and Livestock issued its National Agricultural Development Framework to which the Bank had provided some assistance.</li><li>The Kabul River Basin study (World Bank 2010d) prepared by the Bank in collaboration with the Ministry of Energy and Water is being used as a model for studies of Afghanistan's other river basins.</li><li>The follow-up Bank technical assistance program continues to support the further strengthening of the Ministry of Energy and Water's staff capacity for long-term water resource management and development on a broad front.</li></ul>
Source: IEG evaluation.	

2002 and 2009, grape exports declined 9.6 percent per year while raisin exports increased at an annual rate of 2.9 percent. However, in 2009 raisin exports of about 33,000 tons were only 60 percent of the average annual raisin export of about 56,000 tons during the 1980s.

Since 2002, the national sheep flock increased 3.6 percent per year, but this rise was from an all-time low of 8.8 million sheep, compared with a historical level of around 15 million. Despite the recent increase in numbers to 12.5 million, the longer-term declining trend almost certainly reflects deterioration in the quality of rangelands and in the environment.

The agriculture sector's growth after 2002 (albeit uneven from year to year) in large part reflects a rebound after the decline during the previous two decades of conflict. Agriculture has the potential for further substantial and sustained growth if the enabling conditions for production, such as a stable socioeconomic environment, effective and well-maintained irrigation infrastructure, reliable rural roads, improved technology, agricultural inputs and agricultural support

Figure 4.1 Trends in Wheat Area Harvested and Production (2002–10)

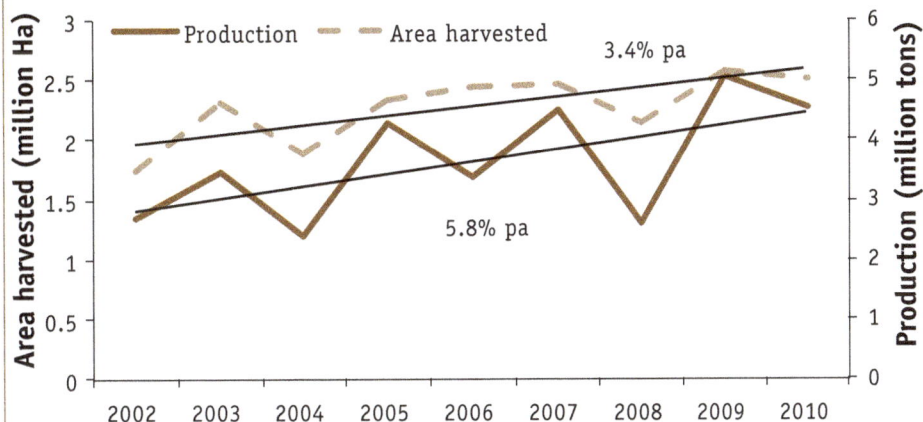

Source: FAOSTAT.

services (research, extension, input delivery systems, and credit facilities), sound stewardship of the environment, and efficient marketing systems are in place.

Irrigation will be an important contributor to future growth. The Bank and development partners have contributed to an improved understanding of Afghanistan's water resources since 2000, mainly through the multisector study of the Kabul River Basin by a government/Bank team that evaluated options for water resource management in the basin. Another advance in this field was the considerable improvement in the managerial and technical capacity of staff in the Ministry of Energy and Water (MEW). This has improved its

Figure 4.2 Trend in Wheat Yield (2002–10)

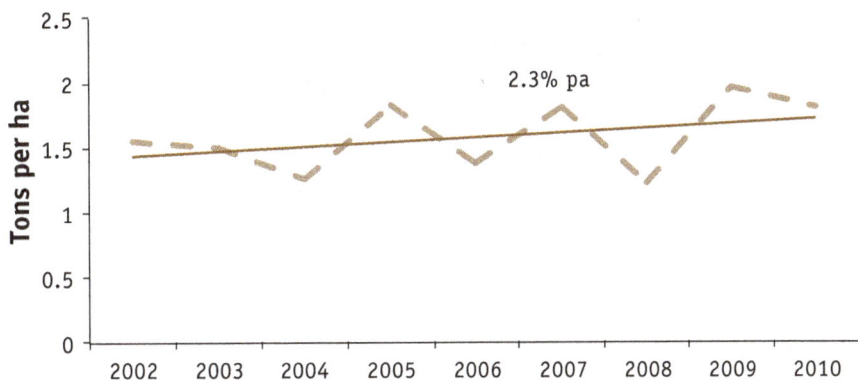

Source: FAOSTAT.

Figure 4.3   Trends in Grape and Raisin Exports (2002–09)

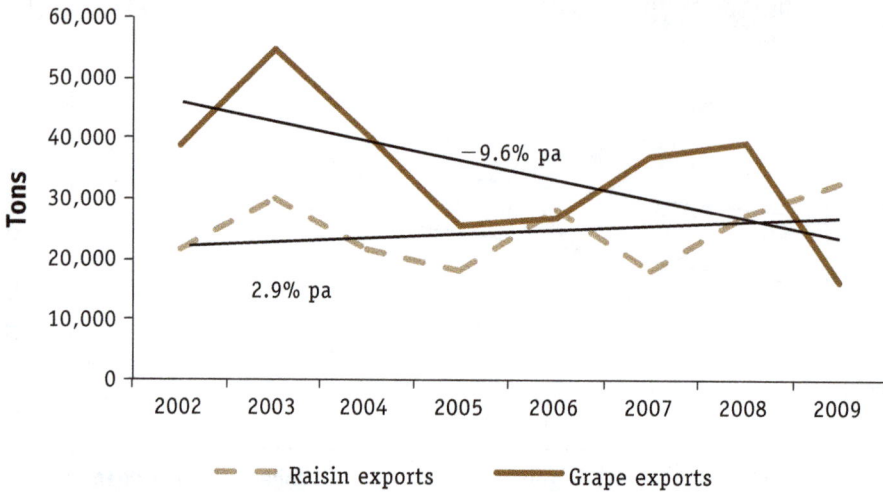

Source: FAOSTAT.

capacity to formulate water resources policy and the competence to interpret the countrywide hydrological measurements made under the EIRP, and laid the basis for much more rapid water resource planning and development for irrigation in the future.

WORLD BANK GROUP CONTRIBUTION

The Bank's program sought to stimulate Afghanistan's agricultural potential by providing some of the enabling conditions for growth and improvement of rural livelihoods. However, only two projects had a substantial record during the 10-year review period for this assessment: the previously mentioned EIRP and the Horticulture and Livestock Project. Of the other two relatively small operations completed—the Food Crisis Response Project ($8 million) and the Avian Flu Project ($5 million)—only the first was able to achieve its objectives. Other projects in the sector were a rural enterprise development project providing support to village-based enterprise activities and small and medium-size enterprise development in FY10 and two irrigation projects that were approved in FY11, but these have not yet achieved evaluable outcomes. The rest are four small but important technical assistance activities aimed at capacity building with total commitments of $1.2 million, some of which are still under implementation.

The EIRP, approved in November 2003, financed the rehabilitation of water supplies to numerous small-scale irrigation systems as well as the installation of meteorological stations. The original aim was to rehabilitate about 1,280 irrigation schemes covering about 280,000 hectares in numerous small- and medium-scale schemes and five large schemes, as well as 70,000 hectares of incremental irrigated area. The project was also designed to rehabilitate hydrometeorology stations in and adjacent to the project area. The main intended outcome was increased wheat yields. However, the project design was too ambitious and complex for Afghanistan's limited implementation capacity and it made little progress over the next two years.

In 2006 the project was restructured to streamline appraisals for irrigation subprojects. In addition, the number of small irrigation schemes to be rehabilitated was reduced and the hydrometeorological measurement component was dropped.[14] The improved design accelerated the pace of implementation, and additional financing of $25 million was approved in 2007. As implementation improved, two additional grants led to an increase in the number of irrigation schemes covered and a reintroduction of the meteorological measurements stations,[15] bringing the total IDA grant to $126.5 million when the project closed.

Given the project's emphasis on the rehabilitation and construction of main irrigation infrastructure (World Bank 2010, p. 3), an improvement in productivity was almost inevitable, because in many cases crops were de facto rain-fed before the improvement to irrigation water supplies. The project has closed, but an Implementation Completion Report is not yet available. The most recent estimated target for the rehabilitation was 602,000 hectares, which would be 19 percent of the area under irrigation in Afghanistan. A Bank report from end 2011 reported that the project also resulted in 156,000 hectares of additional irrigated area, somewhat above the revised target of 145,000 hectares (Matsumo 2011).

An interim assessment of productivity increases based on monitoring and evaluation surveys in December 2008 showed that yield increases were high: 53 percent for wheat (from a base of 1.7 tons per hectare at appraisal to 2.6 tons per hectare) and 67 percent for maize (from a base of 0.6 tons per hectare at appraisal to 1.0 ton per hectare). However, questions remain about the extent to which these high yields can be attributed to the rehabilitation of main irrigation canals compared with the effect of other factors such as repairs to on-farm irrigation systems by farmers, increased fertilizer use, improved seeds, and better crop management. The latest project report estimated 750,000 beneficiaries. The Food Crisis Response Project also provided $8 million for rehabilitation of small-scale community irrigation systems implemented under the umbrella of NSP II.

The Emergency Horticulture and Livestock Project, approved in 2006, supported rehabilitation and development of vineyards and orchards and provided support services for horticulture and livestock producers. However, implementation was slowed by delays in procurement due to inexperience in the implementing ministry. The project also had an overly ambitious structure and design. In November 2006 key outcomes were reduced to increased productivity of perennial and annual horticulture crops (15 percent increase in target orchards) and poultry, and a reduced mortality of cattle by 5 percent and of sheep by 10 percent. The area of orchards to be established was cut from 5,000 hectares to

3,000 hectares. The revisions resulted in a substantially reduced scope for the project.

Early results from the Emergency Horticulture and Livestock Project show incremental productivity for some horticultural crops, but rehabilitation and development costs as well as overhead costs[16] were high, and nomadic livestock herders had not benefited. In total, the area of new orchards established (about 3,000 hectares) accounted for less than 10 percent of the total orchard area in Afghanistan. There was also little impact from this project on the welfare of nomadic herdsmen *(kuchi)*, the poorest rural group, whose incidence of poverty was 54 percent in 2007/08, and whose livelihood depends almost exclusively on livestock. During the evaluation period, IFC supported improvements in processing and marketing of raisins, although the focus of IFC's work was not in one of the Bank-assisted project areas. IFC has agreed to expand its support to the dried fruits industry.

Gender impacts were positive. Twenty-five thousand women (100 percent of the target group) were assisted in establishing semi-intensive poultry units. Sixty-six percent of them adopted improved poultry husbandry practices, exceeding the target of 60 percent. Ninety-four percent of the poultry units have started a second cycle independently, suggesting high levels of sustainability of the benefits for women. Although the outcome of the avian flu project was less than satisfactory, it trained women communicators, and school programs did help to increase women's awareness of controlling such infections among domestic poultry and preparing for, controlling, and responding to possible human infections. Given that women constitute the majority of backyard poultry producers, this helped them to protect one of their few independent sources of income.

EIRP and the two Horticulture and Livestock Projects were the main agricultural projects under implementation in the agriculture sector for the first 10 years of Bank assistance, but much of the agricultural growth occurred before these projects got well under way. By the time the EIRP was restructured in 2006, average yields for rain-fed and irrigated wheat had already reached close to 2.0 tons per hectare. The EIRP therefore was not a major factor in the substantial growth rate of national wheat production shown in figure 4.1. However, with EIRP, future volatility of wheat production will probably be lower than in the past. The growth in raisin exports shown in figure 4.3 also occurred well before the effective implementation of the Emergency Horticulture and Livestock Project in 2009.

Policies and strategies for growth in the agriculture sector were not systematically addressed. While EIRP and the Horticulture and Livestock projects, together with additional projects approved in FY10 and FY11, were important, many policy and strategic issues in the agriculture sector needed to be addressed, such as sequencing of investment programs, land rights, prospects for a sustainable livestock industry, agricultural research and support services, marketing efficiency, export competitiveness, and export-product inspection, as well as forestry and the environment.

Management has informed IEG that the region has discussed the need for an agriculture sector review but has not yet been able to move forward. Such a review is overdue and could provide a broad basis for the Bank's support to the government's agricultural development strategy as well as for the choice and design for investments to achieve improved productivity, increased output, and higher incomes. As discussed earlier, the Bank did contribute to the government's National Agricultural Development Framework. However, during the IEG mission to Afghanistan, many senior government ministers and representatives of partner organizations called for greater Bank contribution to the agriculture sector's future policy and strategy.[17]

In comparison with the agriculture sector, recent analytical work and technical assistance for water resources development has been more strategic. The analysis of institutions in water resources management and the assessment of water resource development options in the Kabul River Basin were well done, and the follow-up technical assistance program funded by the Bank continues to improve the capacity of the MEW staff to undertake future water resource planning and design. This work also stimulated similar studies in the other four main river basins in Afghanistan, and investment prospects are under serious consideration by development partners. It represented substantial progress toward the objective of efficient water resources management in Afghanistan.

Overall, while eventually the irrigation and horticulture/livestock projects made acceptable progress, the absence of a sector review was a major shortcoming that will hamper the planning of the Bank's future assistance to Afghanistan in the agricultural sector. At the same time, the joint Bank–MEW study of water resource management in the Kabul River Basin was a strategic initiative that has strengthened the ability of the ministry to make longer-term investment plans for Afghanistan's irrigation sector.

Overall Assessment

The evaluation's findings on achievement of performance benchmarks listed in the Bank's country assistance strategies (TSSs and ISNs) are summarized in table 4.4.

Risks to Development Outcomes

The risks to development outcomes in this pillar are significant. The Bank's assistance has contributed to short-term job creation but, as evidenced above, has had a modest impact so far on this pillar's core objective of promoting growth in the rural economy and improving rural livelihoods. Lack of a rural access policy and inadequate arrangements for maintenance of rural roads remains a threat to their sustainability.

The NSP has achieved its outputs on a remarkable scale, but its governance objectives will remain at risk until the relationships of the CDCs with higher levels of subnational governance are resolved and a more sustainable model

Table 4.4	Status of Performance Benchmarks for Pillar 2	
Source	**Benchmark**	**Status**
Rural roads		
2006 ISN	3,650 kilometers of new and rehabilitated rural roads	5,900 kilometers rehabilitated by end-2011
National Solidarity Program		
2003 TSS	Number of communities successfully mobilized under the NSP	28,673 communities mobilized by 2011 and 28,456 CDCs formed
2003 TSS	Number of communities receiving block grants under the NSP	27,360 CDCs provided block grants for 59,629 subprojects
2003 TSS	Outcomes achieved by block grants	80 percent of subprojects completed: transport (26 percent), water and sanitation (24 percent), irrigation (19 percent), power (12 percent), and education (10 percent).
2003 TSS	Number of person-days employment provided through public works programs (including women)	8 million person-days provided by rural roads; NSP data unavailable
2006 ISN	NSP reaching 70 percent of the rural population	NSP reached 68 percent by 2009
2009 ISN	Increased allocation of donor and public resources to support rural livelihoods and growth.	Good progress in allocation of ARTF resources for the NSP
2009 ISN	Increased proportion of rural land brought back into productive use	Some progress, but data unavailable
2009 ISN	Increased representation of women in CDCs.	Some progress
2009 ISN	Progress in reducing rural household poverty rates	High variability in poverty across regions and seasons
Agricultural and water resources development		
2003 TSS	Level of agricultural and livestock production	Some progress in availability of veterinary services after slow start
2006 ISN	Incremental milk value from dairy processing of $23 million	Not implemented—only a study undertaken
2006 ISN	Incremental value from semi-intensive poultry of $10 million	Good progress reported in backyard poultry units, benefiting women
2006 ISN	3,600 hectares of orchards rehabilitated, 1,500 hectares of new orchards established	Some progress after slow start: project needed restructuring
2006 ISN	Horticultural exports increased by 30 percent	Some progress, but no evidence to attribute this progress to the Emergency Horticulture and Livestock Projects
2009 ISN	Increased agricultural productivity	After a difficult start and restructuring, EIRP has contributed to 25 percent increase in wheat yields in project irrigation systems
2009 ISN	Progress toward achieving food security	Some progress, but continued dependence on weather because many irrigation systems still need rehabilitation. Household surveys indicate that rural incomes have improved but poverty rates remain high and uneven due to different levels of investment among provinces.

for regular, affordable fiscal transfers and services to local communities is put in place. Agricultural and water resources interventions have been slow to respond to the country's needs, and still lack the kind of strategic analysis needed to stimulate future investments on the scale needed to ensure sustained agricultural growth.

The sustainability of rural roads is a particular problem that so far has no long-term solution. While the Ministries of Public Works and Rural Rehabilitation and Development have recently made agreements with CDCs to maintain some stretches of rural roads, the effectiveness of these arrangements has yet to be evaluated. A sustainable arrangement for maintaining the rural roads infrastructure remains a major challenge.

The risks related to the NSP are primarily the risks of institutional sustainability. The NSP's primary objective has been institutional development in the form of the CDCs that were the vehicle for undertaking the subprojects it financed. The most significant contribution of the NSP has been its substantial outreach across all provinces and districts. The economic stimulus created by the NSP grants helped to establish a government presence, but the institutional benefits may be short-lived, unless the CDCs are able to provide more sustainable and diversified services to their members.

While there undoubtedly has been some social capital formation, its efficacy is difficult to verify and is reported to vary considerably across the country.[18] The absence of effective local government organizations renders it impossible for the CDCs to establish formal links with subnational government structures, and functioning as village councils in isolation (as currently proposed) is not viable.

Recognizing the significance of its governance objective, the NSP is being correctly moved to the governance pillar in the 2012 ISN. This may enable more systematic consideration of the links between the NSP and subnational governance institutions. Given the different perceptions and interests of various government agencies, and the divergent approaches being followed by development partners working at the subnational level, reaching consensus on a local government structure does not appear to be feasible in the short run. It is critical, nonetheless, to engage with the government on this subject, perhaps by undertaking analytical work to lay different options on the table. In the interim, until an agreed local government system is in place, at a minimum it would be advisable to help the government develop a viable system for delivery of public services at subnational levels.

The government considers the agriculture sector critical for jobs and food security. Bank-assisted projects in the agriculture and water resources sectors are achieving their objectives—albeit with delays and the need for restructuring—after two-to-three years of meager progress. However, for one Bank project (Emergency Horticulture and Livestock Project), overheads are estimated to be 40 percent of total costs. Such overheads cannot be sustained, and this undermines the prospects for efficiently scaling up the program.

Achievement of the pillar's objectives of growth and improved rural livelihoods will require a significant shift in the strategy, to build a much broader base for agricultural and rural development. There is, so far, neither a substantial overview of the challenges to achieving broad-based growth in the sector nor a vision for agriculture's future competitiveness. Hence, the basis for future investments and marketing chains is lacking. In addition, the MAIL still has significant capacity constraints. A more sustained partnership between the Bank and this ministry on policy and strategic issues would strengthen its capacity and benefit Afghanistan's agricultural development.

On balance, this pillar's program has government and community ownership, is of sound technical quality, and has had a positive impact on government institutions. At the same time, the Bank's investment programs have been costly and the NSP faces institutional challenges in the future. For the investment programs there can be valid concerns about sustained support through the government budget, unless the ARTF can support these programs in the foreseeable future. For the NSP, unless institutional challenges are recognized and addressed, political uncertainties may undo the achievements of the CDCs.

Notes

1. Both the 2004 strategy "Securing Afghanistan's Future" (Islamic Republic of Afghanistan and others 2004) and the subsequent "Afghanistan National Development Strategy" (Islamic Republic of Afghanistan 2007) identified irrigated agriculture as the main source of growth for the economy.

2. Water is an extremely scarce resource in Afghanistan. The Bank's direct assistance in domestic water supplies has been small, although NSP provided substantial support for improvement of water supplies in rural communities. The U.S. government is by far the largest donor financing access to safe drinking water, irrigation, and water sector management.

3. The Bank-supported NEEP program followed an earlier rural infrastructure project Emergency Community and Public Works Empowerment Program (ECEPWP).

4. Data are from the Program Report January 2012 from the NSP website http://www. nspafghanistan.org.

5. The midline survey report for Afghanistan NSP was conducted in 2007 and 2009, measuring after two years of implementation (Beath and others 2010). The evaluation follows a randomized design across 500 villages in ten districts. A follow-up survey was planned in spring 2011, but the survey was delayed and findings are not yet available.

6. Researchers such as Jennifer Brick have questioned the NSP's governance impact while acknowledging its contribution to local infrastructure.

7. Murtazashvili (2009) dissertation compares the role of the CDCs with traditional *shuras* and *jirgas* and finds that the CDCs do not play a significant role in dispute

resolution while the traditional organizations do so, especially in connection with local land disputes. Traditional organizations also contribute to a sense of personal safety and security while there is some evidence that the existence of CDCs is associated with an increasing incidence of conflict, possibly due to disagreements over use of the additional resources being injected into local communities. Also see Brick 2008a.

8. This could be due to a time difference in the start of NSP activities in the two provinces or it could be a variance in other economic activities between the two provinces. Without the benefit of on-site visits the survey was unable to distinguish the effects of NSP from those of other development interventions.

9. The district *shuras* are being created under the National Area-Based Development Program, implemented by MRRD with UNDP support.

10. The ICR for NSP II acknowledges the additional role of the facilitating partners but this is based on feedback provided by the IEG evaluation team to the ICR team. Due to this endogeneity effect, this fact has not been taken into account by the CPE.

11. The paper (World Bank 2011a) analyzes the policy issues and challenges arising out of the existence of parallel organizations—District Development Assemblies (DDAs) and Afghanistan Social Outreach Programme (ASOPs)—at the subnational level. The DDAs were established by MRRD under UNDP's National Area-Based Development Program. The ASOPs were established as district-level councils by the Independent Directorate of Local Governance and comprise primarily traditional authorities such as wealthy landowners, religious leaders, and tribal leaders. The overlap and competition among them has prevented an agreement between MRRD and the Independent Directorate of Local Governance on district-level governance. "The two councils are an almost perfect case study of the fragmented, inconsistent and donor-driven nature of subnational governance in the country" (World Bank 2011a, p. 7). However, donor support for ASOP, which was motivated primarily by security concerns, is unlikely to be extended.

12. A SIGAR study reports that social mobilization, overseeing elections, and training of CDCs by the facilitating partners costs 19 percent while other administrative costs are 9 percent (SIGAR 2011, p. 6). The Bank estimates that 15 percent is spent on social mobilization and capacity building of CDCs and 13 percent is for the costs and fees of the facilitating partners.

13. A Comprehensive Agriculture and Rural Development Program (CARD) was proposed, composed of 15 subprograms of which the most prominent component was a continuation of the NSP. The other 14 programs covered national food security, area-based development, horticulture, livestock, rural access, rural water supply and sanitation, irrigation, national resources, national surveillance (household surveys), rural electrification, rural enterprise, research and extension, emergency response system, and capacity building.

14. See restructuring project paper for the Emergency Irrigation Rehabilitation Project (World Bank 2006).

15. The important hydrometeorological component was subsequently partly reinstated using more simple technical approaches. There had been no hydrometeorological measurements in Afghanistan for 30 years; these measurements were therefore critical for the future negotiation of water rights and the management of water resources in Afghanistan.

16. An Aide Memoire for an Implementation Support Mission by the Bank in September 2011 summarized the total costs for the project and showed that implementation management support for the project accounted for 41 percent of the total cost of $70.7 million.

17. It is recognized that the Bank completed a series of three studies of the drug industry in Afghanistan (see box 4.1 as well as appendixes D and E).

18. Researchers such as Jennifer Brick have questioned the NSP's governance impact while acknowledging its contribution to local infrastructure. A 2012 study by AREU indicates, however, that at least in the case study villages, NSP has led to empowerment of women.

References

Beath, Andrew, Fotini Christia, Ruben Enikolopov, Shahim Ahmad Kabuli. 2010. "Randomized Impact Evaluation of Phase-II of Afghanistan's National Solidarity Programme (NSP): Estimates of Interim Program Impact from First Follow-UpSurvey. " Available at : http://nsp-ie.org/reports/.

Brick, Jennifer. 2008a. "Final Report: Investigating the Sustainability of Community Development Councils in Afghanistan." Report prepared for the Japanese International Cooperation Agency. Available at: http://jen.murtazashvili.org/ wpcontent/uploads/2011/06/CDC-Sustainability-Final-Report-AREU-FINAL.pdf.

———. 2008b. "The Political Economy of Customary Village Organizations in Afghanistan." Paper prepared for the Annual Meeting of the Central Eurasian Studies Society, Washington, DC, September 2008. Available at: http://www .bu.edu/aias/brick.pdf.

Buddenberg, Doris, and William Byrd (eds). 2006. Afghanistan's Drug Industry: Structure, Functioning, Dynamics, and Implications for Counter-Narcotics Policy. United Nations Office on Drugs and Crime (UNODC) and The World Bank. Available at: http://www.unodc.org/pdf/Afgh_drugindustry_Nov06.pdf.

Byrd, William, and Christopher Ward. 2004. Drugs and Development in Afghanistan. Social Development Papers, Conflict Prevention and Reconstruction Paper No. 18. Washington, DC: World Bank.

Chemonics International, Inc. 2006. "The Afghanistan Ministry of Agriculture, Animal Husbandry and Food Master Plan." Prepared for USAID and presented to His Excellency Obaidullah Ramin. Chemonics International, Inc., Washington, DC.

Echavez, Chona R. 2012. Gender and Economic Choice: What's Old and What's New for Women in Afghanistan. Kabul: Afghanistan Research and Evaluation Unit.

Ecorys. 2012. *Evaluation of Norwegian Development Cooperation with Afghanistan 2001–2011*. Prepared for the Norwegian Agency for Development Cooperation Evaluation Department. Oslo: Norad.

FAO (Food and Agriculture Organization of the United Nations) 2004. *Afghanistan: Survey of the Horticulture Sector.* Rome: FAO.

Hazell, Peter, and Joachim von Braun. 2006. "Aid to Agriculture, Growth, and Poverty Reduction." *EuroChoices* 5(1): 6–13.

Islamic Republic of Afghanistan and the World Bank. 2005."National Employment Program: Final Review Report." World Bank, Washington, DC.

Islamic Republic of Afghanistan. 2008. *Afghanistan National Development Strategy 1387–1398 (2008–2014): A Strategy for Security, Governance, Economic Growth & Poverty Reduction.* Kabul.

———. 2010. *Poverty Status in Afghanistan.* Washington, DC: World Bank.

Islamic Republic of Afghanistan, ADB (Asian Development Bank), United Nations Assistance Mission to Afghanistan, UNDP (United Nations Development Program), and the World Bank Group. 2004. "Securing Afghanistan's Future: Accomplishments and the Strategic Path Forward." A Government/ International Agency Report, March 17, 2004. Prepared for International Conference, March 31, 2004. Available at: http://www.cmi.no/afghanistan/?id=5&Government-of-Afghanistan.

Mansuri, Ghazala, and Vijayendra Rao. 2012. *Localizing Development: Has the Participatory Approach Worked?* World Bank Policy Research Report. Washington, DC: World Bank.

Matsumo, Jan. 2011. *Afghanistan – Emergency Irrigation Rehabilitation Project: P078936– Implementation Status Results Report: Sequence 16.* Washington, DC: World Bank. Available at: http://documents.worldbank.org/curated/en/2011/12/1554797-af-emergency-irrigation-rehabilitation-project-p078936-implementation-statusresults-report-sequence-16.

Murtazashvili, Jennifer Brick. 2009. "The Microfoundations of State Building: Informal Institutions and Local Public Goods in Rural Afghanistan." Ph.D. dissertation, University of Wisconsin, Madison. (Published 2011. Madison, WI: ProQuest, UMI Dissertation Publishing.)

SIGAR (Special Inspection General for Afghanistan Reconstruction). 2011. *Audit of National Solidarity Program.* SIGAR Audit 11-8, Economic and Social Development/ NSP. Arlington, VA: SIGAR.

Torabi, Yama. 2007. *Assessing the National Solidarity Program: The Role of Accountability in Reconstruction, Afghanistan 2007.* Kabul: IWA; London: Tiri. Available at: http://tiri.org/docs/rniss/cs/afghan_nspcs.pdf.

USAID (U.S. Agency for International Development) and Checchi and Co. Consulting. 2007. "Midterm Evaluation: Alternative Livelihoods Program, USAID/Afghanistan. USAID, Washington, DC.

Ward, Christopher, David Mansfield, Peter Oldham and William Byrd. 2008. Afghanistan – Economic Incentives and Development Initiatives to Reduce Opium Production. Washington, DC: World Bank and DFID. Available at: https://openknowledge.worldbank.org/bitstream/handle/10986/6272/424010fullrepo1mIncentives01PUBLIC1.pdf?sequence=1.

World Bank. 2006. Afghanistan – Emergency Irrigation Rehabilitation Project. Washington, DC: World Bank. Available at: http://documents.worldbank.org/curated/en/2006/10/7131617/afghanistan-emergency-irrigation-rehabilitation-project.

———. 2007. "A Policy Note on Rural Access in Afghanistan." Washington, DC: World Bank.

———. 2010. "Afghanistan—On-Farm Water Management Project." Project Information Document, Report No. AB5688. Washington, DC: World Bank.

———. 2011a. "Afghanistan—World Bank Country Brief." Washington, DC: World Bank.

———. 2011b. "District Governance in Afghanistan: DDAs and ASOPs – Policy Issues and Challenges." World Bank Discussion Paper, Washington, DC: World Bank.

———. 2012. *Interim Strategy Note for the Islamic Republic of Afghanistan for the Period FY12–FY14.* Report No. 66862-AF. Washington, DC: World Bank.

Chapter 5

Supporting Growth of the Formal
Private Sector

Context

At the end of 2001, the economy of Afghanistan was dominated by the informal sector, which was estimated to account for 80–90 percent of total economic activity. The lack of market institutions and depleted human capital were major constraints to the development of formal private sector businesses. Physical infrastructure, most of which was destroyed during the conflict or dilapidated due to poor maintenance, had to be rebuilt or rehabilitated, and a modern financial system developed almost from scratch. Pervasive corruption and power structures that emerged during the conflict period represented distortions to competition and efficient functioning of markets. Critical to putting in place the preconditions for a formal market economy is a functional, effective, and accountable state, which was itself weak. Establishing the foundation for sustained private sector–led growth was, and continues to be, a development challenge.

Bank Group support to private sector–led growth mirrored government priorities. The 2002 TSS (World Bank 2002) focused on emergency infrastructure projects to aid economic recovery. The 2003 TSS (World Bank 2003) envisioned a more comprehensive program; one of its four focus areas was enabling private sector development, which covers the business climate, the financial sector, infrastructure, and trade with "illustrative" outcome benchmarks. The 2006 ISN (World Bank 2006a) gave greater emphasis to the rural economy, recognized the difficulties in establishing a property rights regime, and identified mining as a priority sector. The 2009 ISN (World Bank 2009) articulated a three-pronged strategy[1] to support the private sector, which continued to be small and informal, with a limited contribution to growth. Over the period 2002–11, Bank Group activities to promote private sector growth were concentrated in the following areas:

- Improve the investment climate and develop the financial sector to enable expansion of existing businesses and encourage new private sector investments.

- Develop the hydrocarbon and mining and the telecommunications sectors by establishing the institutional framework needed to attract private investment.

- Contribute to the rehabilitation of power and urban roads to improve access by businesses.

- Improve urban management to improve services to support growth of population and businesses in urban centers.

Investment Climate

In 2002, most of Afghanistan's production capacity had been destroyed. Many skilled workers and managers had fled to other countries. Many traditional industries, such as carpet making, had closed and moved to neighboring countries, while others had shut down due to lack of inputs. The poor state of infrastructure had blocked distribution channels. Outside of agriculture, the private sector was dominated by informal, family-owned microenterprises, mainly in trading or provision of basic services. There were few small and medium-size enterprises, and only a handful of large firms. The 2005 Investment Climate Assessment recommended four categories of actions to support private sector development (PSD) through improvements in (i) access to inputs, including developing the financial system, pursuing privatization, upgrading infrastructure services, and strengthening property rights; (ii) flow of information; (iii) provision of business services; and (iv) government capacity to formulate and implement PSD policies and programs.

In its strategy documents, the government has always recognized that sustained growth would depend on the emergence of a vibrant private sector that would provide jobs and generate the revenues needed by the public sector. PSD was one of the three pillars of the government's National Development Framework (NDF), approved in 2002, and a major item in the *Securing Afghanistan's Future* report of 2004 (Islamic Republic of Afghanistan and others 2004). Both the 2006 *Interim Afghanistan National Development Strategy* (I-ANDS) (Islamic Republic of Afghanistan 2006)[2] and the 2008 *Afghanistan National Development Strategy* (ANDS) (Islamic Republic of Afghanistan 2008) had PSD as a subpillar under the category "Economic and Social Development."

The I-ANDS identified the constraints to PSD, but did not have concrete plans to address bottlenecks, which were related to structural issues and weak institutions (reform of state-owned banks and enterprises, enforcement capacity, and the justice system), the poor regulatory framework, the lack of skilled human resources, and dilapidated infrastructure. The ANDS had 12 sector strategies and a general PSD strategy, though how to achieve the goals of these strategies was often not specified and needed to be developed. The government's PSD strategy has three main components: (i) establishment of an enabling environment for private sector and trade development; (ii) development of national resources and infrastructure; and (iii) promotion of increased investment from domestic and foreign investors. The strategy was not accompanied by a results framework or monitoring and evaluation system.

WORLD BANK GROUP OBJECTIVES

The initial focus of the Bank Group was to improve the legal and regulatory framework for private investment, gain knowledge about the investment climate, upgrade the telecommunications system, and provide direct investment in, or guarantees to, private firms through IFC and MIGA. During the ISN periods, the Bank Group began to provide support to specific sectors, such as extractive industries and agribusiness; address the lack of support services through the expansion of industrial parks; and improve private sector skills. In addition, the Bank Group continued to work on reducing the regulatory cost of doing business and on strengthening institutions such as the Ministry of Commerce and the Afghanistan Investment Support Agency (AISA). The World Bank, IFC, and MIGA employed a whole range of instruments (see table 5.1), although donors—especially USAID—spent more resources to support various initiatives in PSD.

The climate for private investment continues to be very challenging. Deteriorating security conditions during the latter part of the evaluation period had a significant impact on new investments. But other components of the investment climate are also inhospitable to business development. The cost of doing business is very high in Afghanistan, driven by regulatory and institutional weaknesses. The *Doing Business* (Doing Business, various years) reports show little or no improvement in any of the indicators except for starting a business (see table 5.2).[3] While many laws have been passed, enforcement and adjudication of disputes are lacking, with low capacity and credibility of institutions such as the judiciary. Investor protection is one of lowest among countries surveyed by Doing Business.

More fundamentally, there is a lack of clarity with respect to property rights, especially land ownership and tenure. Noteworthy initiatives such as establishing alternative dispute resolution mechanisms[4] and industrial estates,[5] which could have provided interim relief to some of the fundamental weaknesses in the investment climate, have yet to produce results. Of major concern is the 2008 Investment Climate Assessment (World Bank 2008) finding of serious decline in business perceptions of policy enforcement and crime prevention, as well as an increase in informal payments required to secure contracts, compared with the 2005 Investment Climate Assessment (World Bank 2005).

The government's objective to use the private sector as the driver of sustained growth remains elusive, with donor-funded construction and basic trading as the main nonagricultural private sector activities. As noted in the 2008 Investment Climate Assessment, private industry's share of the economy and

Table 5.1	Summary Results of Pillar 3—Investment Climate
Results associated with Bank Group goals	**Bank Group contribution to results**
Bank Group Objectives: Improve the business regulatory and legislative framework; facilitate foreign direct investment; enable establishment of industrial parks; and reduce cost of doing business.	
• Investment climate continues to be challenging due to security and governance issues. • While many laws and regulations have been enacted, institutions to enforce these are weak and lack credibility. • Property rights, specifically land tenure, are unclear, with lack of adjudication process; the Doing Business Investor Protection Index is 1 on a scale of 010. • Cost of doing business continues to be high, with no progress in the areas of construction permits, electricity connections, and trade procedures.	• World Bank AAA improved knowledge about the private sector but had little by way of results. • World Bank private sector development project did not result in a successful industrial park as intended. • Investment guarantee project mobilized about $100 million in foreign direct investment, mainly in telecommunications. • IFC investments supported foreign direct investment in a hotel and telecommunications. • Ongoing IFC work on licensing reform may show results in the future.

Table 5.2	Doing Business Indicator for Afghanistan, 2007–12						
		Doing Business Report					
Doing Business area		2007	2008	2009	2010	2011	2012
Starting a business							
Procedures (number)		4	4	4	4	4	4
Time (days)		9	9	9	7	7	7
Dealing with construction permits							
Procedures (number)		12	12	12	12	12	12
Time (days)		334	334	334	334	334	334
Getting electricity							
Procedures (number)		11	9	9	9	9	9
Time (days)		252	250	250	250	250	250
Trading across borders							
Documents to export (number)		10	10	10	10	10	10
Time to export (days)		67	67	74	74	74	74
Cost of export (US$ per container)		2,180	2,180	2,680	3,030	3,545	3,545
Documents to import (number)		10	10	10	10	10	10
Time to import (days)		71	71	77	77	77	77
Cost to import (US$ per container)		2,100	2,100	2,600	3,000	3,830	3,830
Protecting investors							
Strength of investor protection index (0–10)		1	1	1	1	1	1

Sources: Doing Business Surveys, 2007–2012.

household income is small and inflows of foreign direct investment other than in the telecommunications and the mining and hydrocarbons sectors declined significantly after 2006. In contrast, domestic investments have been more resilient (table 5.3).

The IFC portfolio has remained at about $90–95 million since 2009, with a net commitment of $105 million at the end of FY11. Three of the five MIGA guarantees under the Small Investment Program were cancelled due to poor business outcomes, mainly as a result of a difficult investment climate. While improvement in security conditions is a necessary condition for PSD, other elements of the business climate would need to be in place to promote sustainable private sector–led growth and change an economic structure that is dominated by small and informal businesses, which continue to experience difficulties in expanding markets and operations.[6]

Nonetheless, there are some positive outcomes in several sectors. The telecommunications industry is growing, driven by private investment. There have been large foreign investments in the mining and hydrocarbon sector, setting the stage for large-scale development of natural resources as a potential driver of growth. There are reports of some improvement in agribusiness, such

Table 5.3	Initial Investments of New Firms Registered with AISA (2003–11)								
	2003	2004	2005	2006	2007	2008	2009	2010	2011
Investment ($ millions)									
Total	722	657	565	1,180	647	392	517	466	495
Foreign	483	235	177	409	207	109	76	56	55
Domestic	239	422	389	770	439	284	441	410	440
Number of employees (000)									
Total	255	90	87	68	47	80	53	48	46
Foreign	171	35	15	25	9	37	7	9	4
Domestic	84	55	72	43	38	44	46	39	42

Source: Afghanistan Investment Support Agency.

as in the dried fruit industry, which has a significant share of exports. Overall, despite the entrepreneurship and dynamism exhibited by existing businesses, private sector expansion and entry have been constrained by an investment climate that is one of the most difficult in the world.

WORLD BANK GROUP CONTRIBUTION

During the FY02–06 period covered by the TSSs, the Bank Group pursued activities that reflected the strengths of each Bank Group institution. The World Bank completed the 2005 Investment Climate Assessment (World Bank 2005), which generated knowledge about the private sector and was an important input to both government strategies and donor programs. IFC supported the first large foreign direct investment—the Kabul Serena Hotel—in the country since the Bank Group's re-engagement in Afghanistan. The objective was to attract further foreign investment by demonstrating the feasibility of conducting business in the country. However, the project suffered losses due to both implementation and security issues—and an IEG evaluation rated the project less than satisfactory for development outcomes.

IFC implemented several Advisory Services projects, including the pilot Afghanistan Horticulture Export Clusters Development Project, which succeeded in introducing innovations that improved productivity in the dried fruit industry in Kandahar. The World Bank approved an Investment Guarantee Facility, which was managed by MIGA. The $12 million facility leveraged about $100 million of foreign investment, mainly for a single telecommunications transaction. Because of the large presence of donors supporting PSD, including in the drafting of commercial laws and regulations, the World Bank did not have grant operations or nonlending technical assistance (NLTA) projects to support investment climate improvements during the period covered by the TSSs.

During the FY07–11 period, Bank Group support to PSD was fragmented and ad hoc, without a clearly articulated assistance strategy that took into account the large donor presence. During the period covered by the ISNs, the main instrument to support private sector development was the World Bank's Private Sector Development Support Project to develop an industrial park and provide capacity-building assistance to the Afghanistan Investment Support Agency and the Ministry of Commerce.

The industrial park[7] component, which was meant to help alleviate the problems of lack of access to land and infrastructure as well as inadequate business support services, was not yet operational at the time of project closing. As a result, the planned follow-up to the project to develop a second industrial park did not materialize. The Private Sector Development Support Project was technically flawed and the industrial park was constrained by inadequate power and water supply—the Implementation Completion Report rated outcomes as unsatisfactory and Bank performance as moderately unsatisfactory.

The World Bank completed another Investment Climate Assessment in 2008 (World Bank 2008), which was followed by a study of the construction industry as part of a growth study series. However, follow-up initiatives to help address the issues raised in the reports were slow in coming and did not match the scale of the problems. The New Business Development Project (FY11) is expected to provide immediate support to small and medium enterprises, but there is no long-term solution to the problem of lack of skills in the private sector. Ongoing IFC work on licensing reform would help reduce the cost of doing business and is well received by the government. There are discussions of Bank Group support to reforming the judicial system and developing alternative dispute-resolution mechanisms. But overall, progress in addressing critical constraints to PSD—unclear property rights, notably with respect to land and land tenure;[8] no credible institutional mechanism for adjudication of commercial disputes;[9] the prevalence of corruption;[10] and policy and regulatory unpredictability—remains slow, with a lack of systematic and coordinated efforts by the Bank Group and other development partners to address these weaknesses.

Financial Sector

At end-2001, the formal financial sector was virtually nonoperational. The central bank was weak and operating under an outdated 1994 Law on Money and Banking; there was no regulatory or supervisory capacity to monitor banks, and no technological resources to undertake modern-day conventional central banking functions. The banking sector consisted of six state-owned commercial and development banks that were physically destroyed, technologically outdated, and operationally nonfunctional. There was little public confidence in the financial system. The principal sources of credit were shopkeepers, traders, landlords, family, and friends. Lack of capital was a key constraint to micro, small, and medium enterprise growth. NGOs provided a limited amount of microfinance but those microfinance programs were largely unsustainable. In 2002, NGOs had a total outstanding loan portfolio of only $1 million—a tiny percentage of potential demand—and served only 12,000 clients. The informal financial system was the only reliable, safe, and inexpensive means of transferring funds into Afghanistan and between its provinces. Money-exchange dealers provided a diverse range of financial and nonfinancial services, including foreign exchange transactions, funds transfers, and trade finance.

WORLD BANK GROUP OBJECTIVES

The TSSs focused on: (i) strengthening the microfinance industry to improve access by enterprises and (ii) strengthening the institutional and operational capacity of the Afghanistan Central Bank (DAB). The 2003 TSS also envisioned World Bank support for the development of the banking and nonbanking system, mainly through ESW and NLTA, including the development of a medium-term financial sector strategy with the MOF and development partners. The ISNs focused on: (i) access to finance, especially for micro, small, and medium enterprises; and (ii) strengthening key financial sector foundations such as banking supervision, credit management, and banking management skills. The 2009 ISN included a financial sector operation to help achieve Bank Group objectives in the sector.

RESULTS

With the introduction of new laws on banking and the central bank, there has been rapid growth of the formal banking system—12 domestic banks have been registered under the new regime and five branches of foreign banks have opened. Deposits and assets have increased by over 50 percent annually since 2006 and credit to the private sector more than doubled during 2006–11, with a decline in 2012 in the wake of the crisis brought on by problems with Kabul Bank.[11]

However, the financial infrastructure remains undeveloped—accounting and auditing standards and practices are inadequate, credit information is not readily available, property rights are unclear, and contract enforcement is problematic. Credit and risk management skills are weak and lending is generally relationship-based, resulting in banks with poor governance and problematic loan portfolios. In addition, DAB supervisory capacity could not keep up with banking growth, with inexperienced regulators deeply in need of training and oversight. The IMF has reported that banking supervision lacks the political support to enforce compliance with existing regulations. Because growth of bank lending portfolios has not been accompanied by development of financial infrastructure and regulatory capacities, the result has been the exposure of the economy to significant risks (see summary results in table 5.4).

In microfinance, there has been significant growth in lending, with a total outstanding loan portfolio of about $130 million at end-2010, representing about 260,000 borrowers. The Microfinance Investment Support Facility for Afghanistan (MISFA) was set up as an apex facility in 2003 at the invitation of the government as a vehicle through which the Afghan government and donors could channel technical assistance and funding for the microfinance sector; the mandate has more recently been expanded to include small and medium enterprises.

MISFA has reported disbursing about $1 billion in microfinance loans cumulatively. MISFA had a loan portfolio of about $60 million to its microfinance

Table 5.4	Summary Results of Pillar 3—Financial Sector
Results associated with Bank Group goals	**Bank Group contribution to results**
Bank Group Objectives: Support the microfinance industry; develop the banking system; strengthen DAB capacity; and introduce leasing.	
• Microfinance lending has grown during the past 10 years with restructuring of the industry. • Bank lending to the private sector grew, though portfolio risks remain high. • Financial infrastructure and capacity to support risk-based lending are still undeveloped. • DAB capacity has improved generally, but supervision capacity needs review. • Lack of a leasing law has impeded the development of a leasing sector.	• The Bank Group supported development of the microfinance sector through World Bank projects and IFC advisory and investment projects, with a significant contribution to development and restructuring of the sector. • Bank Group work (World Bank operation and IFC Advisory Services) on financial infrastructure and capacity building has yet to show results (with the exception of microfinance) beyond the approval of a regulatory framework for financial infrastructure.

institutions (MFIs) and FMBA (First Microfinance Bank of Afghanistan) as of March 2011. In effect, MISFA provided funding for about half of the outstanding microfinance loans. Two studies (Greeley and Chaturvedi 2007; AMMC 2009) estimate that more than 80 percent of loans were used to start or expand businesses, and that each borrower generated 1.5 jobs.

A 2009 impact assessment (AMMC 2009) indicates that microfinance activities have had a positive impact on the lives of women borrowers and their families. Seventy percent of microfinance clients are women, although the survey also found that 80 percent of loans to women were used by men. Nonetheless, women clients reported improved roles in contributing to business decisions and a positive impact on women clients' participation in the household economic decision making on food, utilities, health, education, and clothing. Improvement was also seen in client savings, with 69 percent of clients saving money, compared to only 34 percent before taking the loan.

During the past three years, the microfinance industry has been going through a major restructuring, and many MFIs became insolvent due to inability to sustain their operations. Were it not for the growth in lending by the IFC investee company FMBA, the microfinance industry portfolio would have declined during the past three years. The number of MFIs supported by MISFA has shrunk from 16 to 7 with the exit or consolidation of MFIs that were not performing well. MISFA, which has been playing an active role in the restructuring of the microfinance industry,[12] has been reporting positive financial results and will not require additional funding for the next two years.[13] The emergence of leasing as an additional instrument to support the private sector has been held up by the delay in approval of a leasing law. Lack of enabling legislation on leasing has prevented IFC from investing in the sector.

WORLD BANK GROUP CONTRIBUTION

The early activities of the Bank Group supported the microfinance industry and improved knowledge of the financial sector. In microfinance, the Bank Group took a two-pronged approach. First, the World Bank supported the transformation and funding of MISFA with nonlending technical assistance in FY03 and the Afghanistan ARTF Microfinance Project in FY04. A follow-up project supporting MISFA in FY08—Expanding Microfinance Outreach and Improving Sustainability—focused on sustainability of MFIs by helping them achieve operating self-sufficiency. Second, IFC supported the establishment of a commercial bank specializing in microlending.

IFC's structured system for results measurement facilitates monitoring and attribution of results of Advisory Service projects. IFC's Advisory Service project—Afghanistan: Feasibility Study for the Establishing a Microfinance Institution—led to the establishment of the FMBA, the first private sector bank registered under the new regime, supported by an FY03 investment and a large technical assistance program for capacity building. FMBA now accounts for almost half of microlending (figure 5.1). Another IFC Advisory Services project—the "Afghanistan Housing Finance/Microfinance Study"—resulted in the introduction of a housing microfinance product in FMBA, supported by an IFC loan and technical assistance. FMBA also developed a product targeted to women following the IFC Advisory Services project: "FMBA Outreach to Women Entrepreneurs." With the success to date of FMBA, IFC helped introduce a new mechanism for funding (through deposits) and delivering microfinance services.

To gain sector knowledge after a long absence, in FY04 the World Bank produced an ESW product—The Financial Sector Study (World Bank 2004a). IFC helped the government develop the legal and regulatory framework for leasing through an Advisory Services project, the "Afghanistan Leasing Project," which led to the revisions to the Tax Law. Though IFC had worked with both the government and Parliament on drafting of the Leasing Law, this critical piece of legislation has

| Figure 5.1 | Growth of Microfinance Portfolio |

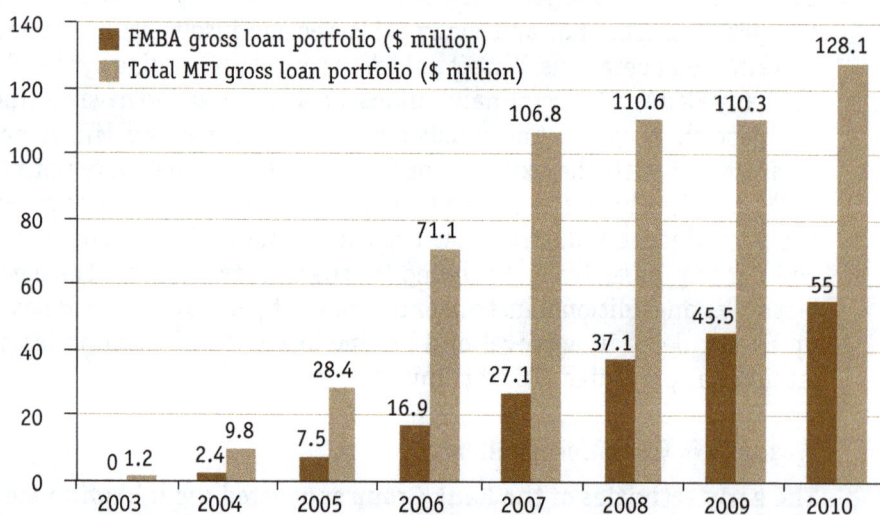

Source: MixMarket at: http://www.mixmarket.org/.

| Box 5.1 | Results Measurement System for Advisory Services at IFC |

In 2006, IFC introduced standardized procedures for approval, supervision, and completion of Advisory Services projects. The process integrates results measurement into every stage of the project life cycle, from concept development to completion.

Project approval documents contain a description of the Advisory Services project's objectives, strategic relevance, and IFC's additionality. The approval document also has to include a results framework with the indicators to be tracked through subsequent supervision reports.

- All projects must select indicators from a list of corporate standard indicators that IFC has developed for each business line and product, and establish baseline data and targets for those indicators.

- A regional monitoring and evaluation officer vets the framework and indicators before approval.

- Advisory Services projects undergo semiannual supervision that reports on the progress of project activities, project results, and financials.

- At completion, the Advisory Services team provides a self-assessment of performance for all Advisory Services projects in a Project Completion Report. Advisory Services projects are rated for development effectiveness and IFC's role and contribution; the development effectiveness rating is based on strategic relevance, results (outputs, outcomes, and impacts), and efficiency.

- IFC's Development Effectiveness Unit (reporting to the executive vice president) reviews final Project Completion Reports and provides its own ratings for each Advisory Services project.

- IEG validates project results for a stratified random sample of Advisory Services projects. IEG, the Advisory Services project team, and IFC's Development Impact Unit follow the same guidelines for rating Advisory Services projects.

- IEG produces a Biennial Report on Operations Evaluation, which assesses the adequacy, coverage, and quality of the monitoring and evaluation system in IFC.

Project information and supporting documentation are stored in the Advisory Services Operational Portal. The operational portal is an interactive IFC application that houses Advisory Services project data and project templates and generates review and approval processes. The system facilitates portfolio data aggregation and reporting on key output, outcome, and impact indicators and efficiency of services.

Source: IEG.

yet to be enacted. IFC also provided technical assistance to the Afghanistan Finance Company, which was establishing leasing operations.

Bank Group support for financial infrastructure and skills development did not come until late in the evaluation period; many of these activities should have been started earlier. In FY09, the World Bank approved the Afghanistan Financial Strengthening Project to enhance the supervision capacity of DAB and establish a Public Credit Registry, Collateral Registry, and the Afghanistan Institute of Banking and Finance. Two IFC Advisory Services projects complemented the World Bank operation: Public Credit Registry Afghanistan (FY09) and Afghanistan Secured Lending Project (FY09). While the IMF[14] and donors have been active in their support to DAB, there has been less donor activity around financial infrastructure, hence the relevance of Bank Group activities in this area.

The World Bank also provided technical assistance—Anti-Money Laundering and Combating Financing of Terrorism (AML/CFT) Financial Analysis/Investigation Capacity Building Program (FY09)—to establish capacity for AML/CFT in DAB (Pierre-Laurent and others 2009). This NLTA is highly relevant in the Afghanistan context and is well received by both DAB and donors. Finally, the World Bank completed the ESW Housing Finance in Afghanistan: Challenges and Opportunities (World Bank with others 2008), but this has not resulted in implementation of recommended reforms or design of follow-up Bank Group initiatives to help the government address the critical issues in housing, land tenure, and land titling identified in the study.

Mining and Hydrocarbons

Afghanistan has a rich endowment of mineral and energy resources, but production has been far short of potential. Mineral production in 2002 was limited to small coal operations, limestone from three operating cement plants, construction materials, and artisanal production of gemstones and dimensional stones. Hydrocarbon production consisted of natural gas in the Sheberghan area and very limited production of oil in Sar-i-Pol. There were identified deposits of minerals that had not been exploited, among them, the world-class Aynak copper and Hajigak iron ore deposits. The Ministry of Mines, which has oversight responsibility for the sector and had 4,000 employees, was in dire need of capacity building and institutional reform. There were also several state-owned enterprises, none of which was operating on a commercial basis.

The government viewed the mining and hydrocarbon sector as a significant potential source of revenue, as well as a major source of employment in remote areas. The government elaborated its sector strategy in two documents: (i) Oil, Gas and Mining Sector Vision and (ii) "National Extractive Industries Excellence Program" (Islamic Republic of Afghanistan 2010b). The strategy pursued the following goals: (i) fully developed sector policies and legislative reform to support sector growth; (ii) strong regulatory environment for responsible sector management, including environmental and social performance; (iii) modernized and strong Ministry of Mines, able to deliver results; (iv) an enabling business environment to attract private sector investment; and (v) reliable and updated geological information to support sector growth. The government has requested donor support to implement the strategy.

WORLD BANK GROUP OBJECTIVES

During the review period, the Bank Group aimed to support the establishment of the appropriate legal and regulatory regime to support private investment in the sector and the building of capacity in the Ministry of Mines to enable policymaking, regulatory enforcement, and private investment promotion. These objectives would be achieved through a mix of AAA and grant operations. The main benchmark for success was the establishment of the legal and regulatory framework for the sector. The 2012 ISN (World Bank 2012b) goes further in envisaging the natural resources sector as a cornerstone of the Bank's efforts to support growth by leveraging investments in the extractive industry to create resource corridors for broader economic development.

RESULTS

A Minerals Law and a Hydrocarbon Law were approved in 2005, with regulations finalized in 2008 (table 5.5). Enforcement, though improving, is still weak and will have to respond to the rapidly developing environment in the sector. One of the significant developments in the mineral sector has been the government's successful tender of the Aynak copper deposit, with technical assistance from the World Bank. The successful conclusion of the main agreement has resulted in a payment of $80 million to the government, as the first tranche against a total signature bonus of $808 million for the right to develop the deposit. The government has also awarded the concession for exploration of the Hajigak ore deposit, reportedly the largest in Asia. Annual benefits during the next 30 years from the development of the Aynak and Hajigak deposits could reach 11 percent of 2008 gross national income in terms of national income, 55 percent of 2008–09 revenues in terms of fiscal revenues, and four times the 2009 amount in terms of exports based on World Bank projections. Annual direct employment in the mines was estimated at around 6,400 (World Bank 2011).

Progress in the hydrocarbon component has been slower than in minerals, with disagreements among donors on the appropriate focus of developing the sector. The Hydrocarbon Law and regulations had to be modified to attract foreign investment, essentially by correcting the balance between oil and gas. The government recently awarded a contract for the development of certain oil and gas resources in the Amu Darya Basin; the value of the contract is much smaller than the ones for the mines. A tender for the exploration, development, and production of hydrocarbons in the Afghan-Tajik Basin in Northern Afghanistan has been issued. In March 2009, the government endorsed the Extractive Industries Transparency Initiative, signaling its commitment to transparent and accountable sector governance.

WORLD BANK GROUP CONTRIBUTION

Initial World Bank activities in the sector consisted of participation in a number of studies and workshops. The World Bank prepared a multivolume study of Afghanistan's oil and gas infrastructure development in FY05, which identified and evaluated viable investment options for the rehabilitation and development of oil and gas. The World Bank provided technical assistance for the preparation of the Hydrocarbon Law and sector-related amendments to the Income Tax Law. The Bank also provided technical assistance and policy advice in FY05 to assist the government in the drafting of hydrocarbon regulations and the development of a model production-sharing contract for oil and gas.

To support the government's goal of providing a transparent and efficient regulatory environment for the extractive industries sector, the World Bank approved the first Sustainable Development of Natural Resources Project in 2006, which provided capacity-building assistance to the Ministry of Mines.

Table 5.5	Summary Results of Pillar 3—Energy and Mining
Results associated with Bank Group goals	**Bank Group contribution to results**
Bank Group Objective: Develop the legal and regulatory regime to enable private investment; and improve capacity of the Ministry of Mines.	
• Large foreign investments in two mines approved. • Legal and regulatory regime is basically in place. • Ministry of Mines capacity has improved.	• World Bank AAA helped develop the laws and regulations in the sector. • World Bank operations and advice supported capacity building.

By focusing on solid minerals and oil, the project complemented assistance being provided by other donors—the ADB in natural gas, the British Geological Survey in geological data compilation and capacity strengthening of the Afghan Geological Survey, the U.S. Trade and Development Agency in cement, and the U.S. Geological Survey in coal.

In 2011, the World Bank approved the second Sustainable Development of Natural Resources Project, which focused on improving enforcement of sector laws and regulations. As the initial contracts for the development of mines were being awarded, the World Bank produced a major study on the mining sector, "The Afghanistan Mining Sector as a Driver of Sustainable Growth: Benefits and Opportunities for Large-Scale Mining" (World Bank 2011), which discussed options for maximizing benefits from mining.[15] The study concluded that the sector could stimulate the industrialization process and lead to broad-based inclusive growth by: (i) integrating infrastructure investments in the sector with the needs of other sectors in the economy; (ii) developing linkage industries, particularly in mining supply firms; and (iii) ensuring that mining communities receive their fair share of the social and economic benefits from mining operations. The study drew lessons for Afghanistan from international experience on maximizing socioeconomic benefits from large-scale mining, including from World Bank and IFC projects.

The Bank Group[16] is currently helping the government leverage the mining investments toward creating a growth corridor with a follow-up NLTA approved in FY12,[17] essentially implementing the findings from the mining ESW (box 5.2). The "resource corridor initiative" has become a critical pillar of the government's growth strategy as well as a major component of the recent Bank Group ISN.[18] If fully developed, the mining sector could eventually contribute 2–3 percent to GDP, although its direct employment effect is expected to be modest (World Bank 2012a, pp. 26–27) In this sector, the World Bank has accompanied an appropriate mix of instruments with sustained policy and technical dialogue with counterparts to get the results achieved thus far.

Information and Communications Technology

There were only two telephones per thousand people in Afghanistan in 2002, compared with 24 in Pakistan, 35 in Tajikistan, and 68 in Uzbekistan. Only one out

The Bank Group's work on the private sector in Afghanistan provides a window on the complementarity of World Bank, IFC, and MIGA activities.

In the ICT sector, the World Bank played a significant and influential role in assisting the government to restructure and liberalize the sector. Through grant operations and nonlending technical assistance, the World Bank helped in the establishment of the institutional framework that would attract private investment. An IFC investment and MIGA guarantees supported the entry and expansion of a third cellular operator to increase competition and expand coverage from 50 percent to 80 percent of the population. The MIGA- and IFC-supported company is now among the three largest in the country in market share and subscribers.

In microfinance, the World Bank focused on MISFA to increase microfinance funding and improve sustainability of MFIs, which were established by NGOs. IFC investment and technical assistance supported the establishment of a new commercial bank, which provided an additional mechanism for mobilizing funds and delivering microfinance services. The IFC investee bank now accounts for almost half of the microfinance portfolio.

The Financial Sector Strengthening Project is a joint World Bank and IFC operation, with the World Bank supporting capacity building in DAB to improve off-site banking supervision and IFC focusing on improving the financial infrastructure. IFC has deployed Advisory Services projects to establish a credit information bureau and collateral registry, and bring IFC experience in other countries.

The current resource corridor initiative utilizes skills and experience not only from different units within the World Bank but also from IFC, which has experience in small and medium enterprise linkage programs in its mining and infrastructure investments.

of 625 Afghan citizens had access to telephone service. Communications between provinces was extremely limited and effectively nonexistent in smaller towns. There was no service provider for Internet and data services. Afghan Telecom was the single service provider for decades, and the telecommunications infrastructure was one of the least developed in the world. The government objective was to establish a stable telecommunications policy and regulatory environment, in order to attract private and foreign investment in Afghanistan. The benchmark was to have a national telecommunications network in place by end-2010, with more than 80 percent of Afghans having access to affordable telecommunications and more than $100 million per year of public revenues. Afghan Telecom was to be privatized in keeping with the government's 2003 Telecom and Internet Policy.

WORLD BANK GROUP OBJECTIVES

The 2003 TSS described a Bank Group program of AAA and grant operations (ARTF and the Public-Private Infrastructure Advisory Facility) that would help the government implement the new telecommunications policy that supported the introduction of private sector–led competitive provision of infrastructure and services. The World Bank would also support the rollout of communications services to meet public and private sector communications needs. The 2006 ISN anticipated a reduced role for the Bank Group given the success of the sector in attracting private investment. The 2009 ISN included ICT in the broad-based work on infrastructure by the Bank Group and noted the planned additional IFC investment in one of the telecommunications companies.

RESULTS

Since 2002, Afghanistan has made considerable progress in expanding access to telecommunications services and improving international connectivity. Afghanistan currently has five nationwide mobile service providers plus three regional licensees, and the overall mobile telephony market is quite competitive, contributing to the lowering of prices from $1 per minute in 2002 to $0.22 per minute in 2010. Private sector entry has been made possible by the establishment of an enabling policy and a legal and regulatory framework (table 5.6), including the establishment of the Afghanistan Telecommunications Regulatory Agency.

Afghan Telecom, which was decoupled from the Ministry of Communications and Information Technology (MOCIT), is currently financially viable, with privatization plans awaiting implementation. A high-capacity fiber optic backbone network now connects 20 of the 34 provinces and provides international connectivity to neighboring countries. There are more than 18 million mobile phone subscribers with coverage of about 80 percent of the total population. Moreover, there has been an increased use of ICT to improve governance in the public sector, productivity in the private sector, and services by both government and businesses.

WORLD BANK GROUP CONTRIBUTION

Bank Group engagement in the ICT sector started early, with technical assistance in FY03 to help in the drafting of various laws and regulations. The NLTA was followed by the Emergency Communications Development Project, which was approved in FY04 to: (i) carry out expansion of the government communications network; (ii) improve capacity of MOCIT to create an enabling environment for private sector investment; and (iii) improve postal services.

The Afghanistan Telecommunications Regulatory Agency was established with World Bank advice and support for capacity building. An IFC investment—its largest in Afghanistan—and a MIGA guarantee supported the entry of the third mobile telephone operator, which introduced competition to what was then a duopoly and increased coverage at a time when only about 50 percent of the population had access. The World Bank also provided advice on the privatization of Afghan Telecom, which has yet to be implemented, though a decision has been made by the government to go ahead with the sale of 60 percent of the company. Donor activities—by USAID, ADB, UNDP, and the International Telecommunications Union —were mainly in the financing of telecommunications infrastructure managed by Afghan Telecom and support in technical aspects such as spectrum management and engineering issues.

Subsequent World Bank support was delivered through rapid-response NLTA as well as continuing dialogue through frequent missions by regional and

Table 5.6	Summary Results of Pillar 3—ICT
Results associated with Bank Group goals	**Bank Group contribution to results**
Bank Group Objectives: Develop legal and regulatory regime for private investment; improve policy and regulatory capacities; support privatization of Afghan Telecom; and enable increased utilization of ICT applications.	
• Sector is now dominated by private sector. • Privatization of Afghan Telecom approved by the government. • Eighty percent mobile phone geographical coverage with prices declining and ICT applications increasing. • Legal and regulatory regime in place. • Improved capacity in the Ministry of Communications and Information Technology and Afghanistan Telecommunications Regulatory Agency. • Increased use of ICT in public sector governance.	• World Bank nonlending technical assistance and operations helped develop the legal and regulatory regime and improve policy and oversight capacities of government offices. • IFC investment and MIGA guarantees supported private investment in the sector.

headquarters staff. The World Bank provided NLTA in FY08 for the development of an ICT strategy. During FY09–11, the World Bank continued to provide technical assistance in various areas: (i) Afghanistan NLTA: Telecommunications Sector (FY09), to help develop options for managing the fiber optic network, design programs for effective utilization of the Telecommunications Development Funds, and help build capacity of the Afghanistan Telecommunications Authority to address regulatory issues; (ii) Remote Asset Monitoring and Verification (FY10) to improve monitoring and verification of irrigation infrastructure; (iii) Broadband to Educational Institutions Program (FY10) to help design a pilot for provision of high-quality and reliable broadband Internet connectivity to educational institutions; and (iv) Mobile Applications in Afghanistan: Mainstreaming Across Government and Developing the Ecosystem (FY10), to support government efforts to mainstream use of mobile telephone–based applications to help expand the reach of public services and strengthen program management through improved supervision and data collection.

In FY11, the World Bank approved the ICT Sector Development Project, which would support expansion of connectivity, mainstreaming in the use of mobile applications in strategic sectors in government, and support for the development of the local information technology industry. The Bank Group has been a major contributor to the development of the sector, with the World Bank, IFC, and MIGA playing complementary roles. The World Bank has provided sustained support to the MOCIT and the Afghanistan Telecommunications Regulatory Agency. The World Bank is now focusing on enhancing the use of information technology applications to improve productivity in various sectors.

Power

In 2002, the power network was in a dilapidated state and in urgent need of rehabilitation. Access to power was only about 6 percent, one of the lowest in the world. Only 234,000 customers were connected to the public grid, of which approximately 30 percent were in Kabul. The other provinces had even less access, and rural areas were virtually unserved. The existing facilities provided unreliable service, with power available for only a few hours a day. The countrywide power utility, Da Afghanistan Breshna Moassese (DABM), a department of the Ministry of Energy and Water (MEW), suffered from overstaffing and lacked skills to run a modern system. Revenues were limited by the lack of efficient billing and collection systems. Technical and nontechnical losses were about 30–40 percent due to overloaded facilities and lack of customer supervision. With the exception of cities, which were supplied with diesel generators, electricity tariffs were well below the cost of supply.[19] The Investment Climate Assessments identified access to electricity as one of main constraints to PSD.

The government strategy articulated in the I-ANDS focused on overcoming power shortages, first, by cross-border power purchases, and then by rehabilitation and establishment of major hydropower schemes. The strategy aimed to ensure that power reached the rural areas, as well as to enhance capacity to maintain infrastructure and manage services. The power strategy articulated in the ANDS supports: (i) commercially and technically efficient energy delivery; (ii) reformed sector governance; (iii) establishment of a market-based enabling environment to facilitate private investment; (iv) diversification of energy resources for long-term, low-cost energy, energy security, and clean energy use; and (v) intersectoral supporting linkages including comprehensive system-based planning. The government would provide the basis for a transition from public to private provision, which would require new institutional arrangements.

Commercialization of DABM has been ongoing since 2006, and an Inter-Ministerial Commission for Energy was established in 2006 to coordinate policy and planning. Targets were: (i) by end-2010, electricity would reach at least 65 percent of households and 90 percent of nonresidential establishments in major urban areas and at least 25 percent of households in rural areas; and (ii) by end-2010, at least 75 percent of the costs would be recovered from users connected to the national power grid.

WORLD BANK GROUP OBJECTIVES

The TSSs focused on supporting rehabilitation through investment projects and providing advice through policy dialogue in the following areas: the future strategy for the sector, immediate investment needs, subsidy and tariff issues, and rural access. The 2006 ISN mentioned continued support to the sector, with two project-specific benchmarks: (i) 94 megawatts of hydropower capacity rehabilitated; and (ii) 25,000 new connections in Kabul, and the medium-voltage network in Kabul and Mazar-e-Sharif rehabilitated. The 2009 ISN mentioned power as part of the broad-based work to improve infrastructure services, and had as a benchmark progress in the corporatization and commercialization of the public power utility.

RESULTS

There has been progress in increasing total electricity supply through both imports and rehabilitation of infrastructure. A number of electricity projects have been implemented in rural areas, benefiting at least one million people. The Inter-Ministerial Commission for Energy has been set up to coordinate energy-related issues within the government and with donors. There has been a restructuring of DABM, with the establishment of vertically integrated Business Units, which were expected to improve operation on a commercial basis with separate accounts. However, progress in improving billing and collection performance has been slow, and an appropriate pricing policy, which is critical to achieving full cost recovery, has yet to be established.

The restructured Da Afghanistan Breshna Shirkat (DABS), successor to DABM, faces many challenges, among them the scarcity of skilled Afghan labor. Metering usage, while increasing, continues to be a constraint to billing and collection performance. There has been a lack of progress in the establishment of an enabling environment for private sector participation (table 5.7). Nonetheless, through donor-financed system rehabilitation and electricity imports from Turkmenistan, there has been progress toward improving access to power.

WORLD BANK GROUP CONTRIBUTION

During the TSS period covering FY02–06, there were two World Bank power operations. The Improvement of Power Supply of Kabul Project (FY03) supported rehabilitation of hydropower stations in Sarobi and Mahipar, rehabilitation of transmission lines, additional street lighting, and rehabilitation of the electricity network. The Emergency Power Rehabilitation Project (FY04) supported rehabilitation and expansion of the distribution network in Kabul, rehabilitation of the Naghlu hydropower plant and the transmission line from Naghlu to Kabul, commercialization of DABM, and technical assistance to MEW and DABM. A World Bank nonlending technical assistance to the power sector in FY04 provided advice on sector policy and corporatization of DABM, produced a power sector reform roadmap, and held an energy workshop. While donors had a major share of financing of overall sector investments, the World Bank played

Table 5.7	Summary Results of Pillar 3—Power
Results associated with Bank Group goals	**Bank Group contribution to results**
Bank Group Objective: Support rehabilitation of power sector including capacity building and advice on sector policy.	
• Based on the 2010 Investment Climate Assessment, power supply remains a major constraint to private sector development. • The power utility company (DABS) continues to suffer from weak capacity.	• The World Bank is not a major player in the sector; World Bank projects focused on power distribution systems in latter part of the evaluation period. • World Bank AAA and operations supported initial reorganization of DABS. • Current portfolio of World Bank projects facing difficulties and may need to be restructured. • World Bank AAA helped develop a power sector road map early in the evaluation period, but the World Bank role at the strategic level has diminished since then.

a major role in defining sector strategy and reform, restructuring DABM, and coordinating donor activities during the TSS period.

World Bank activities during the ISN period were relevant. During the ISN period covering FY07–11, the World Bank began to focus on supporting investments in power distribution, which has lagged behind the progress made on the transmission side and was given less emphasis by donors. The World Bank financed the Kabul-Aybak and Mazar-e-Sharif Power Project (FY08) to support rehabilitation of old and dilapidated infrastructure in Kabul and Mazar-e-Sharif, build a 220/20 kilovolt substation at Aybak and support institutional capacity building for operation and maintenance of distribution systems. The World Bank also financed the Afghanistan Power System Development Project (FY09), which would build on previous projects and rehabilitate distribution network and transmission switchyards and provide capacity building to executing agencies, support the establishment of a unit promoting energy efficiency and demand-side management, help implement some pilots, and improve collection of energy usage information. The World Bank also completed several AAA projects: (i) Kabul Household Energy Survey (FY07) to measure access to electricity (ii) Study of Alternative Options to Increase Electricity Access in Afghanistan (FY09); (iii) Energy Efficient Lighting Options for Afghanistan (FY09); and (iv) Decision Model on Power Sector Deals (FY09).

Implementation has been a challenge in the power sector. Three ongoing power projects in Afghanistan—the Emergency Power Rehabilitation Project; the Kabul, Aybak and Mazar-e-Sharif Power Project; and the Afghanistan Power Sector Development Project—are experiencing implementation issues and may need to be restructured. For 18 months the sector lacked a full-time team leader, putting at risk not only the implementation of physical infrastructure projects, but also critical capacity-building initiatives.

While an in-country presence may be desirable, this is not always possible given the constraints of the Bank's footprint in Afghanistan. However, having a full-time team leader, even if based elsewhere, is essential for effective Bank support. Government dialogue and donor coordination were also adversely affected by the lack of strong World Bank engagement. The World Bank lost the role it had during the TSS period, when the Bank took the lead on sector reform and coordination of donor activities and pushed for the restructuring of DABM. Early Bank advice influenced the government's 2007 power sector strategy, but lack of effective donor coordination subsequently diminished the efficacy of that strategy.

Urban Development

By 2002, urban infrastructure had deteriorated due to lack of maintenance and outright destruction. Roads were in disrepair, and were unable to cope with the increase in vehicular traffic. Street lighting was almost nonexistent. Public buildings had been looted. About a quarter of urban housing had been seriously damaged or destroyed. Urban water supply and sanitation, solid waste management, and storm water drainage facilities were in urgent need of repair.

Few residential buildings had sewage systems, and those that did discharged wastewater directly into rivers without treatment. Water-borne diseases were a major cause of high infant and child mortality rates. At the same time, urban centers were experiencing high population growth, putting even more pressure on improving the delivery of services.

The focus of the government's urban development strategy in the I-ANDS was housing development, in particular land titling to secure property rights of urban homeowners. The strategy was also designed to strengthen the capacity of municipalities to manage urban development and to deliver services effectively and transparently. Benchmarks were: (i) by end-2010, municipal governments would have strengthened capacity to manage urban development and to deliver services effectively and efficiently; (ii) by end-2010, 50 percent of households in Kabul and 30 percent of households in other major urban areas would have access to piped water; and (iii) by end-2010, electricity would reach at least 65 percent of households and 90 percent of nonresidential establishments in major urban areas, with at least 75 percent of the costs recovered from users connected to the national power grid. With respect to the problem of informal settlements, the strategy would achieve phased regularization of tenure for 50 percent of households in informal settlements.

WORLD BANK GROUP OBJECTIVES

World Bank activities focused on two areas. First, it would support rehabilitation of critical infrastructure, mainly roads, water and sanitation, and power (as part of the power portfolio). Second, the Bank would help introduce contemporary techniques of urban planning, initiate programs for community-based upgrading of informal urban neighborhoods, and start modernization of the urban land management system. Third, the 2006 ISN emphasized as a cross-cutting theme the need for greater attention to land issues, which the Investment Climate Assessments identified as one of the top constraints to PSD and which underpin the crisis in urban housing.

RESULTS

There has been significant progress in the rehabilitation of physical infrastructure, most of which was financed by other donors. The Kabul new city master plan and the regional urban development plan have been completed. Urban policies, codes, regulations, and standards are almost complete. An urban development Inter-Ministerial Committee has been put in place to improve coordination and monitoring. However, urban management needs upgrading to implement plans, enforce regulations, and address problems generated by population growth and urban poverty. There has been little progress in resolving housing and land issues (table 5.8).

WORLD BANK GROUP CONTRIBUTION

The Emergency Transport Rehabilitation Project,[20] approved by the World Bank in 2003 and supported by USAID, Japan, Sweden, and Norway, restored road

Table 5.8	Summary Results of Pillar 3—Urban Development
Results associated with Bank Group goals	**Bank Group contribution to results**
Bank Group Objectives: Support rehabilitation of urban infrastructure; introduce contemporary techniques for urban development; and address land issues.	
• There has been significant progress in rehabilitation of infrastructure, though increases in urban population and traffic pose major continuing challenges. • Capacity for urban development remains weak, with authorities unable to deal with the scale of urban issues. • Little progress in addressing land issues, which are critical to mitigation of housing crisis.	• Donors dominate the urban infrastructure rehabilitation; the World Bank had one early road rehabilitation project; World Bank urban water projects focused on institution building. • World Bank Kabul Urban Reconstruction Project (KURP), which addressed urban planning and capacity building issues, had to be restructured. • AAA and KURP covered land and housing issues that remain unresolved.

connections between Kabul and the provinces in the north and the countries along the northern border. The Kabul City Roads and Water Drainage Project (FY04) and the Kabul Urban Roads Improvement Project (FY09) financed repair of major Kabul roads and rehabilitation of drainage structures along repaired roads. World Bank projects were relatively small compared with financing from other donors for rehabilitation of urban infrastructure. The FY04 project was rated satisfactory at completion, while the ongoing FY09 project experienced implementation problems resulting in delays.

The water projects, which had components to deal with institutional and longer-term issues, were relevant given donor focus on physical infrastructure. The Short-Term Urban Water Supply and Sanitation Project (FY05), which aimed to improve water supply and sanitation services and build the technical and institutional foundation for a medium-term urban water supply and sanitation program, was rated unsatisfactory for outcomes in the implementation completion report. The Urban Water Sector Project (FY06), which was restructured and has recently been achieving reasonable implementation progress, had parallel funding by KfW and aimed to: (i) increase access to and reliability of the water supply service in Kabul; (ii) improve capacity of the Central Authority for Water Supply and Sewerage; and (iii) establish the financial sustainability of the Afghan Urban Water Supply and Sanitation Company.

In FY04, the Bank approved the Kabul Urban Reconstruction Project (KURP), which had six components: (i) area upgrading in Kabul; (ii) land tenure regularization; (iii) engineering and management support to urban agencies; (iv) overall capacity building for Kabul municipality; (v) preparation of structure plans and a future urban project; and (vi) main road, drainage, and traffic management in Kabul.

As noted in the Project Paper[21] restructuring the KURP project five-and-a-half years later, the original design was overly ambitious and complex, reflecting lack of knowledge of the sector and overestimation of the capacity and ownership of implementing agencies. In addition, several project components were not aligned with emergency reconstruction priorities. With the restructuring of the project, the land tenure component of the project, which would have developed a methodology and capacity to regularize land tenure on a pilot basis, was dropped, leaving a major gap in addressing a critical factor in the housing crisis. The original KURP had relevant objectives addressing critical needs, but had diminished effectiveness due to poor project design and implementation. The restructured project eventually achieved the physical asset and service delivery outcomes, and the Implementation Status Results Report of May 2012 (Tewari 2012) showed satisfactory ratings for both achievement of project development objectives and implementation progress.

Staffing issues and poor management oversight were contributing factors to the lack of effectiveness. With the placement of a senior staff in the Kabul office, the World Bank is increasing its support to the government to ensure that services are able to meet the increasing demands from urban population and business growth.

World Bank AAA tried to address the knowledge gaps on land issues. The World Bank issued the AAA "Kabul Urban Land Crisis: A Summary of Issues and Recommendations— A Policy Note" in FY07 (World Bank 2006b). The report provided guidance on how to manage three of the most important aspects of land management: (i) development of urban areas using contemporary techniques of planning and regulation; (ii) regulation of tenure in informal areas; and (iii) land rights dispute resolution. Another report—"Land Acquisition in Afghanistan" (FY07; World Bank 2007)—reviewed and assessed the legal framework regulating social safeguards (national and local laws, regulations, procedures, and policies), with special reference to the law and practice of compulsory land acquisition or expropriation. While relevant, these AAA have not resulted in significant progress in addressing land issues, which may require follow-up grant operations or NLTA. The World Bank also provided NLTA—Kabul Historic Conservation in Urban Upgrading (FY10)—to promote the physical, social, and economic development of the old city while safeguarding its heritage.

Overall Assessment of the Growth of Formal Sector Agenda

The outcomes from the Bank Group program in this pillar have been mixed (table 5.9). Bank Group performance and results have been satisfactory or better in three important segments: (i) microfinance, which services a large segment of private business as well as the poor and women; (ii) ICT, which is beginning to have an impact on public and private sector efficiency and governance; and (iii) mining and hydrocarbons, which have potential as drivers of future growth. These are also segments where relatively small Bank Group financing has resulted in significant private sector investments and where the Bank Group had significant inputs in the policy, legal, and regulatory framework as well as related institution building. Bank Group projects that financed rehabilitation of infrastructure have also shown generally satisfactory results, though some projects have experienced or continue to have implementation issues.

Table 5.9	Status of Performance Benchmarks	
Source	Benchmark	Status
Investment climate		
2003 TSS	Quality and functioning of enabling regulations for domestic and foreign investors	Doing Business Indicators show improvement in business entry but lack of progress in other areas
2006 ISN	Two industrial parks operational	Not achieved: no operational industrial park
2006 ISN	Transit times at borders reduced	No reduction in transit times at border
2006 ISN	Reduction in time taken and cost incurred (official and unofficial) to obtain all licenses and permits to open a business	Reduction in time and cost to open a business, but not in other areas
2009 ISN	Progress in facilitating an increase in private sector investment	Little progress has been made in most sectors; the exceptions are mining and ICT
2009 ISN	Increased business and management skills training, including women	World Bank and IFC initiatives contribute to skills development
Financial Sector		
2003 TSS	Regulatory framework, domestic and international payments system operational	Achieved
2006 ISN	Issuance of regulations for licensing and supervision of insurance and nonbanking financial institutions such as leasing and microfinance	Not achieved
2003 TSS & 2009 ISN	Increased access to finance, including microfinance	Achieved
2009 ISN	Adoption of Leasing Law	Drafted but not passed
Mining and hydrocarbons		
2006 ISN	Regulatory environment for minerals/natural resources established	Achieved
Information and communications technology		
2009 ISN	Progress in privatization of Afghan Telecom	There has been a cabinet decision, but privatization has not yet been implemented
Power		
2006 ISN	94 megawatts of hydropower capacity rehabilitated	Ongoing
	25,000 new connections in Kabul city and medium voltage network in Kabul and Mazar-e-Sharif rehabilitated	Achieved
2009 ISN	Progress in corporatization and commercialization of public power utility	Achieved
Urban development		
2006 ISN	Connection of provincial centers to ring road by all-season roads	Achieved
2006 ISN	Road maintenance program in place, operational and routinely included in the budget	Not achieved: not part of program
2006 ISN	15,000 new water connections in Kabul and 20,000 in 15 provincial towns	Ongoing

Bank Group performance and results in the investment climate, power, and urban development have been less than satisfactory. There are various reasons for this. In the investment climate, it has been difficult to develop a focused and relevant program where donor presence is extensive; the only grant operation failed due to poor design and supervision, and, equally important, diverted staff and management attention from addressing other investment climate issues. In the power sector, staffing transition issues weakened project supervision and dialogue with government and donors. In urban development, lack of sector knowledge resulted in poor design of the flagship project. But a common thread has been the lack of progress in addressing fundamental issues such as clarifying property rights, creating institutions, and building capacity and skills.

Looking forward, the Bank Group could build on current successes and strengthen the focus of the program to support private sector growth. Bank Group work on growth corridors and initiatives that promote ICT applications toward improved governance and increased productivity could be major components of a Bank Group PSD program. In addition, Bank Group strategy could have focused on areas that are critical to private sector–led growth: well-defined property rights, establishment of alternate dispute-resolution mechanisms for resolving commercial disputes, institutions with capacity to enforce regulations, and development of skills in both the public and private sectors. Given the importance of addressing complex urban issues that affect urban unemployment and poverty, the Bank Group could review its engagement exercising greater selectivity to enhance effectiveness. The Bank Group program could also consider greater use of NLTA and Advisory Services, which have been effective in providing concrete advice and rapid response to the government.

RISK TO DEVELOPMENT OUTCOMES

The risk to development outcomes for pillar 3 of the ISNs is very high for several reasons. Continuing security concerns have a dampening effect on private sector investment, notably foreign direct investment. Political uncertainty increases risk to the sustainability of current policies and reforms. Corruption increases the cost of doing business and distorts resource allocation. The absence or weaknesses of critical institutions constrain effectiveness of legal and regulatory regimes that are being put in place to promote investments in various sectors. Unclear property rights, notably with respect to land, are impediments to the functioning of markets and the development of many sectors, especially the financial sector, agriculture, and urban development. Lack of skills discourages investment and innovation in the private sector and impacts effectiveness of the public sector. Dependence on foreign aid has placed less emphasis on sustainability issues such as operations and maintenance as well as cost recovery.

Notes

1. These are: (i) address overall constraints to PSD through lending and advisory work; (ii) identify and address specific measures to catalyze business growth; and (iii) invest directly in local companies to help them expand business.

2. Benchmarks were: (i) all legislation, regulations, and procedures related to investment would be simplified and harmonized by end-2006 and implemented by end-2007; (ii) new business organization laws would be tabled in the National Assembly by end-2006; (iii) government's strategy for divestment of state-owned enterprises would be implemented by end-2009.

3. The 2009 ISN stated that World Bank Group efforts to improve the regulatory environment would focus on the Doing Business indicators.

4. The Afghanistan Chamber of Commerce and Industry has requested IFC assistance in developing an ADR mechanism.

5. The World Bank Group had planned to support the establishment of two industrial parks.

6. The ICAs note that while certain factors such as access to land may not be as important with respect to small informal businesses, these factors become binding constraints when small businesses begin to grow.

7. Industrial park development was an important component of the government's PSD strategy. At the time the World Bank project was approved, USAID was developing three industrial parks, which are now operational. The World Bank had planned to develop two additional industrial parks but the World Bank project closed without an industrial park being successfully established.

8. The 2006 ISN had the following statement: "An area of support that warrants greater attention relates to land issues which the ICA identified as the greatest constraint to private sector development, and which underlie the crisis in urban housing."

9. The Afghanistan Chamber of Commerce and Industry has requested IFC assistance in developing an alternate dispute resolution mechanism.

10. See 2009 ISN section on Mainstreaming Governance and Anti-Corruption.

11. See chapter 3 for discussion of the Kabul Bank crisis.

12. In 2010, MISFA established a subsidiary—the Mutahid Development Finance Institution—which would take over the good clients and staff of MFIs that are determined to be unable to achieve sustainability.

13. August 2011 ISR for the Expanding Microfinance Outreach and Improving Sustainability Project.

14. IMF technical assistance to DAB covered monetary policy formulation and implementation, reserve management, banking legislation and regulation development, and banking supervision. IMF also provided assistance in banking crisis management.

15. While the ESW noted the need to manage the macroeconomic impact, including the establishment of an appropriate fiscal regime to deal with the mining revenues,

it does not address macroeconomic and fiscal issues, which are more appropriately dealt with in a Country Economic Memorandum or Public Expenditure Review.

16. Both the World Bank and IFC are involved in this effort, with the World Bank leading the initiative.

17. The NLTA—Afghanistan: Support for Programmatic Resource Growth Corridor Development—was approved in FY12 and was not part of the program covered by the CPE. Nonetheless, the intellectual underpinning of the NLTA was developed during the evaluation period.

18. The ISN covering the period FY12 to FY14 was discussed in the Board on May 2012.

19. See World Bank Project Information Document, Emergency Power Rehabilitation Project, April 15, 2004 (World Bank. 2004. *Afghanistan - Emergency Power Rehabilitation Project*. Washington D.C. - The World Bank. http://documents. worldbank.org/curated/en/2004/04/3303403/afghanistan-emergency-power-rehabilitation-project).

20. While this is not an urban project, it has been included here rather than reviewed as a separate sector.

21. See Afghanistan: Kabul Urban Reconstruction Project Paper Data Sheet, January 28, 2010 (World Bank. 2010. *Afghanistan - Kabul Urban Reconstruction Project: Restructuring*. Washington DC: World Bank). http://documents.worldbank.org/curated/en/2010/01/11847813/afghanistan-kabul-urban-reconstruction-project-restructuring.

References

AMMC (Afghan Management and Consultants). 2009. "Gender Mainstreaming in Afghanistan's Microfinance Sector: An Impact Evaluation." Commissioned by MISFA, Kabul. Available at: http://www.misfa.org.af/?page=publication.

Greeley, Martin, and Mohit Chaturvedi. 2007. "Microfinance in Afghanistan: A Baseline and Initial Impact Study of MISFA." Sussex, U.K.: Institute of Development Studies.

Islamic Republic of Afghanistan. 2006. *Afghanistan National Development Strategy: An Interim Strategy for Security, Governance, Economic Growth & Poverty Reduction*. Kabul.

————. 2008. *Afghanistan National Development Strategy 1387–1398 (2008–2014): A Strategy for Security, Governance, Economic Growth & Poverty Reduction*. Kabul.Islamic Republic of Afghanistan, ADB (Asian Development Bank), United Nations Assistance Mission to Afghanistan, UNDP (United Nations Development Program),and the World Bank Group. 2004. "Securing Afghanistan's Future: Accomplishments and the Strategic Path Forward." A Government/ International Agency Report, March 17, 2004. Prepared for International Conference, March 31, 2004. Available at: http://www.cmi.no/afghanistan/?id=5&Government-of-Afghanistan.

Pierre-Laurent and others. 2009. *Preventing Money Laundering and Terrorist Financing: A Practical Guide for Bank Supervision.*

World Bank. 2002. "Afghanistan—Transitional Support Strategy." Report No. 23822 AF. Washington, DC: World Bank.

————. 2003. "Afghanistan—Transitional Support Strategy:." Report No. 25440 AF. Washington, DC: World Bank.

————. 2004a. The Financial Sector in Afghanistan: Managing the Postconflict Reform Process. Washington DC: World Bank. Available at: http://lnweb90.worldbank.org/Caw/CawDocLib.nsf/vewasiapacific/BA3AEE9915962A5985256F4F007BB62D?open document.

————. 2004b. *Afghanistan - Emergency Power Rehabilitation Project*. Washington DC: The World Bank. Available at: http://documents.worldbank.org/curated/en/2004/04/3303403/afghanistan-emergency-power-rehabilitation-project.

————. 2005.The Investment Climate in Afghanistan: Exploiting Opportunities in an Uncertain Environment. Washington, DC: World Bank.

————. 2006a. *Interim Strategy Note for the Islamic Republic of Afghanistan for the Period FY07–FY08*. Washington, DC: World Bank.

————. 2006b. "Kabul Urban Land Crisis: A Summary of Issues and Recommendations." Kabul Urban Policy Notes Series 1, Washington, DC.

————. 2007. "Land Acquisition in Afghanistan: A Report." Washington, DC: World Bank.

————. 2008. *The Afghanistan Investment Climate in 2008: Growth Despite Poor Governance, Weak Factor Markets, and Lack of Innovation*. Washington, DC: World Bank.

————. 2009. *Interim Strategy Note for the Islamic Republic of Afghanistan for the Period FY09–FY11*. Report No. 47939-AF. Washington, DC: World Bank.

————. 2010. World Bank. 2010. *Afghanistan - Kabul Urban Reconstruction Project: restructuring*. Washington DC: World Bank. Available at: http://documents.worldbank.org/curated/en/2010/01/11847813/afghanistan-kabul-urbanreconstruction-project-restructuring.

————. 2011. "The Afghanistan Mining Sector as a Driver of Sustainable Growth: Benefits and Opportunities for Large-Scale Mining." Report No. 68259. Washington, DC: World Bank.

————. 2012a. *Afghanistan in Transition: Looking Beyond 2014*. Washington, DC: World Bank.

————. 2012b. *Interim Strategy Note for the Islamic Republic of Afghanistan for the Period FY12–FY14*. Report No. 66862-AF. Washington, DC: World Bank.

World Bank, International Finance Corporation, with ShoreBank International Ltd., and CHF International. 2008. Housing Finance in Afghanistan: Challenges and Opportunities. Washington DC. Available at: http://www-wds.worldbank.org/ servlet/WDSContentServer/IW3P/IB/2008/07/14/000334955_20080714044635/ Rendered/PDF/446830ESW0AF0H1B0x0327407B01PUBLIC1.pdf.

Chapter 6

Overall Assessment

The Afghanistan country program operates under extraordinarily difficult circumstances, wherein security conditions pose a continuing challenge to Afghanistan's development and external-partner support. Country risks have been high, both for the government and for development partners. The government has shown its determination to build a modern state out of the ruins and ravages of more than two decades of war. Hence, the Bank Group has a committed partner with the vision to rebuild the Afghan state and modernize Afghan society, capitalizing on the goodwill and development support of the international community.

The commitment of the international donor community also needs to be acknowledged in responding to the huge development needs of the country. The country has benefited greatly from generous donor assistance and a substantial Afghan diaspora, which, with some incentives to return to the country, brought back vital capacity that helped to stimulate this development process. These positive trends have been dampened by setbacks on governance indicators and political economy constraints that will need to be addressed if the development gains are to be sustained.

The work of the World Bank Group and its international partners to move quickly and provide sustained development assistance in a high-risk environment also needs to be commended. Security conditions have worsened since 2007, and staff have had to cope with the pressures of an ongoing conflict, with severe restrictions on personal mobility. Particularly in countries with weak capacity, presence on the ground is often critical to jump-starting development programs. The Bank Group has responded with growing recognition of the challenges faced in FCS and enhanced support for staff to address these challenges. Increasing security risks compelled the country office to take extraordinary measures to ensure the safety of its personnel, substantially raising the cost of the country program. Achieving development results in this context is noteworthy.

Overall Assessment

Overall, Bank Group assistance has achieved substantial progress toward most of its major objectives in Afghanistan since 2001, although country and operational risks to development outcomes remain high. Under each of the major objectives, defined by the three pillars, there have been notable achievements, including some good practice elements, although in some components under the pillars, progress lagged or had shortcomings. Impressive results have been achieved in public financial management (especially fiduciary controls), public health, telecommunications, and community development; substantial outputs have also been achieved in primary education, rehabilitation of rural roads and irrigation systems, and microfinance. All of these were initiated during the initial phase. Some of these, such as public financial management, are long-term programs where the focus on fiduciary controls needs to be complemented by efforts to strengthen budget planning and execution. Bank assistance has also been instrumental in developing the mining sector as a potential engine of growth. However, progress has been much slower in civil service reform, agriculture, and urban sectors and in promoting private sector development.

Although assistance from other donors dwarfs that of the Bank Group, which accounts for less than 5 percent of official development assistance, its ability to complement its financial assistance with AAA and mobilization of donor resources through the ARTF enabled it to play a significant role in many areas. The ARTF, administered by the World Bank, is the largest single source of on-budget assistance to the government and has facilitated effective donor coordination around key institutional reforms and investment programs.

Comments on this evaluation have been received from the Government of the Islamic Republic of Afghanistan and are attached to this evaluation (following appendix K).

Much of the credit for Afghanistan's development trajectory goes to the government's own strategic vision and commitment to change and the willingness of development partners to support the government in this significant turnaround of Afghanistan's history. The government has recast the transition to Afghan responsibility for security in 2014 as the beginning of "the decade of transformation." The international community has pledged to continue support for Afghanistan to realize that vision.

RELEVANCE AND EFFICACY

This evaluation considers the Bank Group's assistance to Afghanistan highly relevant and responsive to client needs, particularly during the initial period of reengagement. The initial strategy responded to the conditions prevalent when the Bank Group reengaged in November 2001, with a transitional government that inherited very weak capacity. The core of the Bank's strategy derives from the needs assessments undertaken in FY02–03 and the strategic vision mapped out by the government in 2004. The focus under the two TSSs was appropriately on building core state institutions, delivery of services to demonstrate the legitimacy of the state, rehabilitating critical infrastructure, and initiating analytical work to build the knowledge base for future development assistance. On these core state functions and delivery of social services the Bank has stayed the course, recognizing that these are long-term endeavors.

Bank Group strategy under the 2006 and 2009 ISNs continued the programs initiated during the previous phase as they were still relevant, but the Bank Group was slow to modify the design of ongoing programs and the components of the pillars to introduce greater realism in the strategic pillars as the context changed. While these programs have been scaled up, risks to development outcomes remain high, due to both country and operational risks.

Aside from the work on the mining sector, which has succeeded in attracting regional investors, the assistance program has not yet evolved beyond the initial foundations for development laid out under the TSSs into a longer-term strategy for sustainable growth. Consequently, both the relevance and the efficacy of Bank Group programs were adversely affected. Subsequent initiatives do not appear to have been derived from a coherent approach that would ensure achievement of the strategic objectives of the ISN pillars. While PFM systems have been put in place and downstream fiduciary controls have created confidence in use of program funds, this has so far not grown beyond financial control measures to effectively influence medium-term expenditure programming, budget preparation and execution, and other upstream aspects of PFM.

The NSP achieved remarkable outreach to a large number of rural communities but has not evolved beyond its project-driven approach to community organization toward economic, social, and governance activities based on more sustainable fiscal transfers to subnational levels and local communities. After stellar portfolio performance during the first few years of the assistance program, when portfolio results were better than the Bank average, implementation quality has suffered and the portfolio at risk has increased substantially.

IFC and MIGA support to an investor in the telecommunications sector has grown over time, but, overall, IFC's investments during the last few years have been lumpy in Afghanistan due to increased uncertainties on the security and political fronts that have not been conducive to private investments. A large, MIGA-supported telecommunications project performed well and was rated high for its development outcome; it contributed to enhanced competition and was highly successful in improving access to telecom services. The project was implemented by a leading mobile telecom operator with prior operational experience in difficult environments. By contrast, several of MIGA's Small Investment Program guarantees have been cancelled because of weak business performance of the insured projects. Security, governance, capacity constraints, and design weaknesses contributed to this deterioration.

The Bank complemented selectivity in lending operations with strategic analytical work in other areas, but knowledge gaps in some key sectors (especially agriculture and urban) have not yet been addressed. The comparative advantage of the Bank lies in its global outlook and its ability to complement lending with knowledge services. Investment in building a knowledge base was appropriately frontloaded, with much greater expenditure on building knowledge during FY02–06 than in FY07–11. And the composition of knowledge products evolved from more ESW during the earlier years toward more technical assistance. The quality of the Bank's AAA drew uniformly high praise from both government counterparts and other donors. The most notable contribution was toward design of the Bank Group's own lending program, although impacts on the government's policies and programs were also evident. In a few sectors, such as telecommunications and mining, the Bank Group's analytical work helped the government mobilize financial support from other partners and the private sector, indicating the value of such strategic analysis in other sectors where the knowledge base remains weak, even if the Bank opts out of financial investments.

The Bank' analytical activities in several cross-cutting areas have had significant influence on government policies and programs and donor activities, but major analytical gaps remain. Analytical work for the strategic needs assessment, gender assessment, social and environmental management, and the economics of transition are successful examples of the Bank's knowledge contributions to the country program. However, the Bank Group and other development partners were unable to anticipate, and have had to adapt to, the governance challenges that have become more acute over the past few years. Although the Bank has played a major role in supporting civil service capacity through the ARTF recurring cost window and several Bank-financed operations, Afghanistan still lacks a strategic human resources plan that matches the growing need for skilled personnel to manage Afghanistan's development. Without a human resources strategy for the civilian sector, including coordinated efforts for higher education and skills development, the government's ability to deliver on its ambitious transformation agenda may be severely cramped after the 2014 transition.

While most of the relevant objectives of the assistance strategy have been met, there is considerable variation within each of the pillars (see appendix A). Under the first pillar, support for PFM was considerably more effective than that for public sector management. Although access to both schooling and public health services has vastly improved, Bank support to the health sector was more effective in achieving and measuring outcomes. In education, substantial strategic and quality gaps remain, and education outcomes are not being assessed. Under the second pillar, the NSP has been effective in achieving its objectives both in terms of physical outputs and in laying the institutional foundations for local governance. Consolidating and sustaining those gains by establishing linkages to other subnational levels and to the market is the challenge of the next phase. Substantial physical progress in the rural roads and agriculture and water resources sectors has been achieved, but overall program impact has not been evaluated and appears to be more muted. Under the third pillar, Bank Group assistance proved highly relevant and effective in ICT and also appears to be highly relevant in the mining sector, with its good future potential as an engine of growth. Bank Group support was also effective in the financial sector, especially in microfinance. But its support to the investment climate, power, and urban sectors has been notably less effective.

Overall, while the country assistance program has achieved acceptable progress toward most of its major relevant objectives, these variations in results reflect, in part, the constraints of working in a conflict environment where the ability of the country team to engage with issues on the ground was increasingly hampered by security restrictions. However, they also appear to reflect a reluctance or inability to reconsider program and strategic design. The first pillar of the two ISNs was conceptually sound and, with further attention to the weaker-performing sectors in the future, is likely to achieve its objectives. However, the strategic objectives of the second and third pillar of the ISNs proved to be overly ambitious; the underlying interventions were not adequate to achieve their higher-order objectives. Nonetheless, at the project level, many of the individual operations within these pillars are likely to achieve their objectives.

Conflicting interests within the country, as well as contradictory advice and competing programs, have undermined the government's ability to develop a clear vision on subnational governance. Substantial investments have been made in village-level infrastructure through the CDCs formed under the NSP. Progress has been more limited in subnational governance, where the government has not yet developed a clear view and approaches and policy advice offered by partner organizations are not consistent. The NSP has created village-level CDCs to manage community projects, and a proposal to recognize the CDCs as Village Councils—the lowest tier of local government—is under consideration. A similar proposal to recognize the District Development Assemblies *(shura)*— formed by representatives of the CDCs with UNDP support—as the local government entity at the district level is meeting resistance. Among donors and government agencies there are divergent views about the need for, and role of, intermediate local government structures. However, in the absence of district or provincial local government structures there is a "missing middle," and without linkages to some form of district- or provincial-level institutions to support the CDCs this investment in social capital is unlikely to be sustained. It is therefore imperative that, at a minimum, the Bank assist the government in reaching agreement on an interim local governance arrangement that enables sustainable public investments and service delivery at subnational and community levels.

Bank engagement in agriculture has been more limited than the demand expressed by government representatives and other key interlocutors. Concern for rural livelihoods and food security renders agriculture a high strategic priority for the government. But the Bank's support to the rural sector still lacks a comprehensive strategy for agricultural development, despite demand for more comprehensive analytical work and systematic engagement from key stakeholders within the government and among donor partners.

Bank Group support for the private sector has had mixed results. Strategic lending by the Bank and IFC complemented by high-quality analytical work, technical assistance, and Advisory Services have led to the rapid spread of mobile phones, the emergence of the mining sector as a key driver of future growth, and consolidation of the microfinance industry. Much of this success has been due to the entrepreneurship of Afghans and the willingness of regional investors to invest in Afghanistan despite the risks. However, growth of the private sector overall has been hampered by the ongoing security challenges, pervasive corruption, infrastructure constraints, and the slow growth of an independent financial sector, which is crowded out by high levels of donor financing and an illicit opium economy. A common thread has been the lack of progress in addressing certain fundamental issues, such as clarifying property rights, strengthening or creating institutions as appropriate, and building capacity and skills. Further improvements in the enabling environment and accountability mechanisms will be needed to enhance the growth of the formal private sector.

Drivers of Success and Weakness

Internal drivers of success included the quality of AAA, customization of design to the country context, and staff capacity. Sound analytical work, either in the form of up-front analysis and judicious use of NLTA, appear to have positively influenced outcomes in public financial management, health, telecommunications, and microfinance sectors and in IFC's Business Advisory Services for horticulture and other business development. The mining sector, likely to have a transformative impact on the economy, stands out as an area where the primary contribution of the Bank was through its knowledge work, which included analytical work, technical assistance, and capacity building.

Contracting out health and microfinance service delivery and community mobilization to NGOs enabled Bank support to the health sector and the NSP to achieve outcomes rapidly. Policy dialogue in the health, telecommunications, and microfinance sectors was facilitated by a realistic assessment of the capacity of the public sector and of the potential of the private and voluntary sectors, as well as acceptance of the comparative advantage of each (with the government in the role of enabler and regulator rather than service provider). Many NGOs had been operating in Afghanistan before and during the Taliban era, and capitalizing on their field presence enabled the Bank Group to accelerate support for the government's strategic priorities. The effectiveness of these programs was enhanced when they were accompanied by clear results frameworks and explicit arrangements for monitoring and evaluation. However, the results vary, with some programs primarily monitoring outputs while others include third-party monitoring of outcomes. Their ability to make course corrections to strengthen program implementation is affected accordingly. The worsening security situation since 2007 has further limited the Bank Group's ability to undertake field supervision. The establishment of clear results frameworks and realistic arrangements for credible monitoring of programs supported by the Bank Group is crucial to demonstrate impact.

The country unit has been mostly successful in mobilizing staff for the Afghanistan country office, with the help of incentives for staff posted in conflict countries, which allowed more intensive support to the client in many sectors. IFC also established a field presence in Afghanistan in 2008, with a country officer co-located with the Bank in Kabul. In core areas, such as PFM, the need for constant support made field presence an imperative. Programs in other sectors—health, ICT, and mining—were effectively designed and managed by task team leaders based elsewhere, but with staff continuity and frequent country visits, indicating that staff decentralization was not always the binding constraint. Nevertheless, unavailability of staff for in-country deployment affected some programs (urban, power), and frequent staff turnover coupled with uneven expertise and experience over time (civil service reform, agriculture, education, NSP) affected others. Heightened security risks in Afghanistan deterred some staff from moving to the country, apparently affecting some sectors. While shorter in-country postings are to be expected in FCS, and recruitment for risky environments will remain a challenge, the experience of some sectors indicates that staff continuity can be maintained from elsewhere. At the same time, the ability of some sectors to deploy experienced staff may have been affected by deskilling over time. While the country office has been strengthened recently by the deployment of a Bank expert on the power sector and an IFC Advisory Services specialist, security constraints limit the overall size of the country office and the Bank Group program will have to rely on a judicious mix of staff posted in country, in neighboring countries, and at headquarters.

EXTERNAL DRIVERS

External drivers of success included strong country ownership, client capacity, and alignment of objectives and approaches in Bank support with partner organizations. Selectivity under the TSSs was driven by priorities clearly articulated by the interim government. Most successful programs have their origins in that period. The subsequent ANDS was more ambitious, with 3 goals and 22 National Priority Programs, which made selectivity more difficult. The government is now attempting to consolidate these into a smaller number of priorities.

Capacity constraints in the civil service were overcome by deploying additional personnel, initially funded by UNDP and subsequently from the ARTF's recurring cost window. Capacity for core functions in apex organizations, especially in the Ministries of Finance and Economy, has enabled improvements in financial management and procurement. Capacity building has been easier where service delivery functions were outsourced (MRRD, MOPH) and the ministry retained responsibility for oversight. This is not feasible in all sectors, but its potential has not been fully used, even in sectors such as agriculture where it may be feasible. International experts gradually gave way to Afghan staff as client capacity increased, though in many ministries capacity depends heavily on a "second civil service" of contracted staff that is paid at a much higher rate than in other countries of the region, owing to skill shortages, insecurity, and competing demands for Afghan staff from other partner organizations. Loss of this second civil service, either because of deteriorating security or because of a decline in aid over the upcoming transition, could substantially undermine government capacity.

Alignment of donor objectives, as in the ARTF, is also a strong determinant of success. The ARTF has evolved into an effective instrument for resource mobilization and coordination among development partners. The Bank's role in the development and administration of the ARTF has enabled it to mobilize substantial financing from partners to provide on-budget resources to the government. In turn, the attractiveness of the Bank to ARTF contributors stems both from the fact that Bank-administered resources are on-budget and support the government's own programs, and from the Bank's exacting fiduciary safeguards, which the development community highly esteems.

ARTF resources are allocated only to programs where there is agreement on objectives and program design, such as with the Incentives Program, the NSP, basic health, and education (EQUIP). Pooling of resources increases leverage and accountability, and the ARTF has been very successful in mobilizing and using resources effectively. It also allows the scaling up of programs piloted with Bank resources through support for on-budget programs, increasing country ownership. But it comes with demand for better documentation and supervision to justify financing decisions and rising expectations of greater voice from the government and financing partners. About half of ARTF funds have been used effectively to scale up programs initially piloted with Bank financing, thereby reducing the risk to contributing development partners. Conditionality associated with the Incentives Program within the recurrent cost window also creates an incentive for the government to address difficult reforms while enabling development partners to sustain a more coherent and influential dialogue with the government on vital reform areas.

Chapter 7
Lessons and Recommendations

Lessons for Fragile and Conflict-Affected Situations

Although Afghanistan's history and challenges are somewhat unusual, given the enormous impact of international actors since 1979, the experience of the past 10 years offers a few important lessons of broader relevance to other FCSs:

- In countries with weak capacity, partnerships with civil society organizations and the private sector can play an important role in augmenting capacity and delivering services rapidly and at scale, particularly in countries where such organizations exist. However, it may be necessary to invest in strengthening the capacity of such organizations and, particularly in post-conflict countries, helping them to evolve beyond humanitarian priorities alone toward a development agenda.

- The use of Bank resources or other grants to pilot and initiate implementation of investment projects can play a valuable role in overcoming initial teething problems and facilitate resource mobilization to scale up tested, ongoing operations through multidonor trust funds.

- Multidonor trust funds have been used to finance recurrent costs of the government during the early phase of recovery in several FCS. The establishment of the Incentives Program is an innovation that proved to be effective in aligning government priorities and those of development partners to support critical state-building reforms. This would not have been possible through a development policy grant, where the policy dialogue tends to be more restrictive.

- Gender mainstreaming is feasible even in FCSs with severe cultural constraints on gender equity if addressed systematically. Coming after more than two decades of civil war and severe restrictions on females since 1995 under the Taliban, reversing the status of women and providing them with social and economic opportunities was a key concern of the government and its international partners. Recognizing the cultural constraints of the country context, the Bank Group mainstreamed gender within all relevant programs. While social discrimination and restrictions on mobility of women and girls remains a substantial concern in Afghanistan, substantial results in terms of service delivery and increasing economic and social opportunities for women illustrate what can be achieved when ownership of gender issues is an integral part of the country program.

- The performance of different sector programs suggests that an early focus on results and monitoring is necessary and feasible even in FCSs with travel restrictions and security constraints, and adds considerable value. The Afghanistan program made effective use of third-party monitoring in several sectors to compensate for the lack of in-country capacity and travel restrictions due to security constraints on field supervision. Outcome monitoring was used more restrictively, limiting the ability of other sectors to adopt a learning-process approach to improve program effectiveness.

- Continuity, experience, and quality of staff are necessary conditions for program effectiveness; location in-country is desirable but not always essential. Some of the most successful programs were designed during the initial years of Bank engagement in Afghanistan by staff that were not based in the country but had in-depth knowledge and experience in their sectors and the commitment to provide the sustained support needed to design and launch those programs. In-country support was more essential for building client capacity during program implementation. But for program design or redesign, in-country presence is not a substitute for experience, as long as staff continuity can be maintained.

- In FCS contexts, the Bank Group needs to lay the foundations for a longer-term strategy early during the recovery phase; the use of emergency procedures can help expedite project processing to address urgent needs but should not obscure the need for long-term strategic planning or for complying with Bank requirements. During subsequent phases of a program, when the urgency no longer exists, emergency procedures should be invoked selectively when there is an operational need that cannot be met through normal project processing. Emergency procedures should not be invoked simply to avoid Bank requirements during project preparation since they would, in any case, need to be addressed during implementation.

- Bank Group AAA can play a critical role in filling knowledge gaps, particularly in FCS contexts, which often lack a good knowledge base. Preserving institutional knowledge by documenting country experience and analytical products on key sector issues and the underlying drivers of political economy is vital to making them available to future members of the country. This is particularly important in FCS countries, where staff turnover is higher than in other countries.

Recommendations

While considerable progress has been achieved in many areas, significant challenges remain in others. Risks to sustainability of development gains remain high. This evaluation's findings lead to the following recommendations for the World Bank:

- **Engage the government on the need for a comprehensive, long-term human resources strategy for the civilian sectors at different levels of government, and provide assistance, in collaboration with other partners, to develop such a strategy.** Development of a strategy would entail: helping the government undertake systematic analysis of the Afghan labor market and civilian human resource needs for the next decade; strengthening coordination among development partners to ensure greater coherence in the provision of higher education and skills training; development and implementation of a plan to produce adequate numbers of skilled graduates through local and foreign universities and training institutions to meet the essential needs of the public and private sector; and assistance to the government in developing affordable human resources systems to recruit and retain trained staff.

- **Focus on strategic-level analytical work toward long-term development strategies in sectors that are high priority for the government.** Given the Bank Group's comparative advantage in providing knowledge services, use a judicious mix of strategic ESW and NLTA/Advisory Services to respond to country needs in priority areas, even where the Bank Group decides against immediate financial commitments.

- **Engage the government in developing local government institutions to enhance the sustainability of national programs and, in the interim, help the government develop a viable system for service delivery at subnational levels.** Development of such a system would entail: collaborating with multilateral development partners and bilateral agencies supporting local government structures and service delivery at subnational levels and drawing on the Incentives Program to develop and support a joint strategy for local governance with the MOF, MRRD, MAIL, IDLG, and relevant line departments, which would give each of them a stake in the outcome.

- **Advise and support the government in transforming the NSP into a more sustainable financial and institutional model to consolidate its gains.** This would involve: scaling down the size of the second grant under NSP III to a level where the benefits can be shared more widely and equitably and linking the CDCs to higher tier(s) of subnational governance with regular intergovernmental fiscal transfers for public investments and services that can be sustained by the government.

- **Focus Bank Group efforts on strengthening the regulatory environment for private sector investment** through: greater use of analytical work, technical assistance, and Advisory Services to assist the government in establishing property rights, commercial dispute-resolution mechanisms, and institutions with the capacity to enforce regulations; assistance to the government and private sector stakeholders in building coalitions to support the regulatory environment for private sector–led growth.

- As part of their commitment to expand support in fragile and conflict-affected situations, **IFC and MIGA could usefully increase business development efforts targeted to new clients, including investors from the region and the diaspora,** to scale up support to the private sector.

Appendix A

Afghanistan—Summary of World Bank Group Program Outcome Ratings

The evaluation criteria for Afghanistan are the same as for other Country Program Evaluations (CPEs). IEG's CPEs assess and rate the *outcomes* (the "results") *of a given World Bank Group country program relative to its objectives.* This differs from rating the country outcomes of the government or the Bank Group, as well as the performance of either of these. The central question underlying the table that follows is "to what extent did the Bank Group program achieve the outcomes that it set out to achieve?" Distinct ratings and subratings are typically assigned to each "pillar" or set of strategic goals set out in the relevant Bank Group strategy documents. For Afghanistan, the strategic goals are based on the 2006 and 2009 ISNs, although the country program has also been credited for achievements since 2002. Appendix B of the evaluation elaborates on IEG's rating methodology.

World Bank Group strategic and operational goals	Achievement of results associated with World Bank Group goals	World Bank Group contribution to results	World Bank Group outcome ratings
A. Building the capacity of the state and its accountability to its citizens			
Moderately satisfactory: Acceptable progress toward most of its major relevant objectives, with some best practice elements and some shortcomings.			
1. Bank Group's objectives in **public financial management** were to strengthen core systems, heighten fiscal sustainability, improve transparency, and use the budget process to make expenditures at subnational level more effective and equitable.	A relatively strong public financial management framework, impressive revenue growth, and greater assurance that funds provided through budget (including most Bank-managed resources) are used effectively. Less than expected progress in several key areas: • Budget formulation and transparency (making headway but still weak) • Procurement (lack of qualified contractors; lack of financial infrastructure, weak capacity of implementing agencies) • External audit (replacement act for CAO law has been drafted, but has not been approved) • Extending core reforms to line ministries and subnational units. Many steps still to be taken in the public financial management road map to further reduce fiduciary risk.	Extensive AAA, four development policy grants, and three capacity building investments helped to: • Draft new laws and regulations • Provide Implementation sup-port on domestic revenue mobilization, expenditure control, treasury and cash management, and financial reporting • Monitor achievements through Public Expenditure and Financial Accountability Assessment Reports, Public Expenditure Reviews, and other high-quality AAA. The Bank's management of the ARTF gave it leverage to provide significant non-IDA funding through the budget, while ensuring fiduciary rigor. ARTF support improved public financial management by demanding compliance with fiduciary standards, adjusting them to the realities of the country, and training public officials in implementing them. The ARTF Incentive Program also offered incentives for the government to address difficult reforms.	Satisfactory

World Bank Group strategic and operational goals	Achievement of results associated with World Bank Group goals	World Bank Group contribution to results	World Bank Group outcome ratings
2. The Bank Group's objective in **public sector governance** was building a reformed and sustainable civil service accountable to its citizens to provide services that are affordable, accessible, and adequate.	Some progress with statistics, pay and grading, merit-based recruitment, pensions, and other human resources processes, but many challenges remain: • The actual quality of "reformed" human resources processes and related training provided is mixed. • Most of the gains rely on a "second civil service" of well-paid professionals outside the civil service. • Little headway on legal and judicial reform and combating corruption.	Extensive AAA, four DPGs, eight capacity building investments, including funding for very attractive contracts for Afghan consultants in key senior positions helped to: • Draft new policies, laws, and regulations. • Regrade 15 ministries and 248,000 civil service positions. • Strive for civil service appointments to be made on merit basis. • Construct court houses and other basic judicial infrastructure.	Moderately unsatisfactory
3. In the **health** sector, the primary objectives of the Bank Group's program were to promote rapid improvement in service delivery in the health sector.	• Strong strategic vision and policy framework established early in the transition period (2002/3) helped the Ministry of Public Health focus on organizing the sector to ensure delivery of a basic package of health services • Capacity to manage contracting out to NGOs complemented with relatively robust independent monitoring of trends in service access, quality, and utilization through an independent monitoring capacity. The Ministry of Public Health plays strong role in anchoring donor coordination, with three major development partners following complementary approaches to service delivery and system development, now facilitated through ARTF financing. • Measured results show the number of functioning public health care facilities increased from 496 in 2002 to over 2000 in 2011, coverage of basic health services reaching all 34 provinces. From 2002 to 2010, the infant mortality rate fell by 38 percent, under-five mortality fell by 42 percent, and the maternal mortality ratio declined significantly, from an uncertain baseline to about 460/100,000.	• Strategically focused policy dialogue in early stages focused on how to implement a vision that was strongly owned by the government and maintained throughout period. • Flexible and responsive approach to building capacity within the MOH for management of NGOs providing service delivery through a "learning by doing" approach in two supporting investment projects; three complementary AAAs documenting early gains and identifying future policy issues; coordination of donor inputs through complementary approach to IDA and ARTF support to investments. • Bank encouraged and supported independent third-party monitoring of service delivery outputs and outcomes. • IFC investments in a private hospital in FY09 contributed to reaching nearly 8,000 patients in Afghanistan.	Satisfactory

World Bank Group strategic and operational goals	Achievement of results associated with World Bank Group goals	World Bank Group contribution to results	World Bank Group outcome ratings
4. In the **education** sector, the primary objectives of the Bank Group's program were to further increase enrollment at the primary, secondary, and vocational levels, with an improvement in gender parity.	• Achievements in school enrollment across the board in primary, secondary, vocational, and higher education. • Primary school enrollment increased from 1 million students in 2001 to 7.2 million in 2011 (net enrollment rate 50 percent). • Females comprise nearly 40 percent of primary school enrollment. • The Ministry of Education and Ministry of Higher Education developed national strategies, though the Higher Education strategy has not yet been approved by the Parliament, with no clear transition strategy. • There have been substantial investments in training teachers and generating more university faculty. • In the area of vocational training, a National Qualifications Framework is under negotiation, and institutions for training have been established.	• Three projects supported the education sector: Education Quality Improvement Program (EQUIP I and II), Strengthening Higher Education Projects (SHEP), and the Afghan Skills Development Project. • All sought to develop sustainable, country-owned and managed projects. EQUIP is aligned with the National Education Sector Strategy and has provided technical support toward achieving student enrollment and teacher training objectives, but education outcomes were not monitored. • While SHEP was slow to get off the ground, in the later period it provided assistance for improving university management and governance, as well as resources for training faculty with partner universities abroad. • The Bank has worked to coordinate the National Qualifications Framework and provide vocational training through the Afghan Skills Development Project.	Moderately satisfactory

B. Promoting growth of the rural economy and improving rural livelihoods

Moderately satisfactory: Acceptable progress toward most of its major relevant objectives; unable to address some key development constraints and high risks to some major development outcomes.

1. The Bank Group's objectives for the **rural roads subsector** were to further rehabilitation of rural access roads and provide employment for poor rural households.	• Of Afghanistan's approximately 40,000 kilometers of rural roads, 10,000 have been rehabilitated since 2001. Close to 60 percent of this work was done with Bank/ARTF assistance. • Provincial Reconstruction Teams and the Commander's Emergency Response Program, both financed by the United States, also provided financial support for rural road rehabilitation, together with the Bank/ARTF-funded National Solidarity Program and a few bilateral donors.	• Three rural road rehabilitation projects (National Emergency Employment Program, National Emergency Employment Program for Rural Areas, and the National Emergency Rural Access Project) were financed by the Bank and the ARTF. Together they rehabilitated close to 5,900 kilometers of rural roads and provided about 8 million days of employment. However, sustainability of rural roads remains a challenge. • The Bank and the government have differed on policy issues for rural roads, such as their width and surfacing.	Moderately satisfactory

World Bank Group strategic and operational goals	Achievement of results associated with World Bank Group goals	World Bank Group contribution to results	World Bank Group outcome ratings
	• The government states it now has the capacity to implement rural road rehabilitation programs itself due to the Bank's support for staff training.	• A policy on the width and surfacing for rural roads could have been resolved five years ago when the government requested Bank advice on rural access policy. The Bank did not respond, and preparation of a rural access policy was stalled. It is being prepared as part of the National Emergency Rural Access Project.	
2. The Bank Group's objectives for the **National Solidarity Program** were to strengthen community-level governance in Afghanistan and to improve the access of rural communities to social and productive infrastructure and services for completing, expanding, and building upon the rollout of the National Solidarity Program across the country.	• Since 2003, the NSP has supported 27,360 Community Development Committees (CDCs), and financed 59,629 subprojects, 80 percent of which have been completed. • NSP grants to communities (assisted by facilitating partners) have improved local capacity to manage the planning, rehabilitation and development of basic public infrastructure in rural areas. • NSP subprojects are primarily for transport (26 percent), water and sanitation (24 percent), irrigation (19 percent), power (12 percent), and education (10 percent). • CDCs have also contributed to building social capital and empowerment of women in rural communities, although results vary across the country.	• Four Bank-assisted NSP projects were implemented, two-thirds of the funding coming from the ARTF. • The NSP's facilitating partners obtained funds from other donors to broaden their activities beyond the NSP's scope. The result has been additional services to communities. • Government and Bank programs are using the CDCs as entry points for other development projects. • The sustainability of the NSP will depend on the transition of CDCs into village councils (envisaged under the constitution). A proposal for this transition is currently under consideration by the government. However, the links with other tiers of subnational governance are still being debated.	Satisfactory
3. The Bank Groups objectives in **agriculture and water resources development** were to promote growth of the rural economy and improve rural livelihoods through rehabilitation of existing traditional irrigation systems, development of rural enterprises; support to the wider agriculture-rural development strategy dialogue and IFC support by scaling up its work in the horticulture sector and more efficient use of Afghanistan's scarce water resources	• Production of Afghanistan's staple food (wheat) increased, albeit with considerable fluctuations, at about 6 percent per year between 2002 and 2010 due mainly to increases in area harvested. Production of other crops also increased but at a slower rate. • The Bank-assisted irrigation project and the horticulture and livestock project did not contribute to the high national growth rate of agricultural production because their effective implementation was delayed by two-to-three years until 2007 and 2009 respectively.	• The completed Emergency Irrigation Rehabilitation Project financed the rehabilitation of water supplies to numerous small to medium-scale irrigation systems as well as the installation of meteorological stations. Incremental wheat yields are reported to be 25 percent since the EIRP got under way after restructuring in 2005. • The ongoing Emergency Horticulture and Livestock Project financed rehabilitation and development of vineyards and orchards, and support services for horticulture and livestock producers. Early results show	Moderately satisfactory

World Bank Group strategic and operational goals	Achievement of results associated with World Bank Group goals	World Bank Group contribution to results	World Bank Group outcome ratings
	• These projects will eventually contribute to improved rural livelihoods, but their impact will be limited because so far they covered only 19 percent of areas currently under irrigation and an even smaller percentage of horticultural areas or livestock production. • Ministry of Agriculture, Irrigation, and Livestock engaged the Bank and many development partners in a dialogue on an agriculture-rural development strategy, which included plans for strengthening the ministry's capacity to provide services to the agriculture sector. • The Bank's analysis of water resource management options in the Kabul River Basin, in collaboration with the Ministry of Energy and Water contributed to capacity building in the ministry and its ability to design additional irrigation projects and formulate water resources policy.	productivity gains for some horticultural crops, but rehabilitation and development costs have been high. • The Bank missed the opportunity to undertake a comprehensive analysis of the agriculture sector to inform the government's agriculture strategy and the design of projects to improve productivity and reduce rural poverty. In 2009 the Ministry of Agriculture, Irrigation, and Livestock issued its National Agricultural Development Framework, to which the Bank had provided some assistance. • The Kabul River Basin study prepared by the Bank in collaboration with the Ministry of Energy and Water is being used as a model for studies of Afghanistan's other river basins. • The follow-up Bank technical assistance program continues to support the further strengthening of the Ministry of Energy and Water staff capacity for long-term water resource management and development on a broad front.	

C. Supporting growth of the formal private sector (including infrastructure)

Moderately satisfactory: Acceptable progress toward most of its major relevant objectives, with best practice development impact in one area, but unable to address some key development constraints

1. The Bank Group's objectives in the area of **investment climate** were to: (i) improve the business regulatory and legislative framework; (ii) facilitate foreign direct investment; (iii) enable establishment of industrial parks; and (iv) reduce the cost of doing business.	• Investment climate continues to be challenging due to security and governance issues. • While many laws and regulations have been enacted, institutions to enforce these are weak and lack credibility. • Property rights, specifically land tenure, are unclear, with lack of adjudication process; the Doing Business Investor Protection Index is 1 on a scale of 0–10. • Cost of doing business continues to be high, with no progress in the areas of construction permits, electricity connections, and trade procedures.	• World Bank AAA improved knowledge about the private sector but had little by way of results. • A World Bank private sector development project did not result in a successful industrial park as intended. • Investment guarantee project mobilized about $100 million in foreign direct investment, mainly in telecommunications. • IFC investments supported foreign direct investment in a hotel and telecommunications. • Ongoing IFC work on licensing reform may show results in the future.	Moderately unsatisfactory

World Bank Group strategic and operational goals	Achievement of results associated with World Bank Group goals	World Bank Group contribution to results	World Bank Group outcome ratings
2. Bank Group objectives in **financial sector development** were to: (i) support the microfinance industry; (ii) develop the banking system; (iii) strengthen DAB capacity; and (iv) introduce leasing	• Microfinance lending has grown during the past 10 years with restructuring of the industry. • Bank lending to private sector grew, though portfolio risks remain high. • Financial infrastructure and capacity to support risk-based lending are still undeveloped. • DAB capacity has improved generally, but supervision capacity needs review. • Lack of a leasing law has impeded the development of a leasing sector.	• Bank Group supported development of microfinance sector through World Bank projects and IFC advisory and investment projects with significant contribution to development and restructuring of the sector. • Bank Group work (World Bank operation and IFC Advisory Services) on financial infrastructure and capacity building has yet to show results (with the exception of microfinance) beyond the approval of a regulatory framework for financial infrastructure.	Moderately satisfactory
3. The Bank Group's main objectives in **energy and mining** were to: (i) develop the legal and regulatory regime to enable private investment; and (ii) improve capacity of the Ministry of Mines.	• Large foreign investments in two mines approved. • Legal and regulatory regime is basically in place. • Ministry of Mines capacity has improved.	• World Bank AAA helped develop the laws and regulations in the sector. • World Bank operations and advice supported capacity building.	Satisfactory
4. The Bank Group's main objectives in **ICT** were to: (i) develop the legal and regulatory regime to enable private investment; (ii) improve policy and regulatory capacities; (iii) support privatization of Afghan Telecom; and (iv) enable increased utilization of ICT applications.	• The sector is now dominated by private sector. • Privatization of Afghan Telecom approved by the government. • Eighty percent mobile phone geographical coverage with prices declining and ICT applications increasing. • Legal and regulatory regime in place. • Improved capacity in the Ministry of Communications and Information Technology and Afghanistan Telecommunications Regulatory Agency. • Increased use of ICT in public sector governance.	• World Bank nonlending technical assistance and operations helped develop the legal and regulatory regime and improve policy and oversight capacities of government offices. • IFC investment and MIGA guarantees supported private investment in the sector.	Highly satisfactory
5. The main objectives of the Bank Group in the **power** sector were to: (i) support rehabilitation of the power sector including capacity building; (ii) provide advice on sector policy.	• Based on the 2010 Investment Climate Assessment, power supply remains a major constraint to private sector development • The power utility company (DABS) continues to suffer from weak capacity.	• The World Bank is not a major player in the sector; World Bank projects focused on power distribution systems in latter part of the evaluation period. • World Bank AAA and operations supported initial reorganization of DABS. • Current portfolio of World Bank projects facing difficulties and may need to be restructured.	Moderately unsatisfactory

World Bank Group strategic and operational goals	Achievement of results associated with World Bank Group goals	World Bank Group contribution to results	World Bank Group outcome ratings
		• World Bank AAA helped develop a power sector road map early during the evaluation period, but the World Bank role at the strategic level has diminished since then.	
6. The main objectives of the Bank Group in the **urban** sector were to: (i) support rehabilitation of urban infrastructure; (ii) introduce contemporary techniques for urban development; and (iii) address land issues.	• There has been significant progress in rehabilitation of infrastructure, though increases in urban population and traffic pose major continuing challenges. • Capacity for urban development remains weak, with authorities unable to deal with scale of urban issues. • Little progress in addressing land issues, which are critical to mitigation of housing crisis.	• Donors dominate the urban infrastructure rehabilitation; the World Bank had one early road rehabilitation project; World Bank urban water projects focused on institution building. • World Bank Kabul Urban Reconstruction Project (KURP), which addressed urban planning and capacity building issues, had to be restructured. • AAA and KURP covered land and housing issues that remain unresolved.	Unsatisfactory

Overall Bank Group program outcome rating

Moderately satisfactory: Acceptable progress toward most of its major relevant objectives, with some best practice elements; unable to address some key development constraints, and high risks to some development outcomes

Appendix B
Guide to IEG's Country Program
Evaluation Methodology

This methodological note describes the key elements of IEG's Country Program evaluation (CPE) methodology.[1]

CPEs rate the outcomes of Bank Group assistance programs, not the clients' overall development progress.

A Bank Group assistance program needs to be assessed on how well it met its particular objectives, which are typically a subset of the client's development objectives. If a Bank Group assistance program is large in relation to the client's total development effort, the program outcome will be similar to the client's overall development progress. However, most Bank Group assistance programs provide only a fraction of the total resources devoted to a client's development by development partners, stakeholders, and the government itself. In CPEs, IEG rates only the outcome of the Bank Group's program, not the client's overall development outcome, although the latter is clearly relevant for judging the program's outcome.

The experience gained in CPEs confirms that Bank Group program outcomes sometimes diverge significantly from the client's overall development progress. CPEs have identified Bank Group assistance programs that had:

- Satisfactory outcomes matched by good client development
- Unsatisfactory outcomes in clients that achieved good overall development results, notwithstanding the weak Bank Group program
- Satisfactory outcomes in clients that did not achieve satisfactory overall results during the period of program implementation.

Assessments of assistance program outcome and Bank Group performance are not the same.

By the same token, an unsatisfactory Bank Group assistance program outcome does not always mean that Bank Group performance was also unsatisfactory, and vice-versa. This becomes clearer once we consider that the Bank Group's contribution to the outcome of its assistance program is only part of the story. The assistance program's outcome is determined by the *joint* impact of four agents: (i) the client; (ii) the Bank Group; (iii) partners and other stakeholders; and (iv) exogenous forces (such as events of nature, international economic shocks, and the like). Under the right circumstances, a negative contribution from any one agent might overwhelm the positive contributions from the other three, and lead to an unsatisfactory outcome.

IEG measures Bank Group performance primarily on the basis of contributory actions the Bank Group directly controlled. Judgments regarding Bank Group performance typically consider the relevance and implementation of the strategy; the design and supervision of the Bank Group's lending and financial-support interventions; the scope, quality, and follow-up of diagnostic work and other analytic and advisory activities (AAA); the consistency of the Bank Group's lending and financial support with its nonlending work and with its safeguard policies; and the Bank Group's partnership activities.

Rating Assistance Program Outcome

In rating the outcome (expected development impact) of an assistance program, IEG gauges the extent to which major strategic objectives were relevant and achieved, without any shortcomings. In other words, did the Bank Group do the right thing, and did it do it right? Programs typically express their goals in terms of higher-order objectives, such as poverty reduction. The country assistance strategy (CAS) may also establish intermediate goals, such as improved targeting of social services or promotion of integrated rural development, and specify how they are expected to contribute toward achieving the higher-order objective. IEG's task is then to validate whether the intermediate objectives were the right ones and whether they produced satisfactory net benefits, and whether the results chain specified in the CAS was valid. Where causal linkages were not fully specified in the CAS, it is the evaluator's task to reconstruct this causal chain from the available evidence and assess relevance, efficacy, and outcome with reference to the intermediate and higher-order objectives.

For each of the main objectives, the CPE evaluates the relevance of the objective; the relevance of the Bank Group's strategy toward meeting the objective, including the balance between lending and nonlending instruments; the efficacy with which the strategy was implemented; and the results achieved. This is done in two steps. The first is a top-down review of whether the Bank Group's program achieved a particular Bank Group objective or planned outcome and had a substantive impact on the country's development. The second step is a bottom-up review of the Bank Group products and services (lending, analytical and advisory services, and aid coordination) used to achieve the objective. Together these two steps test the consistency of findings from the products and services and the development impact dimensions. Subsequently, an assessment is made of the relative contribution to the results achieved by the Bank Group, other development partners, the government, and exogenous factors.

Evaluators also assess the degree of client ownership of international development priorities, such as the Millennium Development Goals, and Bank Group corporate advocacy priorities, such as safeguards. Ideally, any differences in dealing with these issues would be identified and resolved by the CAS, enabling the evaluator to focus on whether the tradeoffs adopted were appropriate. However, in other instances the strategy may be found to have glossed over certain conflicts or avoided addressing key client development constraints. In either case, the consequences could include a diminution of program relevance, a loss of client ownership, and/or unwelcome side-effects, such as safeguard violations, all of which must be taken into account in judging program outcome.

Ratings Scale

IEG utilizes six rating categories for *outcome,* ranging from highly satisfactory to highly unsatisfactory:

Highly satisfactory:	The assistance program achieved at least acceptable progress toward all major relevant objectives, and had best practice development impact on one or more of them. No major shortcomings were identified.
Satisfactory:	The assistance program achieved acceptable progress toward all major relevant objectives. No best practice achievements or major shortcomings were identified.
Moderately satisfactory:	The assistance program achieved acceptable progress toward most of its major relevant objectives. No major shortcomings were identified.
Moderately unsatisfactory:	The assistance program did not make acceptable progress toward most of its major relevant objectives, or made acceptable progress on all of them, but either (i) did not take into adequate account a key development constraint or (ii) produced a major shortcoming, such as a safeguard violation.
Unsatisfactory:	The assistance program did not make acceptable progress toward most of its major relevant objectives, and either (i) did not take into adequate account a key development constraint or (ii) produced a major shortcoming, such as a safeguard violation.
Highly unsatisfactory:	The assistance program did not make acceptable progress toward any of its major relevant objectives and did not take into adequate account a key development constraint, while also producing at least one major shortcoming, such as a safeguard violation.

The **institutional development impact (IDI)** can be rated at the project level as *high, substantial, modest,* or *negligible.* IDI measures the extent to which the program bolstered the client's ability to make more efficient, equitable, and sustainable use of its human, financial, and natural resources. Examples of areas included in judging the institutional development impact of the program are:

* The soundness of economic management
* The structure of the public sector, and, in particular, the civil service
* The institutional soundness of the financial sector
* The soundness of legal, regulatory, and judicial systems
* The extent of monitoring and evaluation systems
* The effectiveness of aid coordination
* The degree of financial accountability
* The extent of building capacity in nongovernmental organizations

- The level of social and environmental capital.

IEG is, however, increasingly factoring IDI ratings into program outcome ratings, rather than rating these impacts separately.

Sustainability can be rated at the project level as *highly likely, likely, unlikely, highly unlikely,* or, if available information is insufficient, *non-evaluable.* Sustainability measures the resilience to risk of the development benefits of the country program over time, taking into account eight factors:

- Technical resilience
- Financial resilience (including policies on cost recovery)
- Economic resilience
- Social support (including conditions subject to safeguard policies)
- Environmental resilience
- Ownership by governments and other key stakeholders
- Institutional support (including a supportive legal/regulatory framework and organizational and management effectiveness) and resilience to exogenous effects, such as international economic shocks or changes in the political and security environments.

At the program level, IEG is increasingly factoring sustainability into program outcome ratings, rather than rating it separately.

Risk to Development Outcome. According to the 2006 harmonized guidelines, sustainability has been replaced with a "risk to development outcome," defined as the risk, at the time of evaluation, that development outcomes (or expected outcomes) of a project or program will not be maintained (or realized). The risk to development outcome can be rated at the project level as *high, significant, moderate, negligible to low,* or *non-evaluable.*

Appendix C
Afghanistan—List of Approved Projects,
World Bank, IFC, and MIGA, FY02–11

Project ID	Project name	Approval fiscal year	Status	Total project commitment (US$ millions)	IDA credit commitment (US$ millions)	IDA grant commitment (US$ millions)	
PILLAR 1: Building the capacity of the state and its accountability to its citizens							
P078618	Programmatic Support for Inst Bldg	2005	Closed	80.0	80.0		
P090829	Programmatic Support for Inst Bldg II	2006	Closed	80.0		80.0	
P102709	Programmatic Support for Inst Bldg III	2007	Closed	80.0		80.0	
P086228	ARTF Civil Service Capacity Bldg	2005	Closed	13.0			
P106170	ARTF Management Capacity Program	2007	Active	15.0			
P121883	Strengthening National Statistical System	2011	Active	14.0			
P077896	Emergency Education Rehabilitation and Development	2002	Closed	15.0		15.0	
P083964	Education Quality Improvement Program	2005	Closed	79.0		35.0	
P106259	Education Quality Improvement Program II	2008	Active	115.1		30.0	
P089040	Strengthening Higher Education Program	2005	Active	45.0		40.0	
P121805	Strengthening Higher Education Additional Financing	2010	Active	20.0		20.0	
P102573	Skills Development Project	2008	Active	29.0		20.0	
P091081	ARTF Strengthening Financial Capacity	2004	Closed	9.1			
P099980	Public Financial Management Reform	2007	Active	33.4		33.4	
P091258	ARTF Recurrent and Capital Costs	2002	Active	2,295.3			
P078324	Health Sector Emergency Rehabilitation	2003	Closed	60.1		59.6	
P098358	Afghanistan Health (supplement)	2006	Closed	30.0		30.0	
P110658	Afghanistan Health (supplement II)	2008	Closed	20.0		20.0	
P101502	HIV/AIDS Prevention Project	2008	Active	10.0		10.0	
P112446	Strengthening Health Activities for the Rural Poor (SHARP)	2009	Active	64.0		30.0	
P120669	SHARP Additional Financing	2010	Active	49.0		49.0	
P120565	Support to Basic Package of Health Services	2010	Active	17.7			
P091259	ARTF Feasibility Studies Facility	2003	Closed	18.5			
P077417	First Emergency Public Administration Project	2002	Closed	10.0		10.0	
P082610	Second Emergency Public Administration Project	2003	Closed	11.4		8.4	
P084736	Public Administration Capacity Bldg Project	2005	Closed	27.0		27.0	
P097030	Civil Service Reform Project	2007	Active	20.4		20.4	
P107372	Judicial Reform Project	2008	Active	27.8			
P107921	Strengthening Institutions DPG	2009	Closed	35.0		35.0	
P113421	Pension Administration and Safety Net	2010	Active	7.5		7.5	
P083906	Emergency Customs and Trade Facilitation	2004	Active	31.0	31.0		
P114572	Emergency Customs and Trade Facilitation Additional Financing	2009	Active	6.8		6.8	
P112872	Customs Reform and Trade Facilitation 2	2010	Active	50.5		50.5	
PILLAR 1 TOTAL				3,419.5	111.0	717.6	

Trust fund commitment (US$ millions)	Date, revised closing	Sector Board	Latest DO	Latest IP	IEG rating
	3/20/2005	Economic Policy			S
	9/30/2006	Economic Policy			S
	3/21/2008	Economic Policy			S
13.0	2/28/2010	Economic Policy			U
15.0	12/31/2011	Economic Policy	MU	MS	
14.0	2/29/2016	Economic Policy	MS	MS	
	6/30/2006	Education			MS
44.0	3/31/2009	Education			MU
85.1	9/1/2012	Education	MS	MU	
5.0	6/30/2013	Education	MS	MS	
	6/30/2013	Education			
9.0	2/28/2013	Education	MS	MU	
9.1	2/28/2006	Financial Management			
	12/31/2011	Financial Management	S	S	
2,295.3	2/28/2013	Financial Management	S	S	
0.5	6/30/2009	Health, Nutrition & Population			S
	6/30/2009	Health			
	6/30/2009	Health			
	6/30/2012	Health	S	MS	
34.0	9/30/2013	Health	S	MS	
	9/30/2013	Health			
17.7	3/14/2013	Health	MS	MS	
18.5	2/28/2010	Poverty Reduction	MS	MU	
	9/30/2005	Public Sector Governance			MS
3.0	9/30/2008	Public Sector Governance			MS
	6/30/2009	Public Sector Governance			S
	7/31/2011	Public Sector Governance	MU	MU	
27.8	6/30/2011	Public Sector Governance	MS	MS	
	8/31/2010	Public Sector Governance			MS
	12/31/2013	Social Protection	S	MS	
	12/31/2010	Transport	S	S	
	12/31/2010	Transport			
	6/30/2014	Transport	S	S	
2,590.9					

Project ID	Project name	Approval fiscal year	Status	Total project commitment (US$ millions)	IDA credit commitment (US$ millions)	IDA grant commitment (US$ millions)	
PILLAR 2: Promoting growth of the rural economy and improving rural livelihoods							
P078936	Emergency Irrigation Rehabilitation	2004	Active	40.0	40.0		
P105492	Emergency Irrigation Rehabilitation Supplemental	2007	Active	25.0		25.0	
P110893	Emergency Irrigation Rehabilitation Supplemental II	2008	Active	28.0		28.0	
P112873	Emergency Irrigation Rehabilitation Additional Financing	2009	Active	33.5		33.5	
P099893	Building Capacity for Land Conflicts	2005	Closed	0.3			
P084329	Emergency National Solidarity Project (NSP)	2004	Closed	290.4		95.0	
P094735	Emergency National Solidarity Supplemental	2005	Closed	28.0		28.0	
P086270	Emergency National Solidarity Supplemental II	2006	Closed	40.0		40.0	
P102288	NSP II	2007	Closed	583.9		120.0	
P112869	NSP II Additional Financing	2009	Closed	75.0		75.0	
P117103	National Solidarity Program III	2010	Active	290.0		40.0	
P098256	Horticulture and Livestock Productivity Project	2006	Closed	54.3		20.0	
P100935	Avian Flu	2007	Closed	13.0		8.0	
P111337	Strengthening Results-based M&E	2008	Active	0.3			
P111353	Capacity Building for Impact Evaluation	2008	Active	0.4			
P111191	Statistical Capacity Building	2008	Closed	0.2			
P113199	Food Crisis Response Project	2009	Closed	8.0			
P110407	Rural Enterprise Development Program	2010	Active	46.0		30.0	
P122235	Irrigation Restoration and Development	2011	Active	97.8		97.8	
P120398	On-Farm Water Management (OFWM)	2011	Active	42.0			
P077533	Emergency Community Empowerment Project	2002	Closed	45.5		42.0	
P082472	National Emergency Employment Program for Rural Access	2003	Closed	58.8	20.4	18.8	
P091036	ARTF National Emergency Employment Program	2003	Closed	61.6			
P103343	National Emergency Rural Access Project	2008	Active	192.0		112.0	
P118828	National Emergency Rural Access Project Additional Financing	2011	Active	40.0		40.0	
PILLAR 2 TOTAL				2,094.0	60.4	853.1	

Trust fund commitment (US$ millions)	Date, revised closing	Sector Board	Latest DO	Latest IP	IEG rating
	3/31/2011	Agriculture and Rural Development	S	S	
	12/31/2011	Agriculture and Rural Development			
	12/31/2011	Agriculture and Rural Development			
	12/31/2011	Agriculture and Rural Development			
0.3	4/26/2009	Agriculture and Rural Development		S	
195.4	3/31/2007	Agriculture and Rural Development			MS
	3/31/2007	Agriculture and Rural Development			
	3/31/2007	Agriculture and Rural Development			
463.9	9/30/2011	Agriculture and Rural Development	S	S	
	9/30/2011	Agriculture and Rural Development			
250.0	9/30/2015	Agriculture and Rural Development	S	S	
34.3	12/31/2011	Agriculture and Rural Development	S	S	
5.0	3/31/2010	Agriculture and Rural Development			U
0.3	6/8/2011	Agriculture and Rural Development		MS	
0.4	6/8/2011	Agriculture and Rural Development		S	
0.2	8/31/2010	Agriculture and Rural Development			
8.0	9/30/2010	Agriculture and Rural Development	S	S	
16.0	1/1/2015	Agriculture and Rural Development	MS	S	
	12/31/2017	Agriculture and Rural Development			
42.0	6/30/2014	Agriculture and Rural Development			
3.5	12/31/2004	Social Development			S
19.6	12/15/2009	Transport			S
61.6	3/31/2009	Transport			MS
80.0	12/31/2010	Transport	MS	MS	
	12/31/2013	Transport			
1,180.5					

Project ID	Project name	Approval fiscal year	Status	Total project commitment (US$ millions)	IDA credit commitment (US$ millions)	IDA grant commitment (US$ millions)
PILLAR 3 World Bank: Supporting growth of the formal private sector						
P083908	Emergency Power Rehabilitation Project	2004	Active	125.0	105.0	
P091060	ARTF Improvement of Power Supply	2004	Closed	7.4		
P098118	Natural Resources Development	2006	Active	30.0		30.0
P116651	Sustainable Development of Natural Resources Additional Financing	2009	Active	10.0		10.0
P118925	Sustainable Development of Natural Resources Project II	2011	Active	52.0		52.0
P106654	ARTF Kabul-Aybak MazareSharif Power Project	2008	Active	57.0		
P111943	ATRF Power System Development	2009	Active	60.0		
P078069	Afghanistan Reconstruction Trust Fund	2002	Active	4.6		
P078452	FSD Afghanistan Work (CGAP Microfinance Framework)	2003	Active	0.0		
P091264	ARTF Microfinance	2004	Closed	184.3		
P091809	First MicroFinance Bank of Afghanistan-JSDF Capacity Building	2004	Closed	0.7		
P088719	Investment Guarantee Facility	2005	Active	5.0	5.0	
P090928	PSD Support Project	2007	Active	25.0		25.0
P104301	Microfinance Project	2008	Active	30.0		30.0
P110644	Financial Sector Strengthening Project	2009	Active	8.0		8.0
P118053	New Market Development	2011	Active	22.0		22.0
P083720	Emergency Communications Development	2004	Closed	22.0	22.0	
P090933	ARTF Telecommunications	2004	Closed	6.1		
P121755	ICT Sector Development Project	2011	Active	50.5	0.5	50.0
P082078	Creating Future Potential Entrepreneurs	2004	Closed	2.8		
P091039	ARTF Kabul Roads	2004	Closed	3.0		
P078284	Emergency Transport Rehabilitation	2003	Closed	108.0	108.0	
P090390	Emergency Transport Supplemental	2005	Closed	45.0		45.0
P107101	ARTF Kabul Urban Roads Improvement Project	2009	Active	18.0		
P083919	Kabul Urban Reconstruction Project	2005	Active	25.0	25.0	
P111825	ARTF Kabul Urban Reconstruction Project	2008	Active	5.6		
P077779	Emergency Infrastructure Reconstruction	2002	Closed	33.0		33.0
P092162	ARTF Afghanistan Short-Term Urban WSS	2005	Active	41.0		
P087860	Urban Water Sector	2006	Active	40.0		40.0
P091038	ARTF Rural WSSP	2006	Closed	7.7		
P112097	ARTF TA for Water Sector Capacity Building	2009	Active	5.5		
PILLAR 3 WORLD BANK TOTAL				1,034.2	265.5	345.0

Trust fund commitment (US$ millions)	Date, revised closing	Sector Board	Latest DO	Latest IP	IEG rating
20.0	9/30/2012	Energy and Mining	S	U	
7.4	3/31/2009	Energy and Mining			MS
	7/31/2011	Energy and Mining	S	S	
	12/31/2012	Energy and Mining			
	6/30/2016	Energy and Mining			
57.0	9/30/2011	Energy and Mining	MS	U	
60.0	7/31/2012	Energy and Mining	U	U	
4.6	2/28/2003	Financial and Private Sector Development			
	N/A	Financial and Private Sector Development			
184.3	6/30/2010	Financial and Private Sector Development	MS	MS	
0.7	6/30/2008	Financial and Private Sector Development			
	9/30/2011	Financial and Private Sector Development	S	MS	
	6/30/2011	Financial and Private Sector Development	MS	MU	
	12/31/2010	Financial and Private Sector Development	MU	MS	
	6/30/2014	Financial and Private Sector Development	MU	MS	
	2/29/2016	Financial and Private Sector Development			
	9/30/2009	Global ICT			MS
6.1	12/31/2006	Global ICT			
	6/30/2016	Global ICT			
2.8	2/28/2009	Social Protection			
3.0	6/30/2005	Transport			
	2/1/2010	Transport			MS
	6/30/2008	Transport			
18.0	12/31/2010	Transport	MS	MS	
	3/31/2011	Urban Development	MS	MS	
5.6	12/31/2011	Urban Development	MS	MS	
	6/30/2006	Water			S
41.0	12/31/2010	Water	U	U	
	6/30/2012	Water	MS	MS	
7.7	12/31/2009	Water			
5.5	3/31/2011	Water	MS	MS	
423.7					

PILLAR 3 IFC: Supporting growth of the formal private sector

Project ID	Project name	Commitment FY [a]	Status [b]	Total net commitment (US$ millions)	Equity	Loan
11629	Kabul Serena Hotel	2004	Active	7.0		7.0
11550	First Microfinance Bank of Afghanistan (FMBA)	2004	Active	1.0	1.0	
24641	BRAC Afghanistan Bank (BAB)	2007	Active	1.0	1.0	
26827	BAB RI	2008	Active	0.4	0.4	
27680	GTFP AIB [d]	2009	Active	5.0		5.0
27503	ACOMET Family Hospital	2009	Active	4.5		4.5
28138	MTNA Mod	2009	Active	75.0	10.0	65.0
29892	MTNA Mod RI	2010	Active	6.4	6.4	
PILLAR 3 IFC TOTAL				100.3	18.8	81.5

PILLAR 3 MIGA: Supporting growth of the formal private sector

Project ID	Project Name	Issuance FY	Status [e]	Gross Exposure	Net Exposure
6169	Afghanistan Project for Cotton and Oil Development (NAPCOD)	2006	Not Active	0.89	0.80
6938	BRAC Afghanistan Bank	2007	Active	1.61	1.46
6260	Baz International Pharmaceutical Company (BIPC)	2007	Not Active	0.37	0.33
6589	Areeba Afghanistan LLC [f]	2007	Active	74.50	33.53
7476	Geo Building Technologies LLC, Afghanistan	2008	Not Active	0.87	0.87
PILLAR 3 MIGA TOTAL				**78.2**	**37.0**

	Total project commitment (US$ millions)	IDA credit / IFC equity commitment (US$ millions)	IDA grant / IFC loan commitment (US$ millions)
World Bank Subtotal Commitment	6,547.7	436.9	1,915.7
IFC Subtotal Commitment	100.3	18.8	81.5
World Bank and IFC Total Commitment	6,648.0	455.7	1,997.2

Sources: World Bank databases as of July 2011; IFC data, June 16, 2011.

Note: HS = highly satisfactory; S = satisfactory; MS = moderately satisfactory; MU = moderately unsatisfactory; U = unsatisfactory; HU = highly unsatisfactory.

IFC definitions

a. Commitment date (FY): Date (FY) of execution of a legal agreement establishing IFC's obligation to provide [financial product] s to [client] s. Also known as "value date," "effective date," and "execution date."

b. Project Status: Standing of [Project]:

Active = A

Closed; All operational and financial activities, and legal obligations, associated with [project] are completed. For Investment Projects, refer to Project Closure Guidelines. = C

Dropped = D

Hold; [Project] activity has been temporarily stopped. = H

Dummy; [Project] created by mistake. Note that projects created in [iDESK] cannot be deleted. = X

Terminated; For Advisory Services only, [Project] permanently stopped after approval of [AS Implementation Plan]. = T

c. XPSR year is the Calendar year of evaluation. Blank cell means "No IEG evaluation."

d. GTFP AIB is a guarantee. There is no disbursement unless the guarantee is called.

e. "Not Active" means either "Expired" or "Cancelled."

f. The existing guarantee was replaced in FY12 with new and expanded coverage to MTN Dubai Ltd., increasing total MIGA coverage for the project by another $80.4 million. The project name was also changed to MTN Afghanistan.

	XPSR year (CY)[c]	Sector			
	2009	Accommodation & Tourism Services			
	2008	Finance & Insurance			
		Finance & Insurance			
		Finance & Insurance			
		Finance & Insurance			
		Health			
		Information			
		Information			

	PER (FY)	Sector			
		Agribusiness			
		Financial Sector Services			
	2012	Telecommunications Services			

Trust fund commitment (US$ millions)					
4,195.1					
0.0					
4,195.1					

Appendix D

Afghanistan—Analytical and Advisory Work by Cluster, World Bank and IFC, FY02–11

	Product ID	Product name	Delivered to client (FY)	Type	Status	
PILLAR 1: Building the capacity of the state and its accountability to its citizens						
I. Needs Assessment and Strategy Design						
I.1	P076994	Afghanistan Country Strategy Brief	FY02	ESW	Closed	
I.2	P076995	Afghanistan Mine Action Study	FY02	ESW	Closed	
I.3	P076996	Afghanistan Border States Development Framework Approach Paper	FY02	ESW	Closed	
I.4	P077010	Conference on Preparation for Afghanistan Reconstruction	FY02	ESW	Closed	
I.5	P077195	Preliminary Needs Assessment	FY02	ESW	Closed	
I.6	P077532	Comprehensive Needs Assessment	FY03	ESW	Delivered	
I.7	P084187	Afghanistan: State Building, Sustaining Growth, and Reducing Poverty	FY04	ESW	Closed	
I.8	P088249	Afghanistan Recosting	FY04	ESW	Closed	
I.9	P091210	ARTF Support to the Afghan Stabilization Program (ASP)	FY05	TA	Closed	
I.10	P113541	Policy Notes for the New Government	FY10	ESW	Delivered	
I.11	P125680	Afghanistan DeMPA Assessment	FY11	ESW	Delivered	
I. Needs Assessment and Strategy Design Cluster: Subtotal						
II. Gender						
II.1	P078877	Afghanistan Country Gender Assessment	FY05	ESW	Closed	
II.2	P098641	Follow Up On Afghanistan Country Gender Assessment	FY06	TA	Closed	
II.3	P108644	Operationalizing CGA Recommendations in Afghanistan's Economic and Sector Work	FY10	TA	Closed	
II.4	P117322	Understanding the Gender Dimension of Trade Markets in Afghanistan	FY11	TA	Delivered	
II.5	551745	GEM FMFB Outreach to Women Entrepreneurs	FY07	IFC	Closed	
II. Gender Cluster: Subtotal						
III. Poverty and Social Protection						
III.1	P082847	Afghanistan: Labor market and Pensions	FY04	ESW	Closed	
III.2	P083961	Poverty, Vulnerability and Social Protection Study	FY05	ESW	Closed	
III.3	P090943	ARTF National Vulnerability Program	FY06	TA	Closed	
III.4	P092152	Afghanistan Pensions	FY08	TA	Closed	
III.5	P096927	Poverty Monitoring and Evaluation	FY07	TA	Delivered	
III.6	P109706	Poverty Assessment nonlending technical assistance	FY10	TA	Closed	
III. Poverty and Social Protection Cluster: Subtotal						

Sector Board	Output type	Cost of product (US$ '000)	Cluster total	Number of AAA	Pillar total
Economic Policy	Report	0.0			
Economic Policy	Policy Note	16.5			
Economic Policy	Report	34.7			
Economic Policy	Conference / Workshop	0.6			
Poverty Reduction	Report	323.9			
Poverty Reduction	Consultations	498.4			
Economic Policy	Report	216.4			
Public Sector Governance	Report	267.6			
Public Sector Governance	"How-To" Guidance	62.0			
Economic Policy	Policy Note	73.8			
Economic Policy	Report	83.7			
		1,577.6	1,578	11	
Gender and Development	Report	559.4			
Gender and Development	"How-To" Guidance	68.8			
Gender and Development	"How-To" Guidance	245.5			
Agriculture and Rural Development	"How-To" Guidance	218.2			
Access To Finance		13.0			
		1,105.0	1,105	5	
Social Protection	Policy Note	152.1			
Social Protection	Report	268.0			
Social Protection	Institutional Development Plan	69.8			
Social Protection	Institutional Development Plan	329.5			
Poverty Reduction	Institutional Development Plan	237.9			
Poverty Reduction	"How-To" Guidance	564.3			
		1,621.6	1,622	6	

	Product ID	Product name	Delivered to client (FY)	Type	Status	
IV. Public Expenditure Management and Fiduciary Aspects						
IV.1	P078656	Afghanistan Public Finance Management Review	FY06	ESW	Closed	
IV.2	P083984	EMS Discussion Series Workshop	FY03	ESW	Closed	
IV.3	P090079	Reforming Fiscal and Economic Management in Afghanistan	FY04	ESW	Closed	
IV.4	P102707	Afghanistan Public Expenditure Review	FY10	ESW	Closed	
IV.5	P096992	Gap Analysis of Public Sector Accounting and Auditing Standards	FY06	ESW	Closed	
IV.6	P097273	Afghanistan: Consulting Industry Assessment	FY07	ESW	Closed	
IV.7	P098046	Afghanistan: ROSC Accounting and Audit Assessment	FY09	ESW	Closed	
IV.8	P100103	E-Procurement: Readiness Report and Implementation Plan for Afghanistan	FY07	ESW	Closed	
IV. Public Expenditure Management and Fiduciary Aspects Cluster: Subtotal						
V. Public Administration and Governance						
V.1	P078617	Afghanistan Civil Service and Governance Issues	FY04	ESW	Closed	
V.2	P084188	Civil Service Reform Dialogue	FY05	TA	Closed	
V.3	P096938	Capacity Building nonlending technical assistance - Civil Service Reform	FY08	TA	Closed	
V.4	P100960	Afghanistan Public Administration Reform Strategy Report	FY08	ESW	Closed	
V.5	P101117	Anti-Corruption Study	FY09	ESW	Closed	
V.6	P108100	Statistical Capacity Building	FY10	TA	Closed	
V.7	P108913	Subnational Dialogue	FY11	TA	Delivered	
V.8	P113538	Public Administration Reform nonlending technical assistance	FY10	TA	Closed	
V.9	P116050	Afghanistan CGAC nonlending technical assistance	FY09	TA	Closed	
V.10	P120630	AML/CFT Assessment of Afghanistan	FY11	ESW	Active	
V. Public Administration and Governance Cluster: Subtotal						
VI. Social and Environmental Management						
VI.1	P084363	Afghanistan: Capacity Assessment - Social and Environmental Management	FY04	TA	Closed	
VI.2	P090344	Afghanistan: Capacity Building for Social and Environmental Management	FY05	TA	Closed	
VII. Social and Environmental Management Cluster: Subtotal						
VII. Health						
VII.1	P083962	Health Sector Review	FY09	ESW	Closed	
VII.2	P115883	Preparation for a Nutrition Situation Assessment	FY10	ESW	Closed	
VII.3	P125544	Afghanistan Mental Health Policy Note	FY11	ESW	Delivered	
VII. Health Cluster: Subtotal						

Sector Board	Output type	Cost of product (US$ '000)	Cluster total	Number of AAA	Pillar total
Public Sector Governance	Report	598.6			
Public Sector Governance	Conference/Workshop	80.9			
Public Sector Governance	Report	0.0			
Public Sector Governance	Report	141.0			
Financial Management	Report	59.7			
Procurement	Policy Note	33.1			
Financial Management	Report	87.4			
Procurement	Report	68.3			
		1,069.0	**1,069**	**8**	
Public Sector Governance	Report	326.7			
Public Sector Governance	"How-To" Guidance	70.9			
Public Sector Governance	"How-To" Guidance	121.1			
Public Sector Governance	Report	983.6			
Public Sector Governance	Report	460.2			
Economic Policy	"How-To" Guidance	13.9			
Social Development	"How-To" Guidance	763.0			
Public Sector Governance	"How-To" Guidance	149.1			
Public Sector Governance	"How-To" Guidance	29.9			
Financial and Private Sector Development	Report	36.8			
		2,955.2	**2,955**	**10**	
Environment	Knowledge-Sharing Forum	46.6			
Environment	Knowledge-Sharing Forum	140.4			
		187.1	**187**	**2**	
Health, Nutrition and Population	Report	243.6			
Health, Nutrition and Population	Policy Note	293.8			
Health, Nutrition and Population	Policy Note	8.2			
		545.6	**546**	**3**	

	Product ID	Product name	Delivered to client (FY)	Type	Status	
VIII. Education						
VIII.1	P083960	Afghanistan Education Policy Note	FY04	ESW	Closed	
VIII.2	P090844	Skills Development/Vocational Training	FY07	ESW	Closed	
VIII.3	P099777	Strategic Planning Higher Education	FY07	TA	Closed	
VIII.4	P113990	Risk Assessment of Schools/Clinics in Afghanistan and Identification for Mitigatory Action	FY10	TA	Closed	
VIII. Education Cluster: Subtotal						
TOTAL						
PILLAR 2: Promoting growth of the rural economy and improving rural livelihoods						
IX. Agriculture and Rural Development						
IX.1	P089208	Afghanistan National Food Policy Study	FY05	ESW	Closed	
IX.2	P109600	Afghanistan Rural Growth Program	FY08	TA	Closed	
IX.3	P114850	Afghanistan Agricultural Competitiveness Project	FY09	TA	Closed	
IX.4	P085679	Afghanistan Drug Economy	FY07	ESW	Closed	
IX.5	P088250	Afghanistan Drug Economy	FY04	ESW	Closed	
IX.6	P110422	Study on Economic Incentives and Development Initiatives to Reduce Opium Production	FY08	ESW	Closed	
IX.7	P078930	Afghanistan Water and Natural Resource Management	FY04	ESW	Closed	
IX.8	P102575	Afghanistan Strategic Water Planning Support	FY09	ESW	Delivered	
IX.9	P101622	Rural Access Policy Note	FY07	ESW	Closed	
IX.10	P106476	Impact Evaluation for Infrastructure (Evaluation of National Emergency for Rural Access Project)	FY09	IE	Closed	
IX. Agriculture and Rural Development: Subtotal						
PILLAR 3 World Bank: Supporting growth of the formal private sector						
X. PSD Enabling Environment						
X.1	P084820	Afghanistan: Framework for Private Investment	FY05	ESW	Closed	
X.2	P094754	Afghanistan Investment Climate Assessment	FY06	ESW	Closed	
X.3	P097779	Afghanistan Doing Business Indicators 2006	FY06	ESW	Closed	
X.4	P100937	Economic Growth and Private Sector Development Cross Cutting AAA	FY11	ESW	Delivered	
X.5	P105734	Afghanistan: Enabling Environment Conference	FY07	TA	Closed	
X.6	P116955	Afghanistan Enterprise Survey	FY09	ESW	Delivered	
X.7	572747	Licensing Reform in Afghanistan	FY11	IFC	Active	
X.8	P083455	Trade and Regional Cooperation between Afghanistan	FY04	ESW	Closed	
X.9	P090828	Regional Issues in Afghanistan's Development	FY06	ESW	Closed	

Sector Board	Output type	Cost of product (US$ '000)	Cluster total	Number of AAA	Pillar total
Education	Policy Note	98.8			
Education	Policy Note	153.4			
Education	"How-To" Guidance	56.3			
Social Development	"How-To" Guidance	11.6			
		320.1	320	4	
				49	9,381
Agriculture and Rural Development	Policy Note	119.8			
Agriculture and Rural Development	"How-To" Guidance	102.4			
Agriculture and Rural Development	Knowledge-Sharing Forum	205.3			
Economic Policy	Report	81.5			
Public Sector Governance	Policy Note	253.7			
Agriculture and Rural Development	Report	39.8			
Agriculture and Rural Development	Policy Note	41.0			
Environment	Policy Note	306.0			
Transport	Policy Note	65.2			
Transport	Report	88.6			
		1,303.3	1,303	10	1,303
Financial and Private Sector Development	Policy Note	213.0			
Financial and Private Sector Development	Report	145.5			
Financial and Private Sector Development	Policy Note	21.4			
Economic Policy	Report	531.3			
Financial and Private Sector Development	Knowledge-Sharing Forum	209.7			
Financial and Private Sector Development	Report	0.9			
Investment Climate		1,337.5			
Economic Policy	Report	229.9			
Economic Policy	Policy Note	82.9			

	Product ID	Product name	Delivered to client (FY)	Type	Status	
X.10	539172	Kabul University Business Skills Project	FY06	IFC	Closed	
X.11	553807	Business Edge Afghanistan	FY09	IFC	Active	
X. PSD Enabling Environment Cluster: Subtotal						
XI. ICT						
XI.1	P079282	Afghanistan: ICT Policy Advice	FY03	TA	Closed	
XI.2	P108582	Afghanistan nonlending technical assistance: Information and Communications Sector	FY08	TA	Closed	
XI.3	P114808	Information and Communications Sector nonlending technical assistance	FY09	TA	Closed	
XI.4	P117132	Technology Solutions for Asset Verification	FY10	TA	Closed	
XI.5	P118449	ICT Policy nonlending technical assistance	FY10	TA	Delivered	
XI.6	P118896	Afghanistan: M-apps and Rural Livelihoods	FY10	TA	Delivered	
XI.7	P123028	Afghanistan nonlending technical assistance	FY11	TA	Delivered	
XI. ICT Cluster: Subtotal						
XII. Urban Development						
XII.1	P083912	Urban Land Management: The Case of Kabul	FY06	ESW	Closed	
XII.2	P102672	Afghanistan Land Acquisition and Resettlement	FY10	TA	Closed	
XII.3	P109155	Kabul Historic Conservation in Urban Upgrading	FY10	TA	Closed	
XII.4	P121993	Evaluation of Kabul Urban Reconstruction	FY12	ESW	Active	
XII.5	P098172	Kabul University Urban Learning Program	FY06	TA	Closed	
XII.6	P122386	Migration and IDPs in Urban Areas	FY11	KP	Active	
XI. Urban Development Cluster: Subtotal						
XIII. Microfinance						
XIII.1	P081846	Support for Afghanistan Microfinance Fund Project	FY03	TA	Delivered	
XIII.2	507823	Feasibility Study for the Establishment of Microfinance Institution	FY02	IFC	Closed	
XIII.3	520505	Comprehensive Capacity Building for the First Micro-Finance Bank of Afghanistan (FMBA)	FY03	IFC	Active	
XIII.4	537059	Afghanistan Housing Finance/Microfinance Study	FY07	IFC	Closed	
XIII.5	554070	Afghanistan Housing MicroFinance Capacity Building	FY09	IFC	Closed	
XIII. Microfinance Cluster: Subtotal						
XIV. Financial Sector						
XIV.1	P084822	Afghanistan Financial Sector Study	FY04	ESW	Closed	
XIV.2	P103187	Afghanistan Housing Finance Study	FY07	ESW	Closed	

Sector Board	Output type	Cost of product (US$ '000)	Cluster total	Number of AAA	Pillar total
Sustainable Business Advisory		345.9			
Sustainable Business Advisory		1,715.8			
		4,833.8	**4,834**	**11**	
Global Information/ Communications Technology	"How-To" Guidance	109.3			
Global Information/ Communications Technology	Client Document Review	72.1			
Global Information/ Communications Technology	Client Document Review	89.1			
Global Information/ Communications Technology	Institutional Development Plan	20.4			
Global Information/ Communications Technology	Institutional Development Plan	95.3			
Global Information/ Communications Technology	"How-To" Guidance	132.2			
Global Information/ Communications Technology	Institutional Development Plan	56.8			
		575.3	**575**	**7**	
Urban Development	Policy Note	217.8			
Social Development	Institutional Development Plan	152.2			
Urban Development	"How-To" Guidance	67.2			
Urban Development	Report	110.0			
Urban Development	"How-To" Guidance	32.0			
Economic Policy	Study	96.8			
		675.9	**676**	**6**	
Financial and Private Sector Development	"How-To" Guidance	122.1			
Microfinance		85.0			
Commercial Banking - Microfinance and Small Business		940.0			
Access To Finance		49.0			
Access To Finance		360.0			
		1,556.1	**1,556**	**5**	
Financial and Private Sector Development	Report	85.9			
Financial and Private Sector Development	Report	57.2			

	Product ID	Product name	Delivered to client (FY)	Type	Status	
XIV.3	P109382	Afghanistan Capacity Building Program	FY09	TA	Closed	
XIV.4	566127	Public Credit Registry Afghanistan	FY09	IFC	Active	
XIV.5	568128	Afghanistan Secured Lending Project	FY09	IFC	Active	
XIV. Financial Sector Cluster: Subtotal						
XV. Infrastructure						
XV.1	P083910	Power nonlending technical assistance	FY04	TA	Closed	
XV.2	P098795	Kabul HH Energy Survey	FY07	ESW	Closed	
XV.3	P105996	Power nonlending technical assistance	FY09	TA	Delivered	
XV.4	P112866	Energy Assessment	FY09	ESW	Closed	
XV.5	P114423	Study of Alternative Options to Increase Electricity Access in Afghanistan	FY11	ESW	Active	
XV.6	P094632	Infrastructure Rehabilitation Policy Advise and Support	FY05	TA	Closed	
XV. Infrastructure Cluster: Subtotal						
XVI. Energy and Mining						
XVI.1	P081815	Afghanistan Oil/Gas Infrastructure Development	FY05	ESW	Closed	
XVI.2	P094633	Afghanistan: Policy Advise	FY05	TA	Closed	
XVI.3	P118694	The Afghanistan Mining Sector as a Driver of Growth: Opportunities and Challenges of Medium- and Large-Scale Mining	FY11	ESW	Delivered	
XVI. Energy and Mining Cluster: Subtotal						
XVII. Business Development						
XVII.1	539163	Afghanistan Horticulture Export Clusters Development	FY06	IFC	Closed	
XVII.2	552245	Afghanistan Horticulture Export Development Clusters 2	FY07	IFC	Active	
XVII.3	535914	AFC Leasing	FY05	IFC	Closed	
XVII.4	548027	Afghanistan Leasing Project	FY07	IFC	Active	
XVII.5	507693	Hotel Development Opportunities in Kabul	FY02	IFC	Closed	
XVII. Business Development Cluster: Subtotal						
Pillar 3 Subtotal						
TOTAL						

Note: ESW = economic and sector work; IFC = International Finance Corporation; KP = knowledge product; TA = technical assistance.

Sector Board	Output type	Cost of product (US$ '000)	Cluster total	Number of AAA	Pillar total
Financial and Private Sector Development	"How-To" Guidance	118.6			
Access To Finance		388.2			
Access To Finance		311.6			
		961.5	**962**	**5**	
Energy and Mining	Institutional Development Plan	60.6			
Energy and Mining	Policy Note	82.1			
Energy and Mining	"How-To" Guidance	29.1			
Energy and Mining	Policy Note	55.0			
Energy and Mining	Report	199.9			
Energy and Mining	Client Document Review	296.2			
		722.8	**723**	**6**	
Energy and Mining	Report	1,473.2			
Energy and Mining	Client Document Review	240.9			
Energy and Mining	Report	123.6			
		1,837.7	**1,838**	**3**	
Sustainable Business Advisory		320.1			
Sustainable Business Advisory		1,067.6			
Access To Finance		204.6			
Access To Finance		325.0			
City and Business Hotel		43.0			
		1,960.3	**1,960**	**5**	**13,123**
				48	
				107	23,808

Appendix E
AAA Assessment

With a recorded budgetary cost of US$29.6 million, AAA was a major component of the World Bank Group's assistance to Afghanistan during 2002–11. It accounted for over a quarter of the total operational budget for Afghanistan over that period. The AAA portfolio comprised 107 tasks, including economic and sector work, technical assistance, and IFC advisory tasks, covering practically all aspects of the Afghan economy (appendix D).

Besides guiding the design of Bank Group's own financial assistance to Afghanistan, the AAA was intended to help the Afghan government to analyze, design, and implement policies and programs to promote socioeconomic development. The AAA was also an important vehicle for strengthening the capacity of the country's nascent institutions. In addition, the AAA was to provide analytical underpinning to influence the focus and design of overall donor assistance to Afghanistan. The paucity of country knowledge following a prolonged hiatus in country relations, extremely weak capacity of local institutions, and availability of exceptionally large levels of donor assistance due to Afghanistan's role in combating global terrorism gives more than usual importance to AAA in the Bank Group's operational support to the country. Evaluating the extent to which the AAA achieved its intended objectives was therefore an important building block for this CPE.

Evaluation Challenges and Approach

Evaluation of the AAA programs poses important conceptual and practical challenges. Although judgments on the relevance and contributions of AAA products are an integral part of the IEG's country evaluations, IEG does not have an established methodology for evaluating AAA. Systematic evaluation of the AAA programs is constrained by differing governance standards concerning AAA in the World Bank Group. While IFC's advisory tasks are required to have a results framework at inception, followed by self-evaluation at completion, no such requirements apply to the AAA products of the Bank. Since most IEG evaluations are objectives-based, based on validating the findings of management's self-evaluations, IEG methodologies need to be adapted both to discern intended outcomes and results of the Bank's AAA and to supplement the related evidentiary base.[1] Gaps in the institutional memory concerning AAA products and, oftentimes, the sheer volume of the AAA work to be evaluated as part of CPEs pose additional practical challenges for AAA evaluations.

The methodology used in this evaluation took into consideration the above challenges as well as the time and resource constraints linked to the timeline and the overall budget envelope for the Afghanistan CPE. It drew heavily on the findings of past IEG work on knowledge products, including the most recent evaluations on AAA (IEG 2008) and middle-income countries (IEG 2007), as well as the experience with the Quality Assurance Group assessments of AAA during 1998–2009. Key features of the approach used in this evaluation are as follows:

- **Clustering of AAA tasks.** Past evaluations suggest that AAA is more effective when undertaken as part of a sustained engagement that may involve lending, policy dialogue, follow-on AAA, or knowledge work by the client or other partners. To capture this dimension, AAA products need to be evaluated within the context of the country program, rather than as isolated products. To examine synergies and complementarities among the different AAA products and to economize on evaluation resources, in consultation with the Afghanistan Country Management Unit, IEG grouped the 107 AAA tasks undertaken by the World Bank Group into 17 clusters of tasks around common sectoral or thematic foci (appendix D). Many of the AAA undertaken were obviously interrelated or follow-up tasks building on previous AAA work. This quasi-programmatic approach (on an ex-post basis) enabled the evaluation to focus on the totality of the effort by reviewing all the major economic and sector work (ESW) undertaken and related nonlending technical assistance NLTA) in different sectoral/thematic areas over a period of time rather than treating each task as an isolated, free-standing activity and sampling a few of them. The cluster-based analysis also led to better understanding of the synergies among related AAA activities and the collective results of each of these AAA clusters over time.

- **Differentiating between results and Bank performance.** Consistent with the IEG framework for evaluation of lending products, the evaluation of the AAA clusters focused on two aspects: adequacy of the *results (likely to be) achieved* by the cluster and appropriateness of the *Bank performance* in designing and implementing the tasks in the cluster. The dual focus recognizes that while results and Bank performance may often move in tandem, it need not be so in all cases, and the Bank's primary accountability is for its own performance.

- **Identifying AAA results.** Many of the tasks in the Afghan AAA program, especially the older ones, did not explicitly specify a results framework. For those AAA, the evaluation looked for results in one or more of the following results areas implicit in the Bank's country strategy documents for Afghanistan:

  a. Analytical advice and support to the Afghan government to help design policies and programs for jump-starting national reconstruction and development.

  b. Technical assistance to national and subnational public institutions in Afghanistan to strengthen their capacity for design and implementation of development policies, programs, and projects.

  c. Rebuilding the knowledge base about the Afghan economy to provide analytical underpinnings for mobilization and coordination of donor assistance for reconstruction and development.

  d. Underpinning and supporting the design and implementation of the Bank Group's operations and financial assistance to Afghanistan.

  e. Improving the understanding and influencing the behavior of other key stakeholders (for example, the private sector, local and foreign nongovernmental organizations [NGOs], academics) interested in developments in Afghanistan.

- **Benchmarking AAA results.** In assessing results, the evaluators exercised their judgments, taking into account the Afghan context, the complexity of the issues involved, the unforeseen exogenous factors, and the levels of effort made. If a particular result area was not found to be relevant to a specific cluster of AAA tasks, the evaluators marked it as *not applicable*. For tasks with intended results in more than one area, the evaluators assessed each relevant result and weighed the relative importance of different areas to determine the overall achievement of results.

- **Assessing Bank performance.** The assessment of Bank performance evaluated the quality of efforts made by the Bank in delivering a sound program in a cost-effective manner. It looked at five separate aspects:

  a. Relevance and timeliness of the different products in relation to the country needs.

  b. Technical quality of the products in bringing state-of-the-art knowledge adapted to the country circumstances.

  c. Efforts made to ensure appropriate engagement of key stakeholders during task design and implementation.

  d. Efficiency in terms of cost-effective use of task budgets, use of Bank and external knowledge, and adequacy of quality assurance processes.

  e. Dialogue and dissemination, including for capacity-building efforts following task completion.

- **Ratings scale.** Results and Bank performance for each AAA cluster were assessed on a six-point scale, ranging from highly satisfactory to highly unsatisfactory, as in other IEG products.[2]

- **Evaluation processes and instruments:**

  a. The starting points for the cluster evaluations were desk reviews of the key documentation (concept notes, peer review comments, final reports) on the various tasks in the respective clusters. The cluster-specific documentation was augmented with core strategy documents of the Afghan government and of the Bank Group as inputs into judging the AAA impact on government policies and programs and on the Bank's operational programs. Key documentation from various donor group meetings was also made available to the evaluators for assessing the impact of the Bank Group AAA on donor behavior and actions.

  b. Recognizing the gaps in institutional memory concerning the AAA program, a learning week was structured to provide evaluators an opportunity to seek clarifications from the country team on issues that might not be clear from the available documentation. This was supplemented, as needed, with follow-up discussions with relevant task team members. Consultations with key clients and stakeholders through audio/video conferences and through face-to-face meetings during the field visits were a key input for enhancing the robustness of the evaluative findings.

c. To ensure robustness of the evaluative judgments and to minimize subjectivity, each of the cluster evaluations was carried out by a two-person panel of experienced evaluators, of which at least one was a respected specialist in the relevant sectoral/thematic area. For most clusters, one member of each of the AAA assessment panels was also a core member of the CPE team, thereby ensuring synergies and complementarities with other components of the CPE.

d. A short guidance questionnaire was used to systematize the work of the evaluators. The ratings in the guidance questionnaire were complemented by textual comments to elaborate on the basis of the main judgments, especially those concerning the outlier ratings. Where significant variations existed among different tasks of the cluster, the text comments also identified and commented on those differences. Last, the evaluation text distilled any cross-cutting lessons for the future emerging from that evaluation.

e. Quality assurance was provided by a seasoned reviewer who adjudicated any differences among different panelists, reviewed the guidance questionnaires to ensure internal consistency in the assessments with the underlying evidence, and consistency in the use of the rating scale across different AAA clusters.

f. To maximize learning, special attention was paid during the evaluation to tasks within the clusters, where the results were judged to be particularly good or seriously deficient.

Main Findings

Table E.1 provides a summary view of the IEG judgments concerning results and Bank performance related to the 17 clusters. For the AAA program as a whole, IEG rates both aspects as *moderately satisfactory* —acceptable but with significant missed opportunities for doing better.

The results achieved varied considerably among different clusters. The *Health* cluster was by far the best-performing cluster and was commended by IEG evaluators for "solid and important contributions to knowledge of the health and nutrition sectors in Afghanistan providing useful and pertinent recommendations for health and nutrition policy in Afghanistan with explicit links to Afghan National Development Strategy." Commendable results were also noted for clusters related to *Needs Assessment, Gender, ICT, Microfinance, Energy and Mining,* and *Business Advisory Services.* In contrast, the results in clusters related to *Public Administration and Governance, Private Sector Development,* and the *Financial Sector* left much to be desired.

Not surprisingly, the AAA's most notable contributions were toward designs of the Bank Group's own assistance strategies and policy dialogue, underscoring synergies and complementarities between the Bank's lending and nonlending activities. In particular, the Bank's work on Needs Assessment and Strategy was critically important in shaping the Bank's own operations, enabling

Table E.1	AAA Ratings by Clusters and Quality Dimensions					
	R1	R2	R3	R4	R5	Overall Result
I. Needs assessment and strategy design	S	S	MS	S	MS	S
II. Gender	S	S	NR	S	MS	S
III. Poverty and social protection	MS	S	MS	MS	MU	MS
IV. Public expenditure management and fiduciary aspects	MS	MS	MS	MS	NR	MS
V. Public administration and governance	MS	MU	MU	MS	MU	MU
VI. Social and environmental management	MS	MS	NR	MS	NR	MS
VII. Health	HS	S	HS	HS	HS	HS
VIII. Education	MU	MU	MS	MS	MS	MS
IX. Agriculture and rural development	MS	MS	S	MS	MS	MS
X. Private sector development enabling environment	MU	MU	MS	MU	MU	MU
XI. ICT	HS	S	MS	HS	HS	S
XII. Urban development	MS	MS	MS	S	NR	MS
XIII. Microfinance	S	HS	S	S	S	S
XIV. Financial sector	MU	MS	MU	MS	MU	MU
XV. Power	S	MS	MS	MS	MU	MS
XVI. Energy and mining	S	S	S	S	MS	S
XVII. Business development	S	S	NR	S	S	S
Average (MS+S+HS) (percent)	82	82	80	94	64	82
Average (S+HS) (percent)	47	47	27	47	29	41

Note: HU = Highly unsatisfactory

U = Unsatisfactory

MU = Moderately unsatisfactory

MS = Moderately satisfactory

S = Satisfactory

HS = Highly satisfactory

NR = There are substantial gaps in information

R1 = Influence on country policies or programs

R2 = Institutional development impact on national or subnational organizations and programs

R3 = Influence on donor assistance

R4 = Impact on Bank's operations and policy dialogue

R5 = Influence on stakeholders outside the public sector

B1 = Relevance and timeliness

B2 = Technical quality

B3 = Client and stakeholder ownership

B4 = Bank inputs and processes

B5 = Dialogue and dissemination

B1	B2	B3	B4	B5	Overall Result
S	S	MS	MU	S	MS
S	S	MS	MS	MS	MS
S	S	MS	S	S	S
S	MS	MU	MS	MU	MS
MS	MS	MU	MS	MU	MS
HS	S	S	S	MS	S
S	S	HS	S	HS	S
MU	MU	MS	MU	MS	MU
MS	S	MS	MS	S	MS
MS	MS	MU	MU	U	MU
HS	HS	S	MS	S	HS
MU	S	MS	MS	MU	MS
HS	S	S	S	S	S
MS	MS	MS	MU	MS	MS
MU	MS	MU	MU	MU	MU
S	MS	MS	MS	S	MS
HS	S	S	S	HS	S
82	94	76	71	71	82
59	59	29	29	47	35

them to get off to a rapid start and laying the basis for many of the most successful interventions. The exceptional results achieved in the Health sector also underscore the importance of using lending and nonlending instruments in a mutually reinforcing fashion to advance the sectoral agendas. A key exception in this results area was the Bank Group's work to improve the enabling environment for private sector development. The exceptionally challenging country context and security risks are no doubt important factors explaining the lack of progress toward creating a dynamic private sector. Arguably, however, greater strategic coherence in the Bank's AAA as well as better coordination among different parts of the Bank Group could have helped in that regard.

The Bank Group AAA had mixed success in strengthening Afghan policies and institutions. The AAA made significant contributions in several areas, including *ICT, Microfinance, Mining,* and *Poverty Monitoring.*

- In *ICT,* the Bank Group's AAA established a road map to guide Afghanistan toward increased connectivity through a major expansion of the mobile telephone network and commercialization of the Internet service.

- In microfinance, IFC's advisory services were critical to developing the sector by helping establish the First Microfinance Bank of Afghanistan.

- In mining, the Bank's AAA contributed toward a much improved assessment of the country's mineral potential as well as a stronger safeguards and governance framework for developing that potential.

- And finally, the Bank's poverty assessments and related technical assistance added significantly to the capacity of the government to conduct poverty surveys and to use the survey data to analyze poverty and social issues.

The Bank had less success, however, in influencing the policies and programs of the government aimed at curbing corruption and in building sustainable capacity among the Afghan civil service for managing the core functions of the government. Lacking adequate strategic focus, Bank Group's AAA also had little success in strengthening the country's fragile financial sector. The mixed results may reflect the overarching importance in recent years of higher-order political and security agenda, with its emphasis on short-term results that are sometimes incompatible with the sustained efforts required for institutional development.

The Bank Group also had mixed success in influencing the behavior and actions of other donors and stakeholders. Partner feedback during field consultations indicated uniformly high regard for the quality and objectivity of the Bank's analytical work. The Bank's work assessing the economic implications of the coming transition (prepared for the 2011 Bonn Conference) was mentioned by many interlocutors as a good example of what the Bank is uniquely qualified to contribute toward challenges faced by the Afghan government and the donor community. The confidence in the Bank's analytical capacity and its ability to get things done has meant significant support from several donors through trust funds (especially ARTF) managed by the Bank.

The donor community, however, has been less forthcoming on the critical issue of budget comprehensiveness; the Bank's repeated urgings to channel more aid through the government budget has had less impact than hoped for, with 74 percent of documented donor expenditures managed through special donor arrangements. The Bank's recommendations for rationalizing and aligning the mix of ad hoc incentives paid to officials and consultants have also found little resonance with other donors. The mixed results regarding donor behavior suggest the need for the Bank to be more realistic in its expectations in situations such as that found in Afghanistan, where objectives other than sustainable, socio-economic development may be more important drivers of donor decisions and actions.

The sectoral and thematic composition of the AAA was broadly appropriate, leading to generally high ratings for relevance, albeit with some notable exceptions. Where relevance was an issue, it was often due to what the Bank did not do rather than to what it did do. Client consultations in the field suggest that in some areas (for example, education and infrastructure), the Bank missed opportunities to help the government define prioritized investment programs in keeping with available financial and human resources. In education, the AAA program largely overlooked higher education, despite its salience to building a capable workforce to manage the country's reconstruction. Also, the AAA undertaken did not result in actionable recommendations for primary and secondary education. Inadequate attention to improving delivery of municipal services was a major gap in the urban sector AAA. The omission and gaps, in part, reflected lack of clarity among donors about the division of labor as well as inadequate donor coordination.

IEG evaluators noted the generally high technical quality of the Bank's AAA work, indicating the Bank's ability to mobilize teams of knowledgeable professionals to deliver good quality even in challenging country conditions. IEG evaluators found that most of the AAA reports contained sound analysis, had the right emphases, were well written, and had recommendations consistent with the findings and appropriate to the country context. A key factor in assuring quality and relevance of the Bank Group's AAA was inclusion in teams of individuals with intimate understanding of the cultural and socio-political context of Afghanistan.

The Bank was less successful in assuring an adequate level of client and stakeholder involvement during design and implementation of many of its AAA tasks. Contributions of AAA in several clusters (for example, Public Expenditure Management, Public Administration and Governance, PSD, and in several infrastructure clusters) suffered because of inadequate client ownership in defining the AAA agenda and in owning the resulting conclusions and recommendations. While in part this reflected the pervasive weaknesses in the Afghan government in deploying suitable counterparts to work with the Bank teams, inadequate efforts on the part of the Bank teams in dialogue, dissemination, and capacity building also contributed to this problem. Feedback from some of the donors in the field also noted the need for improved dissemination of the Bank's AAA.

Efficient management of the AAA resources was an area of concern in many products and clusters. For several tasks (such as the study of labor markets and pensions), despite intensive follow up, IEG was unable to locate any output related to those tasks. In many tasks, the Bank also failed to recognize adequately the significant inputs and contributions provided by other partners. The fragmentary data available on the Bank's quality assurance processes as well as the managerial attention devoted to AAA tasks suggest that the Bank did not always get full value for the resources spent on the AAA. Management of IFC's Business Advisory Services with a structured instrument for planning, monitoring, and oversight of such activities was a notable exception.

Difficult country conditions and frequent changes to the programs due to exogenous factors accounted for some of the inefficiencies involved in delivering the Bank's AAA program in Afghanistan. The efficiency also suffered, however, from systemic weaknesses in planning and managing AAA in the Bank. The Bank could benefit from adopting some of the processes and instruments used by IFC for managing its portfolio of Advisory Services.

Main Lessons

Key lessons from the AAA review include:

- The need for the Bank to be more realistic in terms of what its support and interventions can accomplish in complex, post-conflict situations.

- In countries emerging from a long period of isolation, the need, early on, for comprehensive reviews of constraints, opportunities, and options in key sectors to help guide government and donor decisions around prioritized agendas of policies and programs.

- Importance of complementing global technical expertise with a good.

- Understanding of the local political, cultural, and institutional context.

- Ensure effective delivery of AAA.

- The need for the Bank to tighten its planning, monitoring, and oversight systems to ensure efficient delivery of its AAA programs.

Notes

1. The Activity Completion Summary – which is not universally completed – does not amount to a self-evaluation because it is mainly an administrative exercise and lacks agreed evaluative criteria.

2. HS= Highly Satisfactory: Best practice for most of the tasks in the cluster and no significant deficiencies in any of the tasks; S = Satisfactory: Satisfactory or better

on all key tasks and no major deficiency in any of the cluster tasks; MS = Moderately Satisfactory: At least Satisfactory on most key tasks, but showing deficiencies and missed opportunities in some tasks; MU = Moderately Unsatisfactory: Significant deficiencies in some key tasks; U = Unsatisfactory: Significant deficiencies in several key tasks; HU = Highly Unsatisfactory: A broad pattern of deficiencies.

Appendix F
Results of Bank Support for
Gender Equality

This note reports the findings of an assessment of the gender dimensions of Bank support for Afghanistan.[1] This assessment examined the relevance of Bank support for gender equality between FY2002 and 2011, the quality of its implementation, and the gender-related results of its operations (operations were selected consistent with the gender strategy reflected in the Bank's country strategy documents).

Gender Equality in Afghanistan

Reforming gender relationships in Afghanistan has historically met with limited success and has been extremely challenging and complex. Although Afghan women obtained gender equality under the 1964 Constitution, the legal system granted differential rights to men and women. The 1977 Civil Code introduced significant reforms, which did not hold up during years of conflict with the breakdown of state functions that followed in the 1980s and 1990s. The 1977 Civil Law was replaced by a largely unreformed Hanafi Family Law, and customary law continued to rule in practice. The legal framework guiding Afghan women's lives has been a combination of elements of civil law, customary law, and Islamic (Hanafi and Shia) Law.

In the post-Taliban years, development efforts to support gender equality have resumed, strengthened by the constitutional mandate for gender equality. Although Afghanistan signed the Convention on the Elimination of All Forms of Discrimination against Women (CEDAW) in August 1980, given the decades of conflict, it was able to accede to the convention only in March 2003. It acceded without any reservations, thus agreeing to be legally bound by all terms of the convention.

As a result of the efforts of the government and its development partners, there was slow but steady progress toward increasing gender equality over the evaluation period (table F.1). Available sector-level data confirms the slow but steady progress. For example, in 2002 there were 50 men in the teacher training colleges and no women. In 2010, there are 1,700 faculty members, of which 23 percent are women. In 2002, there were 450 male students attending teacher training colleges; in 2010, 50,256 students were enrolled in teacher training colleges, of which over 40 percent were female.[2] Nevertheless, as indicated by the Gender Development Index 2011, Afghanistan remains among the bottom 6 countries (141st out of 146 countries), and the lowest in South Asia (table F.2). (In the Human Development Index, it fared better, standing at 172 among a set of 187 countries).

RELEVANCE OF BANK SUPPORT

The World Bank gave significant emphasis to gender issues through its support to Afghanistan. This was reflected in the Bank's Transitional Strategy documents of 2002 and 2003, as well as the World Bank's Interim Strategy Notes of 2006 and 2009. Such support for gender in Afghanistan was substantially relevant because it was: (i) consistent with the Bank's gender policy, (ii) strategic and considered, given the difficult and complex country context; and

Table F.1	Data on Gender Equality		
	2000	2005	2006
Population, total	25,950,816	29,904,962	30,751,661
Population, female	12,511,378	14,425,187	14,835,155
Life expectancy at birth, total (years)	45	47	47
Life expectancy at birth, male (years)	45	47	47
Life expectancy at birth, female (years)	45	47	47
Labor force, total	7,931,764	9,273,559	9,585,133
Labor force, female (% of total labor force)	26	26	26
Primary completion rate, total (% of relevant age group)	..	34	..
Primary completion rate, male (% of relevant age group)	..	48	..
Primary completion rate, female (% of relevant age group)	..	19	..
Fertility rate, total (births per woman)	8	7	7
Births attended by skilled health staff (% of total)	12	..	19
Mortality rate, adult, female (per 1,000 female adults)	408	392	389

Source: World Bank Genderstats.

Note: .. = information not available

(iii) provided for the most part in collaboration with government agencies and local communities.

CONSISTENT WITH THE BANK'S MANDATE

The Bank's support for gender equality in Afghanistan was consistent with its mandate. For the Bank, gender equality is an instrument to help

Table F.2	Gender Inequality Index (GII) Trends, 1995–2011				
Country	1995	2000	2005	2008	2011
Afghanistan	..	..	0.709	0.695	0.707
Bangladesh	0.664	..	0.598	0.602	0.550
India	0.692	..	0.646	0.614	0.617
Nepal	0.724	0.680	0.665	0.563	0.558
Pakistan	0.773	..	0.611	0.600	0.573
Sri Lanka	0.473	..	0.447	0.430	0.419

Source: http://hdr.undp.org/en/statistics/gii/.

Note: .. = information not available

achieve the institutional mandates of poverty reduction and economic growth. The Bank's gender policy aims to "assist member countries to reduce poverty and enhance economic growth, human well-being, and development effectiveness by addressing the gender disparities and inequalities that are barriers to development, and by assisting member countries in formulating and implementing their gender and development goals." Operational Policy 4.20, Gender and Development.

A literature review undertaken for the 2008 Gender evaluation confirms the linkages between gender equality and poverty reduction. The literature suggests that improving gender outcomes in education and health; expanding women's participation in the labor force, entrepreneurship, and access to productive assets; and that strengthening women's voice and rights can lead to better development outcomes across a range of sectors.

CONSISTENT WITH CLIENT PRIORITY

The Bank's approach and strategy in Afghanistan was, overall, responsive to the Afghan context. Gender issues were initially addressed only in sectors and areas where women were already present. Support for gender equality was implemented over time, in an incremental manner, using culturally relevant strategies. For instance, while the initial voting policy did not require female participation under the National Security Program (NSP), later versions called for women to vote, influencing gender and power dynamics within communities. The nature of the support was often left to community groups to decide, thereby avoiding the feeling that gender equality was being imposed by external actors. The Bank's approach was also opportunistic, pursuing gender equality in some provinces, while not making it an issue in others where there was less ownership. This more cautious approach helped to keep gender in the dialogue with specific ministries, and also facilitated a learning spiral for different stakeholders.

Bank support was also consistent with the policies of the Afghan government and other strategic documents of the government, although it may not have been in line with the sentiments of the more conservative segments of society that represented traditional tribal or religious interest groups. The country's National Development Framework (NDF) of 2002 stressed the need to pay special attention to women and girls by enhancing their capabilities and participation at all stages of reconstruction planning and development. It suggested that this would be accomplished partly through increased capacity building by the Ministry of Women's Affairs.[3] The Afghanistan National Development Strategy (ANDS) recognizes the importance of gender equality, and identifies gender equality as one of four cross-cutting issues in its strategy for the nation. The National Action Plan for Women in Afghanistan has been formulated as part of the ANDS. As stated earlier, the government had also acceded without any reservations to CEDAW (Convention on the Elimination of All Forms of Discrimination against Women) in 2003.

The quality of implementation of Bank support for gender quality is assessed utilizing three indicators. These are: (i) sound diagnosis of gender issues in Afghanistan; (ii) gender integration at the project level in a manner consistent with its stated gender strategy; and (iii) collaboration with other development partners in providing such support.

SOUND DIAGNOSTICS

The Bank undertook sound diagnostics as a basis for its engagement on gender issues in Afghanistan. Overall, relevant AAA pieces integrated gender, the analysis was sound, and by and large the reports were sensitive to the country context. As required under Operational Policy 4.20 on Gender and Development, the Bank conducted a country-level gender diagnostic in 2005, which helped to initiate the dialogue in Afghanistan. The gender assessment (World Bank 2005c) identified health, education, and agriculture as priority sectors where gender-responsive interventions were needed. Microfinance was also stressed. Subsequent strategies focused on the gender Assessment's recommendations and laid out a strategy for addressing gender inequalities (box F.1) by increasing focus on gender in key sectors such as health, education, and agriculture. Several other ESWs in the health and economic sectors, both before and after the assessment, were also substantively gender-aware.

Box F.1	Gender Was Consistently Integrated into Country Strategies

The Transitional Support Strategy, or TSS (World Bank 2002), recognized the large gender gaps and emphasized that women and men must be fully engaged in reconstruction and development. Increased employment and school enrolment (including for women and girls) were key desired outcomes. Nonformal education for illiterate and poorly-educated young women was also noted as part of the strategy.

The subsequent TSS (World Bank 2003) envisaged preparation of a Country Gender Assessment to consider how to mainstream gender equity considerations in its assistance program.

The 2006 ISN (World Bank 2006a) announced the delayed launch of the Afghanistan Country Gender Assessment. It proposed to forge entry points for gender mainstreaming in sectors where significant gains were possible, such as education, health, and the civil service, where women already had an acceptable presence. Economic empowerment of rural women was emphasized, as were linkages to programs like the National Solidarity Program (NSP) and Microfinance Investment Support Facility for Afghanistan (MISFA). In urban areas, the focus was intended to be on job creation in industrial sectors where women already had a foothold.

The 2009 ISN (World Bank 2009) reflected the recommendations of the gender assessment and aimed to improve service delivery and to empower women economically in key markets. It supported the government's policy of gender mainstreaming and the National Action Plan for the Women of Afghanistan (2007–17). It emphasized improvement in gender parity through continued delivery of basic services, including in health and education, and strengthening gender mainstreaming into the three pillars of the Afghanistan National Development Strategy (ANDS).

Source: IEG evaluation team.

Relevance of the diagnostic, however, was reduced by the fact that the Country Gender Assessment and other gender-related AAA were prepared entirely by a group of Bank staff and consultants. The inputs from the government appear to have been weak. Although this reflected the weak capacity of government stakeholders during the early years and the ongoing conflict, the question remains of whether, at the cost of quality, greater ownership should have been encouraged. However, Bank staff felt that in the early days, the need was for analysis and information and the tradeoffs made were the right choices.

The lack of clear recommendations in the Country Gender Assessment reduced relevance of the diagnostic. It only suggested "main areas of intervention in support of gender equity and gender mainstreaming," but did not provide clear guidance to Bank staff. This appears to be a missed opportunity that reduced the relevance of the gender assessment, both for the Bank and the country, until later in 2008 when funds were obtained from the Bank's Gender Action Plan to operationalize the assessment's recommendations.

GENDER INTEGRATION AT THE PROJECT LEVEL[4]

Overall, integration at the project level was consistent with the strategy laid out in the Bank's policy, which required attention to gender only in sectors or thematic areas identified in the country strategies (box F.1). There was thus more attention to gender in projects related to health, education, rural enterprise, and microfinance development. There was also significant attention to gender in the financial sector, and some modest attention to issues in pension administration and higher education. The majority of the projects that did not consider gender issues were infrastructure projects, such as power supply provision, road construction, irrigation, and activities associated with customs and trade facilities, or public administration.[5] There is no marked difference in the treatment of gender over the decade, with the Bank's attention to gender issues continuing to focus on the areas mentioned above.

In projects that addressed gender, innovative and culturally appropriate mechanisms were utilized to target women. The Emergency Education Quality Improvement Program (EQUIP), for example, facilitated gender-separate

---

Box F.2   Funds for Sustaining Gender Results on the Ground

An important question that the Afghanistan gender team is unable to answer is whether they will receive budget to sustain and strengthen the operational successes in supporting gender equality. In the past several years, the Gender Action Plan has provided almost half a million dollars for operationalizing the Country Gender Assessment recommendations. Such funding has now stopped. Without funding it will be difficult for the team to take the gender agenda forward. This is particularly so for Afghanistan, where supporting women's empowerment is more expensive than in other countries because of the strict constraints on women's mobility.

community meetings for each affected area to inform the local population about their rights under the project. However, the same project did not ensure separate toilets for boys and girls in mixed schools. The National Emergency Empowerment Program for Rural Access Project utilized innovative solutions such as the production of building materials from women's homes or other socially acceptable locations to facilitate women's participation.

Bank attention to monitoring gender issues in its operations was strong in the case of the human development interventions. Both education and health projects include one or more specific indicators. While the NSP projects assessed the extent of participation of women in community committees, monitoring of gender-disaggregated results was weak in projects in the economic empowerment dimension in general. Microfinance projects were more gender-aware and assessed the extent to which the benefits were reaching women. In recent years, more attention has been paid to ensuring gender-disaggregated indicators, particularly given the pressure from donors and the availability of Gender Action Plan funds to operationalize the Country Gender Assessment.

COLLABORATION WITH OTHER DEVELOPMENT PARTNERS

The Afghanistan Reconstruction Trust Fund (ARTF) is a partnership between the international community and the Afghan government for reconstruction efforts and is administered by the World Bank. Since 2002, 30 donors have been part of this group, and part of the high levels of gender integration in the overall portfolio can be attributed to their focus on gender mainstreaming and monitoring of results. Field visits confirmed the overall satisfaction of other donors on the arrangement and those interviewed felt that although the Bank was slow in taking leadership in this area, more attention is paid to integrating and monitoring gender issues today. (USAID and DFID).

RESULTS OF BANK SUPPORT

The results of 21 projects listed in appendix A were reviewed to better understand the Bank's contribution to supporting gender equality in Afghanistan. The review utilizes the same results framework as the 2010 Gender Evaluation in assessing results, equating gender equality with: (i) strengthened human development, (ii) strengthened economic empowerment of women, and (iii) improved voice of women in development matters.

Overall, the assessment concludes that given the challenges and complexity of supporting gender equality in Afghanistan, the results of Bank support, as well as Bank performance, were commendable. The reasons for this conclusion are provided below.

STRENGTHENED HUMAN DEVELOPMENT

Significant progress has been made in human development in Afghanistan. Education levels improved over the 2002–10 timeframe. Enrollment rates increased, along with the numbers for female teachers trained and female

Table F.3	Bank Support Reviewed for Results	
Dimension	Sum of US$ millions	Count of dimension
Economic empowerment	219.31	9
Human development	167.6	6
Voice and participation	400	6
Total	**786.91**	**21**
Source: IEG evaluation team.		

teachers on the job. The health status of the Afghan population improved significantly through the duration of the World Bank–supported health project (2003–09). Available data trends show reduced maternal mortality rates and fertility rates, and an increase in modern contraceptive prevalence.

Bank support aimed to increase access to education services for girls and close the education access gap across provinces; it was partly successful. For example, the Emergency Education Rehabilitation and Development Project improved the access of women and girls to education. According to the Implementation Completion Report, between 2003 and 2005, enrollment across the country in primary school (grades 1-6), secondary school (grades 7-9), and high school (grades 10-12) grew from 3.1 million to over 5.5 million. It increased from under 839,000 to 1.74 million for females, and for males, from 2.27 million to 3.27 million. However, there were challenges; approximately 30 percent of completed schools that received infrastructure grants did not comply with the gender-equity criteria. Hard-to-access and conflict-afflicted provinces also experienced more implementation obstacles. Nevertheless, the Implementation Completion Report notes that at the provincial level, there is an overall positive degree of association between the EQUIP and improved gender ratio.

In collaboration with other donors, Bank support helped to establish School Management Shura, or Council, for every school under the EQUIP program of the Ministry of Education. Through these shuras, the Ministry aimed to increase awareness of the importance of girls' education and to determine mechanisms for encouraging parents and communities to support the education of girls. Overall, this approach appears to have been successful. Shuras decided to construct boundary walls, provide water, and construct sanitation facilities, all very important in achieving gender equality in enrollments. Sustainability will be an issue because the resources for such participation are likely to be unavailable, and there was inadequate time for such community-level institutions to be established.

There were several other challenges in increasing access of girls to education. For example, EQUIP found it challenging to increase enrollment of girls in schools where provinces were insecure and the probability of conflict was high. Security risks were also associated with the cost-effectiveness ratio, making education access to girls in unsecure regions not only difficult but costly as well. Even though the overall number of female teachers in Afghanistan increased over the years, there was less than a 2 percent increase in females as a percentage of the total teaching force. Their representation increased from 27.75 percent in 2004 to 29.42 percent in 2009. Moreover, retention of girls is an issue, with enrollment figures dropping precipitously after primary school (grade 6), and continuing to decline throughout secondary school.

Education sector projects, however, focused mostly on the supply side of the education sector with investments in teacher training as well as strengthening institutional capacity of the government agencies at the central and provincial levels, NGOs, and school-level administration. Demand-side incentives like providing stipends to girls (planned) or other similar conditional cash transfers were not explored to encourage girls to enroll in schools. Instead, social mobilization and community participation were utilized to encourage households to send girls to school. Given the context, this was a reasonable approach.

Progress in supporting gender equality in the health sector is particularly notable. Maternal mortality in Afghanistan is the second-highest in the world: with a ratio of 1,600 maternal deaths per 100,000 live births, women's survival remains a top priority for the health sector. Data from a 2006 household survey of women in rural areas suggests that utilization of health services is improving but still far too low to put the country on track for reaching Millennium Development Goals 4 and 5.

Through the National Emergency Employment Program for Rural Access (2008), the Bank rehabilitated rural roads and provided better connectivity and access to 23 hospitals. Outpatients utilizing hospital facilities increased by 30 percent, women seeking pre-natal care has gone up by 90 percent, and women seeking delivery care and services doubled during the post-project period. The ratio of women using delivery services and prenatal services from these hospitals has gone up from 41 percent to 51 percent in benefiting villages. Access to female health care workers has increased. Partly due to an effort to train female front-line health workers as part of the support provided to the health sector, the percentage of primary health care facilities with at least one female doctor, nurse, or midwife increased from 26 percent in 2004 to 81 percent in 2007. Other sectors did not adopt such an approach.

Economic Empowerment of Women

One of the achievements of early support provided jointly by the Bank and the Consultative Group to Assist the Poorest (CGAP) was the establishment of an apex microfinance facility called Microfinance Investment Support Facility for Afghanistan (MISFA) (AMMC 2009). MIFSA helped to strengthen institutions as well as empower women. In 2008, MIFSA became a private company that provided support to the 15 microfinance institutions (MFIs) that by July 2007 had disbursed 808,000 loans totaling US$282 million, with a portfolio outstanding of US$87 million. The outstanding loan portfolio was about $130 million at end-2010, representing about 260,000 borrowers. A 2009 impact assessment (AMMC 2009) indicates that the activities have had a positive impact on the lives of women borrowers and their families. Seventy percent of microfinance clients are women. Women clients reported improved roles in contributing to business decisions and a positive impact on their participation in the household economic decision making about food, utilities, health, education, and clothing. Improvement was also seen in client savings, with 69 percent of clients saving money, compared to only 34 percent before taking the loan.

The Bank contributed to enhancing micro-businesses for women. For example, the Horticultural and Livestock Project has made notable progress in the last two years in terms of increasing productivity of women farmers. Sixty-six percent of target farmers (all women) adopted the introduced improved poultry husbandry practices in focus districts (exceeding the target of 60 percent). About 1,050 hectares of new orchards were established in focus districts, which brings the cumulative new plantings to 3,187 hectares (this represented a "household-focused approach" that covered both men and women, and it responded to women's needs in a culturally appropriate manner by supporting economic activities around the household).

The project has so far helped to establish 11,000 women-operated poultry units, which have produced over 13 million eggs since July 2009, with marketing being undertaken at competitive prices through women village group leaders. Ninety-four percent of the poultry units have started a second cycle independently, suggesting high levels of sustainability. This was confirmed during the mission with authorities in MAIL, who noted how the project had benefited women. Similarly although the overall rating of the Avian Influenza Control and Human Pandemic Preparedness and Response Project was not satisfactory, trained women communicators and school programs did help to increase women's awareness of controlling such infections among domestic poultry and preparing for, controlling, and responding to possible human infections. Given that women constitute the majority of backyard poultry owners, this helped to protect one of their few sources to income.

Gender considerations were, however, not integrated into projects dealing with civil administration, as noted in the 2006 ISN. The Programmatic Support for Institution Building supported the preparation of a policy note to enhance the role of women in the civil service and initiated the gathering of gender-disaggregated information in the civil service. This was expected to lead to the development of policy options that would support gender equality. This has not happened according to the IARCSC, but is under consideration.

Increased Voice and Participation

The Bank supported the enhancement of voice and participation of women at the community levels. The National Solidarity Program (NSP) supported equal representation of women in Community Development Councils (CDCs). The NSP's original target for proportion of women participating in CDC elections was 40 percent, but the actual value achieved was 50 percent. On average, 35 percent of CDC representatives are women, and in some regions they constitute 60 percent of the CDC. All in all, about 90,000 women are members of mixed or all-female CDCs. According to stakeholders, such participation has had a significant demonstration effect on community members. Also, female CDCs provided an unprecedented forum for women to discuss shared problems and issues. The first follow-up survey (2009) for the NSP impact evaluation confirms that the program had a positive impact on the role of women in rural communities by increasing women's participation in local governance, enhancing responsiveness of village institutions to women's needs, and by familiarizing women with village leadership.

ENCOURAGED PRODUCTION OF GENDER-DISAGGREGATED DATA

The Bank, along with other donors, supported the government and donors in improving and expanding the National Risk and Vulnerability Assessment—a national household survey—which emphasized issues related to women's well-being. This has facilitated the availability of significant gender-related data, and led to better understanding of gender and poverty issues in Afghanistan. The 2007-08 assessment is the third of three successive rounds of surveys, following the National Risk and Vulnerability Assessments of 2003 and 2005. The assessment is very gender-aware and provides information on demographics by gender and age, as well as gender-based indicators such as spousal age difference based on current age of the wife, fertility rate (children per woman), women's mean age at first marriage, and number of widows. Gender-disaggregated data was collected for labor force characteristics showing unemployment rates and employment to population ratios in urban and rural areas for men and women.

Conclusion

Overall, the assessment concludes that Bank support successfully supported gender equality in a culturally responsive manner. It contributed to improving access of women to health services and increasing girls' access to schooling. Prior to the NSP, it was uncommon to find women in community groups; with the NSP, such participation has become more acceptable and women have a seat at the table (although admittedly their voices are yet to be heard). Despite efforts to enhance women's economic empowerment, results were weaker in this dimension, although projects such as the Horticultural and Livestock Project and the Skills Development Project (still ongoing) are showing considerable promise. Women also obtained access to microfinance, but such support enhanced their social status more than economically empowering them. Given the huge obstacles to gender equality, the prevalence of traditional practices that are inherently biased against women and the continuing conflict in Afghanistan, these achievements in a single decade are considered quite substantial.

Part of the reason for the better results than those seen in other conflict situations is the very low initial conditions that existed in Afghanistan in matters related to gender equality. Another important reason for the effectiveness of Bank support could also be the fact that the Bank adopted programs that involved community groups in making gender-related decisions. Thus, in the education sector, although recognizing that education is a universal human right, Bank support involved community groups at the school level in determining how best to encourage the participation of girls. The NSP encouraged the participation of women at the community level, providing a seat at the table for women. There was also significant effort to train women to reach women within their homes, which in many parts of Afghanistan is the only way of addressing the issue. Leaving the decision to communities may have delivered slower results, but in the long term such processes appear to have generated greater ownership and more sustainable results.

There is, however, no room for complacency. Out of 23.9 million people in Afghanistan, 48.8 percent are female (2009). Females make up 49 percent of the population ages 0–19 and 43 percent of the population 60 years and over. Afghanistan ranks 155 out of 169 countries in the 2010 Human Development Index and the Gender Development Index for Afghanistan is the lowest in South Asia.[6] Much more needs to be done. The Bank will need to continue to strategically nurture its support for gender equality and women's economic empowerment at the country level, while providing adequate funding and support to operational task teams to ensure that this initial contribution to gender equality in Afghanistan is slowly but surely sustained and strengthened in the years ahead.

Lessons

- Sustainable change to gender relationships has to be demanded by internal constituencies. Involving communities and other social/religious leaders and organizations to take a lead in supporting gender equality in Afghanistan enhanced the effectiveness of Bank support.

- Promoting women's empowerment without triggering a political and social backlash will necessitate dissemination of regional best practices, both in- country, in a culturally compatible manner, as well as within the Bank team.

- Addressing gender barriers to access to care can be improved by increasing the number of women health providers and extending services geographically, as well as by pairing couples together as community health workers.

- In post-conflict countries, construction and rehabilitation of roads and other relevant infrastructure can enhance the gender quality of human development services if the roads are built taking into account the accessibility of remote communities to health and education facilities.

Table F.4	List of Closed Projects (for Assessment of Results)	
Dimension	Sum of US$ millions	Count of dimension
Economic empowerment	**219.31**	**9**
ARTF - Rural Water Supply and Sanitation Project	5	1
Creating Future Potential Entrepreneurs	2.84	1
Emergency Infrastructure Reconstruction Project	33	1
Expanding Microfinance Outreach and Improving Sustainability	30	1
First MicroFinance Bank of Afghanistan - JSDF Capacity Building	0.65	1
Horticulture and Livestock Productivity Project	20	1
National Emergency Employment Program - Phase I	61.62	1
National Emergency Employment Program for Rural Access	39.2	1
Public Administration Capacity Building Project	27	1
Human development	**167.6**	**6**
Avian Influenza Control and Human Pandemic Preparedness and Response Project	8	1
Education Quality Improvement Program	35	1
Emergency Education Rehabilitation & Development Project	15	1
Health (supplement II)	20	1
Health (supplement)	30	1
Health Sector Emergency Reconstruction and Development	59.6	1
Voice and participation	**400**	**6**
Emergency Community Empowerment and Public Works Project	42	1
Emergency National Solidarity – Supplemental	28	1
Emergency National Solidarity Project	95	1
Emergency National Solidarity Project (II supplemental)	40	1
Emergency National Solidarity Project II	120	1
NSP II - Additional Financing	75	1
Total	**786.91**	**21**

Source: IEG Evaluation.

Notes

1. This appendix is based on the assessment reported in appendix D of IEG's evaluation of bank support for gender and development (IEG 2010). It also relies on a background paper prepared for this evaluation on gender-related results of Bank support in Afghanistan. In addition, an assessment of results was undertaken for 22 activities that closed during the evaluation period. Views obtained through interviews with several relevant stakeholders as well as Bank staff have also fed into the report.

2. Data provided in a note on "World Bank-Supported Work on Gender in Afghanistan: Afghanistan Reconstruction Trust Fund (ARTF)," Donors Meeting, December 7, 2010.

3. The Ministry of Women's Affairs was established by the Bonn Agreement of December 2001. The interim and transitional governments of Afghanistan gave it the responsibility for leading and coordinating government efforts to advance the role of women so that gender disparities are reduced. Gender focal points were established in other ministries.

4. This is based on a project-level analysis by IEG of 21 closed or completed World Bank projects from FY02–10 across three dimensions of human development, economic empowerment, and voice and participation at the local and national levels. The assessment also examined 20 more recent projects approved between FY09 to FY11 to understand how gender was being integrated into more recent projects.

5. No doubt, these projects would have delivered better results for women and men if gender considerations were integrated into the design of infrastructure projects. The assessment, however, does not consider this necessary because the Bank's policy requires only integration of gender issues in selected areas.

6. See footnote 2.

References

AMMC (Afghan Management and Consultants). 2009. "Gender Mainstreaming in Afghanistan's Microfinance Sector: An Impact Evaluation." Commissioned by MISFA, Kabul. Available at: http://www.misfa.org.af/?page=publication.

World Bank. 2002. "Afghanistan—Transitional Support Strategy." Report No. 23822 AF. Washington, DC: World Bank.

———. 2003. "Afghanistan—Transitional Support Strategy:." Report No. 25440 AF. Washington, DC: World Bank.

———. 2006. *Interim Strategy Note for the Islamic Republic of Afghanistan for the Period FY07–FY08.* Washington, DC: World Bank.

———. 2009. *Interim Strategy Note for the Islamic Republic of Afghanistan for the Period FY09–FY11.* Report No. 47939-AF. Washington, DC: World Bank.

Appendix G
Afghanistan Beneficiary Feedback Survey

This appendix presents data from a survey of World Bank project beneficiaries in two provinces of Afghanistan: Nangarhar and Herat. The survey asked questions of project beneficiaries related to the National Solidarity Program (NSP), education, and health. This appendix first discusses the survey methodology. Second, it presents descriptive information about the respondents. Third, it highlights key findings from the data, and, finally, frequencies are presented by gender, region, and education status of respondents.

Survey Methodology

IEG worked in coordination with a data collection agency between January and March 2012 to conduct a mobile-phone survey of World Bank project beneficiaries in two Afghan provinces: Nangarhar and Herat. The survey involved a three-phased approach, including: (1) the use of a basic mobile short message service (SMS) Survey; (2) a voice-based follow-on survey with respondents; and (3) data entry. IEG worked with the survey firm to design a survey instrument. The survey firm then used a radio-based crowd-sourcing technique integrated into a remote assessment approach.

Radio programming was utilized as a mechanism for advertising the initial assessment in one Pashtun (Nangarhar) and one non-Pashtun (Bagdhis and Herat) region. This involved making arrangements with local radio stations to run advertisements. The approach sought to source respondents who sent SMS responses to a radio-based advertisement aired in both regions. A voice-based follow-on survey using a survey instrument was conducted by calling respondents who opted in to the assessment through the radio-based advertisement. The firm was responsible for (1) translating the survey instrument into Dari and Pashtu; and (2) making arrangements for the follow-on survey. The target number of respondents was 600, 300 from each region. Respondents, listening to the radio, self-selected to participate by opting in to a radio advertisement.

The survey provides one tool to help validate service delivery, since field-based verification was not possible during the IEG's mission, given the security situation in the country. Overall messages in the survey are similar to messages heard from ministries and Bank staff in the field—views reflected in the overall country program evaluation.

Afghanistan Beneficiary Survey Respondents

In total, 664 respondents participated in the survey—298 (45 percent) from Nangarhar and 366 from Herat (55 percent). Overall, the response rate was higher in Herat and it took fewer radio advertisements to meet the goal of 300 relative to responses in Nangarhar. Also, more women participated in Herat. In total, 28 (4 percent) respondents were women and 636 (96 percent) respondents were men. Of the female respondents, only one was from Nangarhar. The remaining 27 were from Herat.

Fifty eight percent (384) of the respondents had graduated from at least the 10th class. Forty-two percent of the respondents (280) did not manage to complete the 10th class. Among women and men in the survey, there are no differences in educational attainment—58 percent of women (17 out of 29) and 58 percent of men (367 out of 635) had completed 10 years of schooling.

As illustrated in table G.1, survey respondents, overall, tend to be young. The majority of respondents (59 percent) are below the age of 25. Among the 28 female respondents 22 were below the age of 25 (11 below the age of 20).

Survey Findings

The survey asked a series of questions related to the NSP, education, health, and rural livelihoods. Overall findings reveal a pattern of much more positive responses from Nangarhar (a Pashtun province in the east) than Herat (a non-Pashtun province in the west). Respondents with more education also provided more positive responses than those who had not completed 10 years of schooling (table G.2). Most of the female respondents were from Herat, and their responses were closer to those from the males from Herat than from respondents from Nangarhar (almost all of who were male). On two indicators—school attendance, and a health facility in their village— women were more positive than men, and on two other indicators— the existence of the NSP and the improvement in agricultural livelihoods— they were within 3 percentage points of male respondents from Herat. On all other indicators men were more positive than women (table G.3), even within the Herat sample.

NATIONAL SOLIDARITY PROGRAM

Overall, 69 percent of respondents reported the NSP in their villages, and 40 percent of respondents reported that that they were members of Community Development Councils (CDCs). In Nangarhar, 73 percent of respondents reported

Table G.1	Respondent's Age	
Age	Total	Percent
Below 20	179	27
20–24	210	32
25–29	107	16
30–34	70	11
35–39	41	6
40–44	26	4
45–49	16	2
50–54	7	1
55 and above	8	1
Total	664	100

NSP activities in their village compared with only 65 percent of respondents from Herat.

These numbers may be somewhat inflated, because fewer respondents reported actually attending CDC meetings. Forty-one percent of respondents report that they have actually attended a CDC meeting. In Nangarhar, 56 percent of respondents report having actually attended a CDC meeting relative to only 28 percent in Herat. In terms of female participation in CDCs, even with a small sample of 29 respondents, there was quite a bit of variation in their answers. Of the 29 female respondents that participated, five (17 percent) reported that they had attended a CDC meeting.

According to respondents, delivery of education, health, and infrastructure to villages has improved across the board in the last five years. This is particularly true for Nangarhar, where more than three-fourths of respondents reported such improvements.

Education

In response to the education questions—80 percent of respondents reported that access to education had improved since the CDC was formed, and 79 percent of respondents reported that the quality of education had improved in the last five years, but responses on access and quality of education were 29 percentage points and 18 percentage points, respectively, lower in Herat than in Nangarhar.

The story on school management committees in villages is weaker. Only 52 percent of respondents reported that there is a school management committees in their village. More respondents in Nangarhar (62 percent) reported the existence of school management committees than in Herat (only 43 percent). These results reinforce what IEG learned during its mission to Kabul in meetings with the Ministry of Education and various stakeholders in the education sector.

Health

In health, 57 percent of respondents reported that there was a health clinic within an hour of their village and 58 percent reported that access to health services had improved over the last five years. In Nangarhar 67 percent of respondents reported a health service center in their village compared to 49 percent in Herat, and 65 percent from Nangarhar reported that access to health services had improved compared to 52 percent from Herat.

It is important to note that among the female respondents, fewer reported that there was a health care facility within one hour (only 52 percent of women respondents). This finding may be the result of female circumstances in Afghanistan. Since most women do not leave home without their husbands they may not be aware of the existence of health facilities. Similarly, while 27 percent of overall respondents (32 percent of respondents in Nangarhar and 23 percent of respondents in Herat) reported that a female health worker had visited their village in the last month, only 14 percent of the female respondents reported the same.

Rural Livelihoods

More than two-thirds of respondents felt that infrastructure and livelihoods had improved over the last five years, responses being 24 percentage points higher in Nangarhar than in Herat for infrastructure and 13 percentage points higher in Nangarhar than in Herat for livelihoods. When asked about their own financial situation, 52 percent of respondents reported that their circumstances had improved in the last five years. Among women, less than a quarter (21 percent) reported that their financial situation had improved. Both this and the health finding suggest that the overall conditions for women relative to men may not be improving as fast.

Equally important, in Nangarhar, 68 percent of respondents reported that they were financially better off than they were five years ago, relative to Herat, where only 39 percent of respondents reported the same. This aligns with other accounts of regional disparities. One common stereotype is that Pashtun provinces, especially those closer to Kabul, are benefiting more from aid services relative to non-Pasthun provinces and those that are farther away from the capital. The findings in this survey comport with this stereotype, and raise questions for further exploration about regional variation in service delivery.

Table G.2	Survey Frequencies (percent)						
				Education		Age	
Question	Total	Herat	Nangarhar	Did not complete 10th	Complet-ed 10th	29 or younger	30 and above
Is there a national solidarity program in your village?	69	65	73	66	71	68	72
Are you a member of the community development council (CDC)?	40	38	42	37	42	36	49
Have you ever attended a CDC meeting?	41	28	56	34	46	39	47
Access to education has improved since the creation of the CDC.	80	83	76	80	80	82	76
In the last five years more children from my village attend school.	79	66	95	74	83	80	75
The quality of education has improved since the creation of the CDC.	79	71	89	76	82	81	74
Does your village have an active local committee to discuss school matters such as quality of education, teacher quality or school construction?	52	43	62	47	55	50	57
Access to health service has improved since the creation of the CDC.	58	52	65	53	61	59	54

(Table continues on the following page.)

Table G.2 — Survey Frequencies (percent) (cont.)

Question	Total	Herat	Nangarhar	Education Did not complete 10th	Education Completed 10th	Age 29 or younger	Age 30 and above
Is there a health facility within an hour's walk of your village?	57	49	67	55	59	59	52
Has a female health worker visited your village in the last month?	27	23	32	26	28	28	23
Infrastructure such as roads, or irrigation or drinking water supply in my village has improved in the last five years.	65	53	79	60	68	66	61
In my village livelihoods (Rozgar) have improved in the last 5 years by increase in agricultural production.	68	62	75	64	71	70	62
I am financially better off today than I was 5 years ago.	52	39	68	43	58	51	54

Note: n = 339 men and 27 women.

Table G.3 — Herat Survey Frequencies by Gender (percent)

Question	Men in Herat	Women in Herat
Is there a national solidarity program in your village?	65	63
Are you a member of the community development council (CDC)?	39	26
Have you ever attended a CDC meeting ?	29	15
Access to education has improved since the creation of the CDC.	83	85
In the last five years more children from my village attend school.	67	59
The quality of education has improved since the creation of the CDC.	72	63
Does your village have an active local committee to discuss school matters such as quality of education, teacher quality or school Construction?	45	22
Access to health service has improved since the creation of the CDC.	53	33
Is there a health facility within an hour's walk of your village?	49	52
Has a female health worker visited your village in the last one month?	24	11
Infrastructure such as roads, or irrigation or drinking water supply in my village has improved in the last five years.	54	48
In my village livelihoods (Rozgar) have improved in the last 5 years by increase in agricultural production.	62	59
I am financially better off today than I was 5 years ago.	40	19

Note: n = 339 men and 27 women.

Appendix H
Engagement with Beneficiaries through Social Media

Methodology and Main Messages

IEG launched a three-month-long social media campaign to engage with broader groups of beneficiaries in Afghanistan for its Afghanistan Country Program Evaluation (CPE). The engagement plan aimed to gather additional information in the form of *qualitative data* that could be triangulated with other sources used in the evaluation. This was particularly important because the mobility of staff going on mission to the country was limited by security concerns. Additionally, using online outreach tools aimed to make the evaluation process participatory and transparent by posting study questions online for public feedback.

To achieve the above-mentioned goals, IEG used its existing Facebook and Twitter accounts to reach out to target groups with key messages and questions. Through these channels, IEG solicited comments from online users, targeting people located in Afghanistan in its Facebook advertisement campaigns and Twitter tags.[1] On twitter, IEG also used dedicated hashtags[2]— #Afghanistan Eval and #Afghanistan.

All of the questions posted on social media channels mirrored main evaluative questions and were asked sequentially, with a week-and-a-half allotted for each question. Questions were asked in several languages —English, Dari, and Pashto—to ensure that the team reached out to people in Afghanistan who have online presence, but do not speak English. The questions were posted both as open-ended queries to solicit descriptive comments and as polls to obtain quantitative data. The questions were grouped under four main themes that closely followed questions asked in the household survey conducted by the evaluation team in Afghanistan with radio and mobile technology. Short messages emerging from the outreach are provided below.

Some of the polls and open-ended questions received a higher number of responses than others. The questions on infrastructure and education received more feedback than questions on health. This could be explained by the particular relevance of the questions to the respondents or the fact that they were asked later in the outreach campaign, by which time the Facebook page had more followers from Afghanistan than it did before.

GENERAL OVERVIEW

In general, both the polls and open-ended questions show that access to education, health, and infrastructure in Afghanistan has improved in the last five years. However, in the open-ended questions the respondents brought up several issues that are hampering this progress, including lack of quality and corruption. Overall, 14 percent of responses indicate that despite greater access to education, health, and infrastructure, the quality of the services provided is low. Complaints about low quality were particularly evident in responses on the questions about education and infrastructure. The same proportion of respondents (14 percent) cited corruption as one of the impediments to sustainable development, with most of these responses attached to the questions on infrastructure. Two respondents commented on the corruption in infrastructure development by saying:

> Six to seven years ago the electricity system was good in Herat and people were happy that at least they have electricity. The water system was also not bad. But, as the time passes works get worse in Afghanistan. The electricity system had gotten worse, which always disturbs the life of the people. The roads also lost for few months after they are made. As long as there are some corrupt people in the government we shouldn't wait and hope for a better situation.
>
> —Facebook respondent from Herat, Afghanistan
> [The comment was translated into English from Dari]

> In our district a clinic was built by the government, but instead of doctors, pharmacists are working there. When they receive the allocated medicines for the clinic from the provincial Public Health and Safety Department, they take those medicines to their private clinics to do their business. When patients go to the clinic they only give them Disprin and Paracetamol tablets. I am a resident of Khust district, Baghlan province. The medical clinic of Tagab Dahna.
>
> —Facebook comment from a user in Kabul, Afghanistan
> [Comment translated from Pashto]

EDUCATION

Users responding to the polls and open-ended questions agreed that in the last five years access to education in Afghanistan has increased. For instance, the poll ran in Dari and Pashto showed that 811 out of 937 agreed that access to education has increased and 126 disagreed. A user commented:

> In terms of education, Afghans have a lot more access than they had 5 years ago. Filing of 160,000 applications for Kankor[3] exam this year could be counted as a success and achievement of Afghans compared to 5 years ago.

At the same time, open-ended responses suggested that even if access increased by having more educational facilities and opportunities to receive education, the quality of education is still an issue. Some users also brought up the issue of admissions to higher education, which is still challenging. Users commented:

> Due to the density of population a lot of people have gotten access to education, but in terms of opportunity and the overall condition of education it is still in the same level as it was in 2006.
>
> —Facebook respondent from Kabul, Afghanistan
> [The comment was translated into English from Dari]

No	
Yes	

0   20   40   60   80   100

Percent (n = 937)

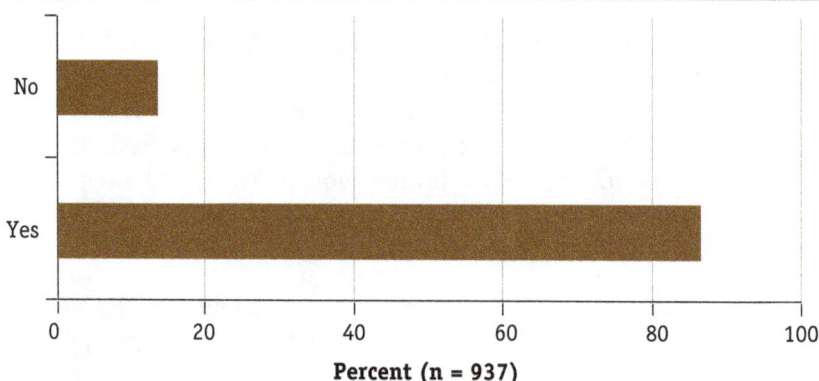

Source: IEG Evaluation Facebook Survey.

I think access has increased, which can be attributed to the growth in services, public demand and awareness, etc. The key question is quality, which is critical to sustainability of growth in access.

—Facebook respondent from Kabul, Afghanistan

Compared to the past few years, now we have more access to [educational] facilities. Regarding education, though the number of people going to school has risen but the education level is declining, because the teachers who are teaching at the schools do not have higher education. Those people who are getting lower scores at Kanqor (general exams for getting admission in University) are admitted to the Education Department to become a teacher. Most of the people who are becoming teachers are due to their lower scores at the exam, as they can't get to any other department.

—Facebook respondent from Sayed Karam, Paktiā, Afghanistan
(currently lives in Italy)
[The comment was translated into English from Pashto]

HEALTH

The polls in English and Dari/Pashto on the availability of a heath facility within one hour's walk collectively gathered 371 responses. The poll was conducted twice, the first time in English, the second time in Pashto and Dari. In the English poll, 30 percent responded *yes,* while 9 percent said *no,* but 61 percent of respondents said *they didn't know,* indicating either that the language barrier was a major issue or that this poll attracted respondents who are not from a village. When the poll was repeated in Dari and Pashtu, 73 percent of respondents said *yes,* 22 percent said *no,* and 6 percent said *they didn't know.* If the two polls are added, 43 percent responded *yes* while 12 percent responded *no.* The remaining were unable to answer the question.

Is There a Health Facility Within One Hour's Walk of Your Village in Afghanistan?

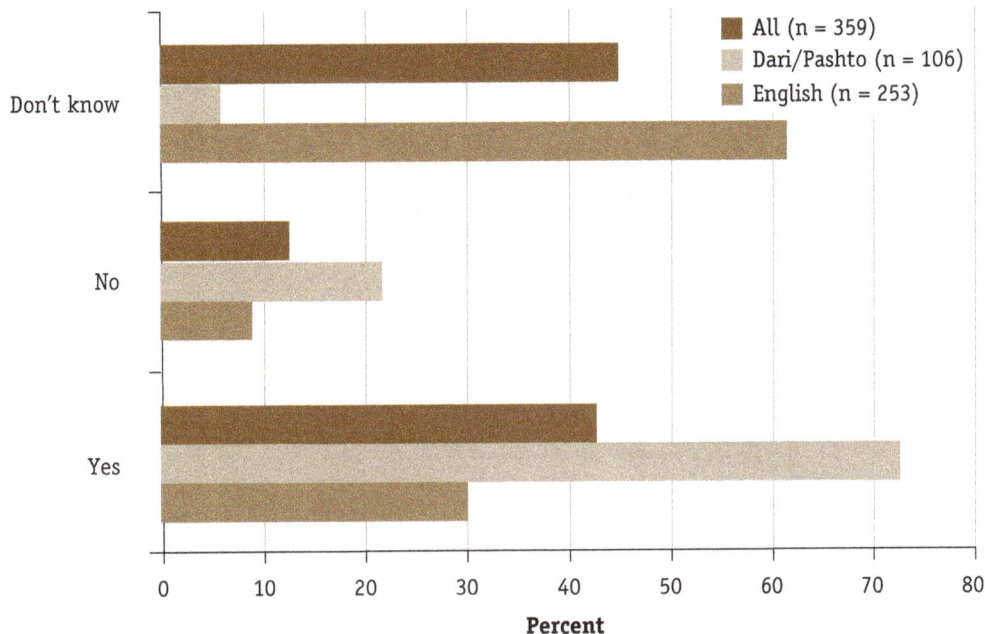

Legend:
- All (n = 359)
- Dari/Pashto (n = 106)
- English (n = 253)

X-axis: Percent (0, 10, 20, 30, 40, 50, 60, 70, 80)

Categories: Don't know, No, Yes

Source: IEG Evaluation Facebook Survey.

Some of the users complained about the quality of the services provided in the health facilities and implementation of promised health projects:

Unfortunately most of these works [health improvement projects] are limited and they remain only on a piece of paper instead of being implemented....A good example is our district, where nothing has been done yet

—Facebook comment from a user from Ahmad Abad district, Paktia province [Comment translated from Pashto]

Another great and interesting way for corruption and taking bribe.

—Facebook comment from a user from Ahmad Abad district, Paktia province, in response to the question whether the access to health facilities in Afghanistan has increased.

Infrastructure

Open-ended responses indicated that there have been improvements made in access to infrastructure in the country in the last five years. For instance, 82 percent of respondents (528 of 643) to the poll on the access to infrastructure said that the access has increased in the past 5 years, and 18 percent responded that it has not.

Figure H.3 — Has Infrastructure in Your Village Improved in the Last Five Years?

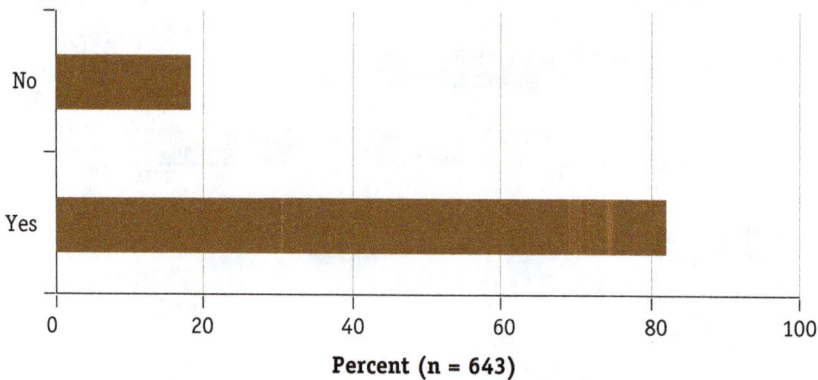

Percent (n = 643)

Source: IEG Evaluation Facebook Survey.

However, the respondents to a similar open-ended question also indicated that new infrastructure lacked the quality needed to be sustainable in the long term. Respondents complained that the new roads are being washed away by rain and other natural forces, and that access to electricity and drinking water is still lagging behind:

> The roads are made at a very expensive cost, but they are useless now because of the poor quality of work. A good example is the road from Mastofiat to Bagh-e-Milat. When the work was completed around 100 meters of the road was destroyed within few days, which they repaired, but it is still in same condition.
>
> —Facebook respondent from Herat, Afghanistan
> [The comment was translated into English from Dari]

> Unfortunately all of [the new] infrastructure that are put in place in Herat couldn't last long, most of them are already destroyed and they are completely useless now. A huge amount of money was spent to pave the roads in Herat, but due to the low quality of materials, unprofessional staff and not using technology that is up to the standard, almost all of the roads are destroyed and Herat's electricity system is also facing problems. All of those electricity generators and transformers that were bought by the government under the name Made in Japan, turned out they were not made in Japan, but rather they were Chinese. After two years all of them are not functioning.
>
> —Facebook respondent from Herat, Afghanistan
> [The comment was translated into English from Dari]

Notes

1. IEG reached out to most active Tweeters on Afghanistan by tagging them through their Twitter handles in its postings and through hashtags.

2. A *Hashtag* is used on Twitter to group content based on a topic, region, country, or other attribute.

3. Standardized exam for higher-education admission in Afghanistan.

Appendix I
Second Civil Service[1]

The approach to public administration reform supported by the Bank used a variety of incentive schemes to motivate key Afghan civil servants and other contracted specialists, offering, inter alia, contract pay rates up to 11 times the highest rate for civil servants (even after pay and grading reform). This is politically and financially unsustainable without donor financing.

These relatively well-paid staff, often referred to as the "second civil service," include over 5,000 key personnel that help adopt many of the structures, processes, and systems recommended in the Bank's AAA and operations. In addition, there are many more contracted staff working in field and support positions. Numbers and dependency vary across ministries and departments, with particularly large dependency in the Ministry of Health (about 18,000 contract staff in addition to 14,400 civil servants) and the Ministry of Rural Reconstruction and Development (about 6100 contract staff in addition to 2900 civil servants).

Among the relatively less-dependent entities is the Ministry of Finance, which has 342 consultants, or about 5 percent of the total 7,100 civil servants, of which about 5,000 have gone through the pay and grading exercise. However, table I.1 indicates that within the Ministry of Finance, the Policy and Budget Departments are much more highly dependent on contracted staff, while other Departments are less so. In the cases of Customs and Revenue, there is credible evidence that some key positions are bought by Afghan civil servants because of their rent-seeking potential: for example, 20 percent or more of provincial customs positions were "purchased" because of the opportunities for rent-seeking. In many cases where contracted staff are carrying out critical functions, these would be difficult to turn over to civil servants at this time.

The support from contracted professionals to the civil service has been a facilitating factor in improved public financial management and revenue collection, improved access to health care, and increased primary school enrollments. It has also contributed to favorable and improving opinion ratings on public administration and government performance.

A design shortcoming of some projects (for example, Emergency Public Administration, Strengthening Financial Capacity) is that operational support and capacity building support were combined, with consultant terms of reference asking them to do both.

Due to the low skill levels of most civil servants, and the urgent requirements of ensuring basic government performance, the objectives of institutional development and knowledge transfer to civil servants were relegated to the background in the interest of providing immediate operational support. This problem has been addressed in more recent projects (Public Financial Management Reform I and II) with separate components for operational support, capacity development, and reform management. Yet Public Financial Management Reform I changed one of its project development objectives from reducing technical assistance by 50 percent to ensuring that there is enough technical assistance to manage the increase of aid using country systems.

Table I.1	Dependency on Second Civil Service in Ministry of Finance, Selected Units, 2012			
Unit	Civil servants	Afghan consultants	Foreign consultants	Dependency ratio[a]
Policy	17	3	18	1.24
Budget	81	69	12	1.00
Customs	194	59	11	0.36
Internal Audit	150	12	4	0.11
Revenues	642	40	18	0.09
Treasury	503	32	4	0.07
Admin	164	2	0	0.01

a. Number of consultants/number of civil servants.

This illustrates the difficult juggling act between transitioning to a more sustainable staffing pattern on the one hand, while being able to carry out technical functions of an acceptable quality on the other.

Another worrying sign is that the numbers of 2010-11 graduates from Kabul University have declined in some vital skill areas (table I.2). The reasons could include disruption of studies due to the deteriorating security and increased opportunities for study in local private universities and abroad. A better understanding of these trends and how to mitigate or take advantage of them is crucial to a transition plan toward sustainable government capacity.

The Capacity Building for Results Project approved by the Bank in 2011 assures funding for up to 2,400 professionals through 2017. This operation has a number of design features intended to address the shortcomings of past support, including joint management by MOF and IARCSC, high-level controls to prevent rent-seeking through recruitment practices, a results-based approach to access funding and assess ministry performance, and predictable levels of funding over a five-year period.

However, there are major shortcomings that remain. In the case of the security sector, there is a transition plan for turning over responsibilities to Afghan forces with agreed dates, numbers of Afghan soldiers, costs, and a process for agreeing on funding. This is not the case in the civilian sector. There has been no detailed planning on how and when Afghanistan will turn over civilian responsibilities from foreign to Afghan contract staff and civil servants, how large a civil service is required, what proportion of Afghan contract staff to civil servants will be needed in the future, what this will all cost, and how it will be paid for. Such planning needs to take into account the minimum requirements for maintaining a functioning government, the scale and capabilities needed to maintain civilian control despite the presence of a very large security sector, and the sequencing of necessary reforms. Both activities in higher education

Table I.2	Graduates of Kabul University, by Discipline		
	2008–09	2009–10	2010–11
Agriculture	927	1,202	1,057
Veterinary	94	50	94
Economy	525	461	458
Management and trade	45	39	
Engineering	705	512	501
Science	485	690	566
Geology	195	132	111
Geology and mine	166	144	60
Chemical technology	26	54	82
General medical faculty	510	351	240
Medical for children	109	86	59
Medical treatment	304	248	156
Stomatology	51	46	80
Nursing			30
Pharmacy	129	85	53

and in technical and vocational training can be more targeted to meeting those needs.

Further, in the transition to the scheduled pullout of foreign forces in 2014 and beyond, there remain multiple risks both to the Capacity Building For Results approach and to sustaining the progress achieved. If high levels of aid continue, donors may bid away top professionals from key government positions, thus reducing the value of Capacity Building for Results incentives for ministry performance. If aid levels are reduced, there may be insufficient financing to support the scheme at the end of five years, although there would also be less pressure from donors bidding away essential government staff. The government is unlikely to take over paying with its own resources thousands of Afghan contract staff at rates many times the amounts paid to civil servants, and far in excess of those in other countries of the region. Inflated pay has clearly been driven by the large scale of the aid effort, and reining in these pay levels remains a key challenge.

There are different categories of staff, presenting different risks. Staff within ministries and not receiving enhanced pay may be reluctant to support the efforts of their much better paid colleagues. Staff in ministries where very few staff are receiving enhanced pay may refuse to cooperate with ministries where larger numbers benefit from high pay.[2]

There is also the challenge of differential pay between Kabul and provincial staff, with delays and uncertainty in payment facing the latter, due in part to lack of consistency between Tashkeels and Takhsis (budget allotments).

While in theory this is a highly centralized system, with 40 percent of civil servants based in Kabul, in practice many subnational jurisdictions are ruled by governors, commanders, and warlords with a combination of de jure and de facto authority based on financial and military strength, as well as personal, factional, and historical loyalties. The Capacity Building for Results provides limited support to all ministries in an effort to stem possible resentment arising among nonparticipating staff but this may not be sufficient to address the magnitude of the problem.

There are additional political risks. The systems put in place with Bank support, while technically more efficient than the patronage-based systems they are meant to replace, may not be resilient enough to withstand expected stresses over the next few years. Afghan politicians may be unwilling to use government funds to pay senior staff at such comparatively high levels. In addition, as foreign forces leave, the regime may find it necessary to roll back the administrative improvements achieved to date, in order to make greater use of public resources to make non-transparent transfers to elite supporters needed to sustain a ruling coalition.

Other donors recognized that this was an exceptionally challenging area to work in, and they wanted the Bank to take the lead. A number of donor projects were aligned with the Bank's recommendations. However, there is no evidence as yet that the Bank's recommendations for rationalizing and aligning the mix of *ad hoc* incentives paid to officials and consultants have been accepted by donors. While government and donors agreed at the 2007 Afghanistan Development Forum on 11 steps to address capacity development, there has been little action because of reform management constraints, poor understanding of specific capacity problems, the one-size-fits all nature of the recommendations, and the fact that neither government nor donors have yet shown the will and discipline to proceed in implementing the steps. The project appraisal document for the Capacity Building for Results Project states that the government will adopt guidelines on donor-financed salaries and allowances, with the agreement of main donors, based on a Presidential Decree and recommendations of the National Technical Assistance Commission to address these issues. The prospects for this being realized are unknown.

Notes

1. As part of the Country Program Evaluation, IEG commissioned a review of the second civil service within selected ministries in 2012. The findings in this appendix are based on the case studies, which covered the Ministry of Finance (MOF), Ministry of Rural Rehabilitation and Development (MRRD), Ministry of Agriculture, Irrigation and Livestock (MAIL), Ministry of Mines (MoM), and Ministry of Public Health (MPH).

2. A Capacity Building for Results provision of limited support to less reform-oriented ministries is intended to address this risk.

Appendix J
Statistical Supplement

Key Development Indicators		Afghan-istan	South Asia	Low income
(2009)				
Population, mid-year (millions)		29.8	1,545	828
Surface area (thousand sq. km)		652	5,131	17,838
Population growth (%)		2.7	1.5	2.2
Urban population (% of total population)		24	29	28
GNI (Atlas method, US$ billions)		9.1	1,534	389
GNI per capita (Atlas method, US$)		310	993	470
GNI per capita (PPP, international $)		860	2,775	1,131
GDP growth (%)		40.8	4.8	6.2
GDP per capita growth (%)		37.1	3.3	3.9
(most recent estimate, 2003–2008)				
Poverty headcount ratio at $1.25 a day (PPP, %)		..	40	..
Poverty headcount ratio at $2.00 a day (PPP, %)		..	74	..
Life expectancy at birth (years)		44	64	57
Infant mortality (per 1,000 live births)		134	56	77
Child malnutrition (% of children under 5)		33	41	28
Adult literacy, male (% of ages 15 and older)		..	72	73
Adult literacy, female (% of ages 15 and older)		..	50	59
Gross primary enrollment, male (% of age group)		127	110	107
Gross primary enrollment, female (% of age group)		84	105	100
Access to an improved water source (% of population)		48	87	64
Access to improved sanitation facilities (% of population)		37	36	35

Net Aid Flows	1980	1990	2000	2009*
(US$ millions)				
Net ODA and official aid	33	122	136	4,865
Top 3 donors (in 2007):				
United States	2	56	2	2,112
European Commission	0	2	18	349
United Kingdom	1	2	13	322
Aid (% of GNI)	0.9	..	16.4	45.7
Aid per capita (US$	2	7	6	168
Long-Term Economic Trend				
Consumer prices (annual % change)	..	..	..	−15.0
GDP implicit deflator (annual % change)	..	..	..	−15.5
Exchange rate (annual average, local per US$)	44.1	50.6	67.7	49.3
Terms of trade index (2000 = 100)	..	..	..	..
Population, mid-year (millions)	15.1	18.6	23.6	29.8
GDP (US$ millions)	3,642	..	2,462	14,483
			(% of GDP)	
Agriculture	..	..	45.2	32.5
Industry	..	..	19.7	22.1
Manufacturing	..	..	15.0	13.3
Services	..	..	35.1	45.4
Household final consumption expenditure	..	..	111.5	88.5
General gov't final consumption expenditure	..	..	7.9	9.0
Gross capital formation	13.9	..	11.6	25.0
Exports of goods and services	10.8	..	30.6	15.6
Imports of goods and services	13.9	..	61.6	47.7
Gross savings	16.6	..	1.6	50.1

Age distribution, 2009

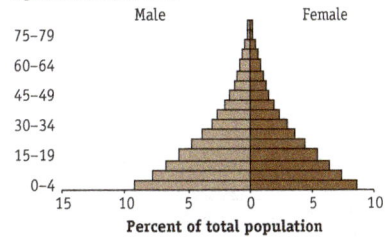

Percent of total population

Under-5 mortality rate (per 1,000)

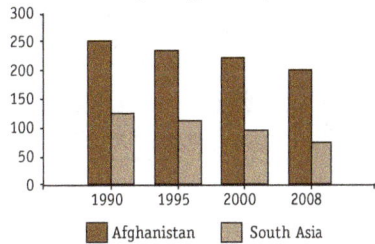

■ Afghanistan   ☐ South Asia

Growth of GDP and GDP per capita (%)

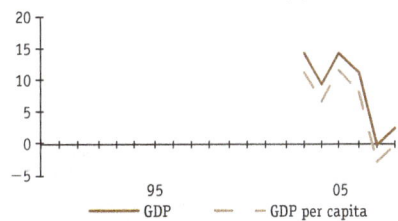

—— GDP   — — GDP per capita

1980–90	1990–2000	2000–09
(average annual growth %)		
2.1	2.4	2.6
..	..	10.5
..	..	4.9
..	..	14.5
..	..	8.7
..	..	13.5
..	..	..
..	..	..
..	..	..
..	..	..
..	..	..

Note: .. = information not available

Balance of Payments and Trade	2000	2009
(US$ millions)		
Total merchandise exports (fob)	1,291	1,835
Total merchandise imports (cif)	1,697	3,280
Net trade in goods and services	−1,363	−6,681
Current account balance	−150	−462
as a % of GDP	−3.5	−3.2
Workers' remittances and		
compensation of employees (receipts)	..	..
Reserves, including gold	425	1,662
Central Government Finance		
(% of GDP)		
Current revenue (including grants)	7.8	18.3
Tax revenue	..	..
Current expenditure	7.9	12.3
Overall surplus/deficit	−0.1	−0.5
Highest marginal tax rate (%)		
Individual	..	..
Corporate	20	20
External Debt and Resource Flows		
(US$ millions)		
Total debt outstanding and disbursed	..	2,328
Total debt service	..	11
Debt relief (HIPC, MDRI)	600	38
Total debt (% of GDP)	..	16.1
Total debt service (% of exports)	..	0.3
Foreign direct investment (net inflows)	..	185
Portfolio equity (net inflows)	..	0

Governance indicators, 2000 and 2009

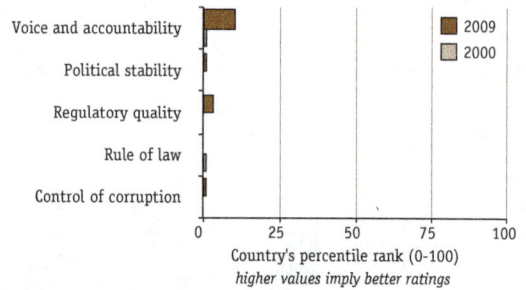

Country's percentile rank (0-100)
higher values imply better ratings

Source: Kaufmann-Kraay-Mastruzzi, World Bank.

Composition of total external debt, 2009 (US$ millions)

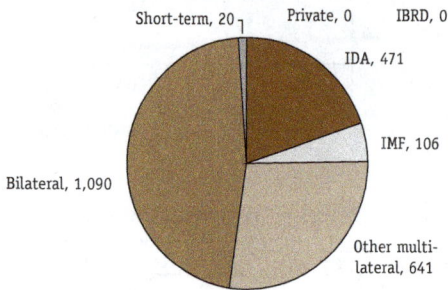

Technology and Infrastructure	2000	2008
Paved roads (% of total)	13.3	29.3
Fixed line and mobile phone		
subscribers (per 100 people)	0	28
High technology exports		
(% of manufactured exports)	..	..
Environment		
Agricultural land (% of land area)	58	59
Forest area (% of land area)	1.6	1.2
Terrestrial protected areas (% of surface area)	..	0.2
Freshwater resources per capita (cu. meters)	2,213	1,895
Freshwater withdrawal (billion cubic meters)	23.3	..
CO2 emissions per capita (mt)	0.03	0.03
GDP per unit of energy use		
(2005 PPP $ per kg of oil equivalent)	..	..
Energy use per capita (kg of oil equivalent)	..	..

World Bank Group portfolio	2000	2009
(US$ millions)		
IBRD		
Total debt outstanding and disbursed	0	0
Disbursements	0	0
Principal repayments	0	0
Interest payments	0	0
IDA		
Total debt outstanding and disbursed	0	471
Disbursements	0	27
Total debt service	0	2
IFC *(fiscal year)*		
Total disbursed and outstanding portfolio	0	12
of which IFC own account	0	12
Disbursements for IFC own account	0	3
Portfolio sales, prepayments and		
repayments for IFC own account	0	0
MIGA		
Gross exposure	0	77
New guarantees	0	0

Private Sector Development	2000	2009
Time required to start a business (days)	–	7
Cost to start a business (% of GNI per capita)	–	30.2
Time required to register property (days)	–	250
Ranked as a major constraint to business	2000	2009
(% of managers surveyed who agreed)		
n.a.	..	..
n.a.	..	..
Stock market capitalization (% of GDP)	..	..
Bank capital to asset ratio (%)	..	..

Note: .. = information not available; n.a. = not applicable.

Millennium Development Goals

	Afghanistan			
With selected targets to achieve between 1990 and 2015 (estimate closest to date shown, +/- 2 years)				
Goal 1: halve the rates for extreme poverty and malnutrition	1990	1995	2000	2008
Poverty headcount ratio at $1.25 a day (PPP, % of population)	..	..	..	..
Poverty headcount ratio at national poverty line (% of population)	..	..	..	42.0
Share of income or consumption to the poorest qunitile (%)	..	..	..	..
Prevalence of malnutrition (% of children under 5)	..	..	..	32.9
Goal 2: ensure that children are able to complete primary schooling				
Primary school enrollment (net, %)	..	28	..	..
Primary completion rate (% of relevant age group)	..	28	..	39
Secondary school enrollment (gross, %)	11	21	13	29
Youth literacy rate (% of people ages 15-24)	..	..	..	..
Goal 3: eliminate gender disparity in education and empower women				
Ratio of girls to boys in primary and secondary education (%)	54	47	0	58
Women employed in the nonagricultural sector (% of nonagricultural employment)	18	..	..	..
Proportion of seats held by women in national parliament (%)	4	..	..	28
Goal 4: reduce under-5 mortality by two-thirds				
Under-5 mortality rate (per 1,000)	250	235	222	201
Infant mortality rate (per 1,000 live births)	167	157	148	135
Measles immunization (proportion of one-year olds immunized, %)	20	41	35	75
Goal 5: reduce maternal mortality by three-fourths				
Maternal mortality ratio (modeled estimate, per 100,000 live births)	1,700	1,800	1,800	1,400
Births attended by skilled health staff (% of total)	..	..	12	24
Contraceptive prevalence (% of women ages 15-49)	..	..	5	15
Goal 6: halt and begin to reverse the spread of HIV/AIDS and other major diseases				
Prevalence of HIV (% of population ages 15-49)	..	..	..	..
Incidence of tuberculosis (per 100,000 people)	190	190	190	190
Tuberculosis case detection rate (%, all forms)	18	4	18	55
Goal 7: halve the proportion of people without sustainable access to basic needs				
Access to an improved water source (% of population)	..	3	21	48
Access to improved sanitation facilities (% of population)	..	29	32	37
Forest area (% of total land area)	2.0	1.8	1.6	1.2
Terrestrial protected areas (% of surface area)	..	..	..	0.2
CO2 emissions (metric tons per capita)	0.1	0.1	0.0	0.0
GDP per unit of energy use (constant 2005 PPP $ per kg of oil equivalent)	..	..	..	..
Goal 8: develop a global partnership for development				
Telephone mainlines (per 100 people)	0.2	0.1	0.1	0.3
Mobile phone subscribers (per 100 people)	0.0	0.0	0.0	27.2
Internet users (per 100 people)	0.0	..	0.0	1.7
Personal computers (per 100 people)	..	..	..	0.4

Education indicators (%)

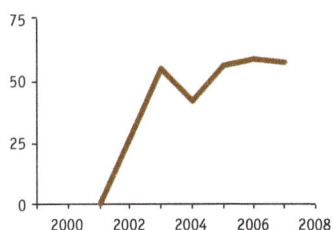

- - - Primary net enrollment ratio (..)
— Ratio of girls to boys in primary & secondary education

Measles immunization (% of 1-year olds)

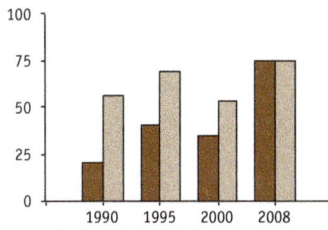

■ Afghanistan ■ South Asia

ICT indicators (per 100 people)

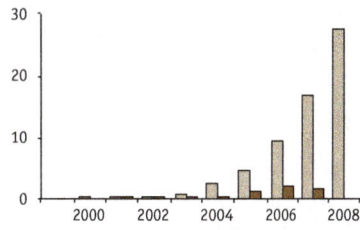

■ Fixed + mobile subscribers
■ Internet users

Note: .. = information not available

Series name	2002	2003	2004	2005	2006	2007	2008	2009	2010
Growth and inflation									
GDP growth (annual percent)		14.3	9.4	14.5	11.2	11.1	3.4	20.4	8.2
GDP per capita growth (annual percent)		11.1	6.4	11.3	8.1	8.1	0.6	17.1	5.2
GNI per capita, Atlas method (current US$)			200.0	230.0	270.0	300.0	290.0	370.0	410.0
GNI per capita, PPP (current international $)	490.0	590.0	650.0	750.0	890.0	970.0	860.0	1,010.0	1,060.0
Inflation, consumer prices (annual percent)				12.7	7.3	8.5	30.6	(8.3)	0.9
Composition of GDP									
Agriculture, value added (percent of GDP)	45.2	46.0	41.6	39.5	32.6	34.5	28.1	31.2	29.9
Industry, value added (percent of GDP)	19.7	18.7	23.4	25.3	28.2	25.8	26.0	21.2	22.2
Services, etc., value added (percent of GDP)	35.1	35.3	35.0	35.2	39.2	39.7	45.9	47.6	47.9
External accounts									
Exports of goods and services (percent of GDP)	30.6	41.9	30.3	25.2	24.2	18.0	15.6	17.0	15.5
Imports of goods and services (percent of GDP)	61.6	90.8	77.6	71.3	67.7	59.0	47.7	59.9	53.6
Current account balance (percent of GDP)									
Present value of external debt (percent of GNI)								5.3	6.5
Total debt service (percent of GNI)					0.1	0.0	0.1	0.1	0.1
Other macroeconomic indicators									
Gross fixed capital formation (percent of GDP)	11.6	16.2	17.4	31.3	34.7	31.9	16.3	15.4	16.3
Gross fixed capital formation, private sector (percent of GDP)	1.1	1.2	8.9	8.7	8.1	7.7	8.0	7.4	
Gross domestic savings (percent of GDP)	(19.4)	(32.7)	(29.9)	(14.8)	(8.8)	(9.1)	(15.8)	(27.5)	(21.8)
Gross savings (percent of GDP)									
Fiscal accounts									
Revenue, excluding grants (percent of GDP)					8.1	7.0	6.9	9.1	
General gov't final consumption expenditure (percent of GDP)	7.9	9.4	9.8	9.7	10.5	10.5	9.1	10.1	10.7
Gross national expenditure (percent of GDP)	131.0	148.9	147.3	146.1	143.5	141.0	132.1	142.9	138.1
Cash surplus/deficit (percent of GDP)					(1.9)	(1.8)	(2.0)	0.2	
Social indicators									
Life expectancy at birth, total (years)	45.8	46.1	46.4	46.6	46.9	47.2	47.5	47.9	
Immunization, DPT (percent of children ages 12-23 months)	36.0	41.0	50.0	58.0	58.0	63.0	64.0	63.0	66.0
Mortality rate, infant (per 1,000 live births)	103.3	103.9	103.6	103.8	103.8	103.7	103.3	103.2	103.0
Out-of-pocket health exp. (percent of private exp. on health)	98.9	98.9	98.9	98.9	98.9	98.9	98.9	98.9	
Health expenditure, public (percent of GDP)	1.5	1.6	2.0	2.1	2.1	1.8	1.6	1.6	
Population growth (annual percent)	2.9	2.9	2.9	2.9	2.8	2.8	2.8	2.8	2.8
School enrollment, primary (percent gross)	63.6	85.7	95.9	89.9	93.8	92.1	94.8	92.4	97.1
School enrollment, secondary (percent gross)		11.8	16.4	17.2	25.7	25.6	34.2	39.7	45.5
School enrollment, tertiary (percent gross)		1.1	1.1					3.3	
Population, total (million)	27.5	28.3	29.1	29.9	30.8	31.6	32.5	33.4	34.4
Telephone lines (per 100 people)	0.1	0.1	0.2	0.3	0.3	0.3	0.3	0.4	0.4
Unemployment, total (percent of total labor force)				8.5					
Poverty headcount ratio at nat'l poverty line (percent of pop.)				33.0		42.0	36.0		
Improved water source (percent of population with access)				41.0			48.0		
Improved sanitation facilities (percent of population with access)				35.0			37.0		
School enrollment, preprimary (percent gross)		0.7	0.7						
Population, female (percent of total)	48.2	48.2	48.2	48.2	48.2	48.2	48.3	48.3	48.3
Population, male (percent of total)	51.8	51.8	51.8	51.8	51.8	51.8	51.7	51.7	51.7

Source: Development Data Platform, World Bank, data as of March 27, 2012.

Table J.3 — Afghanistan and Comparators: Key Economic and Social Indicators, Average, 2002–10

Series name	Afghanistan	South Asia	Low income	Bangladesh	Congo., Dem. Rep	Haiti	Nepal	Pakistan	Tajikistan
Growth and inflation									
GDP growth (annual percent)	11.6	7.4	5.4	5.9	5.6	0.3	3.8	4.9	8.2
GDP per capita growth (annual percent)	8.5	5.8	3.2	4.5	2.6	(1.1)	1.7	3.0	7.0
GNI per capita, Atlas method (current US$)	295.7	814.6	377.6	514.4	134.4	505.0	317.5	774.4	446.7
GNI per capita, PPP (current international $)	807.8	2,382.1	1,019.6	1,372.2	271.1	1,073.3	1,013.3	2,301.1	1,586.7
Inflation, consumer prices (annual percent)	8.6	N/A	N/A	6.9	16.7	14.5	7.2	9.6	11.0
Composition of GDP									
Agriculture, value added (percent of GDP)	36.5	19.4	28.8	20.1	45.8	N/A	35.6	21.6	23.7
Industry, value added (percent of GDP)	23.4	27.3	23.7	27.6	25.3	N/A	17.2	25.8	29.7
Services, etc., value added (percent of GDP)	40.1	53.3	47.4	52.3	28.9	N/A	47.1	52.6	46.6
External accounts									
Exports of goods and services (percent of GDP)	24.3	18.9	20.0	17.5	24.2	13.8	14.0	14.7	33.6
Imports of goods and services (percent of GDP)	65.5	23.0	31.1	23.9	35.3	44.5	31.6	19.2	65.3
Current account balance (percent of GDP)	N/A	N/A	N/A	1.3	N/A	(2.2)	2.2	(2.0)	(3.2)
Present value of external debt (percent of GNI)	5.9	N/A	N/A	16.6	25.4	9.6	21.3	24.0	40.9
Total debt service (percent of GNI)	0.1	2.4	1.6	1.2	5.4	1.4	1.5	2.7	5.6
Other macroeconomic indicators									
Gross fixed capital formation (percent of GDP)	21.2	27.4	20.7	24.1	16.7	N/A	20.6	17.2	14.4
Gross fixed capital formation, private sector (percent of GDP)	6.4	20.3	14.6	18.5	9.5	N/A	17.0	12.8	4.5
Gross domestic savings (percent of GDP)	(20.0)	26.5	10.1	17.7	6.6	(2.7)	9.6	14.2	(15.2)
Gross savings (percent of GDP)	N/A	31.6	23.3	34.0	N/A	25.6	30.4	24.4	8.2
Fiscal accounts									
Revenue, excluding grants (percent of GDP)	7.8	12.5	11.1	10.4	7.9	N/A	12.0	13.8	13.3
General government final consumption expenditure (percent of GDP)	9.7	10.5	10.0	5.4	7.8	8.2	9.3	9.1	16.9
Gross national expenditure (percent of GDP)	141.2	N/A	N/A	106.4	110.1	130.7	117.6	104.6	131.7
Cash surplus/deficit (percent of GDP)	(1.3)	(3.3)	(1.4)	(0.9)	N/A	N/A	(1.2)	(4.1)	(5.6)
Social indicators									
Life expectancy at birth, total (years)	46.8	63.8	56.9	67.1	47.1	60.1	65.8	64.2	65.8

(Table continues on the following page.)

Table J.3	Afghanistan and Comparators: Key Economic and Social Indicators, Average, 2002–10 (cont.)								
Series name	Afghanistan	South Asia	Low income	Bangladesh	Congo., Dem. Rep	Haiti	Nepal	Pakistan	Tajikistan
Immunization, DPT (percent of children ages 12-23 months)	55.4	70.8	74.6	92.9	59.4	57.7	84.1	76.9	86.8
Mortality rate, infant (per 1,000 live births)	103.5	56.8	76.1	47.0	115.4	66.4	49.6	73.7	60.4
Out-of-pocket health expenditure (percent of private expenditure on health)	98.9	84.2	83.7	96.2	84.3	66.0	74.5	80.9	96.7
Health expenditure, public (percent of GDP)	1.8	1.2	2.0	1.2	2.3	1.2	1.8	0.8	1.2
Population growth (annual percent)	2.9	1.5	2.1	1.3	2.9	1.4	2.0	1.8	1.1
School enrollment, primary (percent gross)	89.5	104.3	96.7	101.2	83.0	N/A	115.1	83.7	100.6
School enrollment, secondary (percent gross)	27.0	50.2	34.7	47.8	32.5	N/A	43.6	31.6	83.7
School enrollment, tertiary (percent gross)	1.9	9.9	5.5	7.3	5.2	N/A	5.1	4.1	18.1
Population, total (Million)	30.8	1,493.1	733.8	141.9	59.1	9.5	27.8	161.7	6.5
Telephone lines (per 100 people)	0.3	3.3	1.0	0.7	0.0	1.3	2.1	2.7	4.0
Unemployment, total (percent of total labor force)	8.5	4.6	N/A	4.3	N/A	N/A	N/A	6.3	N/A
Poverty headcount ratio at national poverty line (percent of population)	37.0	N/A	N/A	35.8	71.3	N/A	30.9	26.9	57.5
Improved water source (percent of population with access)	44.5	85.4	62.4	80.0	45.5	61.5	87.0	89.5	68.5
Improved sanitation facilities (percent of population with access)	36.0	34.0	34.8	51.5	21.5	18.0	29.5	43.0	93.5
School enrollment, preprimary (percent gross)	0.7	37.6	12.3	12.1	2.8	N/A	11.9	42.9	8.9
Population, female (percent of total)	48.2	48.5	50.1	49.0	50.3	50.4	50.3	49.0	50.5
Population, male (percent of total)	51.8	51.5	49.9	51.0	49.7	49.6	49.7	51.0	49.5

Source: Development Data Platform, World Bank, data as of March 27, 2012.

Note: N/A = not applicable.

Table J.4 — Afghanistan Agriculture Production, 2002–10 (in tonnes)

Item	2002	2003	2004	2005	2006	2007	2008	2009	2010	Average 2002–10
Cereals (rice milled eqv + (total)	3,607,796	4,236,478	3,405,821	5,263,495	4,458,180	5,602,184	3,666,204	6,299,215	5,733,224	4,696,955
Cereals, total + (total)	3,737,000	4,381,000	3,560,000	5,425,000	4,638,000	5,786,000	3,870,000	6,514,000	5,957,000	4,874,222
Citrus fruit, total + (total)	22,747	20,077	20,260	19,801	10,284	8,709	9,738	7,157	7,500	14,030
Coarse grain, total + (total)	663,000	467,000	707,000	674,000	735,000	750,000	635,000	805,000	753,000	687,667
Barley	345,000	240,000	290,000	337,000	364,000	370,000	333,000	486,000	437,000	355,778
Fruit fresh nes	123,438	100,000	95,644	94,712	95,890	90,326	96,000	80,000	95,800	96,868
Grapes	365,000	365,000	349,100	345,700	350,000	360,000	364,000	394,000	447,400	371,133
Maize	298,000	210,000	400,000	315,000	359,000	360,000	280,000	300,000	301,000	313,667
Potatoes	230,000	350,000	300,000	300,000	300,000	300,800	280,000	302,400	333,600	299,644
Rice, paddy	388,000	434,000	463,000	485,000	540,000	552,000	612,000	645,000	672,000	532,333
Seed cotton	57,000	33,000	28,000	33,000	32,000	35,051	35,000	42,872	53,600	38,836
Vegetables fresh nes	545,941	680,317	600,000	800,000	620,000	650,000	646,000	686,000	836,300	673,840
Watermelons	110,479	129,000	71,000	138,000	200,000	227,206	200,000	250,000	281,900	178,621
Wheat	2,686,000	3,480,000	2,390,000	4,266,000	3,363,000	4,484,000	2,623,000	5,064,000	4,532,000	3,654,222

	Annual growth rate (percent)								Average
	2002–03	2003–04	2004–05	2005–06	2006–07	2007–08	2008–09	2009–10	2002–10
Cereals (rice milled eqv + (total)	17	-20	55	-15	26	-35	72	-9	11
Cereals, total + (total)	17	-19	52	-15	25	-33	68	-9	11
Citrus fruit, total + (total)	-12	1	-2	-48	-15	12	-27	5	-11
Coarse grain, total + (total)	-30	51	-5	9	2	-15	27	-6	4
Barley	-30	21	16	8	2	-10	46	-10	5
Fruit fresh nes	-19	-4	-1	1	-6	6	-17	20	-2
Grapes	0	-4	-1	1	3	1	8	14	3
Maize	-30	90	-21	14	0	-22	7	0	5
Potatoes	52	-14	0	0	0	-7	8	10	6
Rice, paddy	12	7	5	11	2	11	5	4	7
Seed cotton	-42	-15	18	-3	10	0	22	25	2
Vegetables fresh nes	25	-12	33	-23	5	-1	6	22	7
Watermelons	17	-45	94	45	14	-12	25	13	19
Wheat	30	-31	78	-21	33	-42	93	-11	16

Source: FAOSTAT as of February 23, 2012.

Note: Nes = Not elsewhere specified.

Table J.5	Afghanistan Poverty Trends, 2005–10					
	2005	2006	2007	2008	2009	2010
Poverty						
Poverty headcount ratio at national poverty line (percent of population)	33	..	42	36	-	
Poverty headcount ratio at rural poverty line (percent of rural population)	36.2	..	45	37.5		
Poverty headcount ratio at urban poverty line (percent of urban population)	21.1	..	27	29		
Inequality						
GINI index	..	..	..	29.4		
Income share held by fourth 20 percent	..	..	..	24		
Income share held by highest 10 percent	..	..	..	38.7		
Income share held by highest 20 percent	..	..	..	13.1		
Income share held by lowest 10 percent	..	..	..	16.9		
Income share held by lowest 20 percent	..	..	..	22.3		
Income share held by second 20 percent	..	..	..	9		
Income share held by third 20 percent	..	..	..	3.8		

Source: Development Data Platform, World Bank, data as of March 27, 2012.

Note: .. = information not available.

Table J.6				Afghanistan Social Indicators Summary, 2002–10						
Series name	2002	2003	2004	2005	2006	2007	2008	2009	2010	Average
Education										
School enrollment, preprimary (percent gross)	..	0.7	0.7	..	..	..	..	..	..	0.67
School enrollment, primary (percent gross)	63.6	85.7	95.9	89.9	93.8	92.1	94.8	92.4	97.1	89.47
School enrollment, secondary (percent gross)	..	11.8	16.4	17.2	25.7	25.6	34.2	39.7	45.5	27.03
School enrollment, tertiary (percent gross)	..	1.1	1.1	..	..	..	..	3.3	..	1.87
Health										
Life expectancy at birth, total (years)	45.8	46.1	46.4	46.6	46.9	47.2	47.5	47.9	..	46.80
Immunization, DPT (percent of children ages 12–23 months)	36.0	41.0	50.0	58.0	58.0	63.0	64.0	63.0	66.0	55.44
Mortality rate, infant (per 1,000 live births)	103.3	103.9	103.6	103.8	103.8	103.7	103.3	103.2	103.0	103.51
Fertility rate, total (births per woman)	7.4	7.3	7.1	7.0	6.8	6.7	6.6	6.4	..	6.92
Adolescent fertility rate (births per 1,000 women ages 15–19)	161.2	152.7	144.2	135.7	127.2	118.7	114.9	111.0	..	133.19
Births attended by skilled health staff (percent of total)	..	14.3	..	..	18.9	..	24.0	..	..	19.07
Health expenditure, public (percent of GDP)	1.5	1.6	2.0	2.1	2.1	1.8	1.6	1.6	..	1.78
Health expenditure, public (percent of government expenditure)	28.5	24.8	29.3	4.1	4.3	3.7	3.7	3.7	..	12.76
Health expenditure, total (percent of GDP)	7.5	8.4	8.7	8.8	7.8	7.6	7.4	7.4	..	7.93
Population										
Population, total	27.5	28.3	29.1	29.9	30.8	31.6	32.5	33.4	34.4	30.82
Urban population growth (annual percent)	4.3	4.3	4.3	4.2	4.4	4.4	4.4	4.4	4.3	4.34
Rural population growth (annual percent)	2.4	2.4	2.4	2.4	2.3	2.3	2.3	2.3	2.3	2.35
School enrollment, primary, female (percent gross)	39.7	61.7	57.8	66.4	72.3	70.3	74.2	73.8	79.1	66.13
School enrollment, primary, male (percent gross)	85.8	108.2	131.5	111.8	113.9	112.4	114.1	109.8	113.9	111.28
Ratio of female to male primary enrollment (percent)	46.3	57.0	44.0	59.4	63.5	62.6	65.0	67.2	69.4	59.36
Ratio of female to male secondary enrollment (percent)	..	34.9	21.0	32.8	36.7	37.9	43.1	48.9	50.6	38.23

Source: Development Data Platform, World Bank, data as of March 27, 2012.

Note: .. = information not available.

Table J.7	Afghanistan Selected Gender Indicators Summary, 2002–10								
Series name	2002	2003	2004	2005	2006	2007	2008	2009	2010
Fertility rate, total (births per woman)	7.4	7.3	7.1	7.0	6.8	6.7	6.6	6.4	..
Mortality rate, infant (per 1,000 live births)	103.3	103.9	103.6	103.8	103.8	103.7	103.3	103.2	103.0
Life expectancy at birth, female (years)	45.9	46.2	46.4	46.7	47.0	47.3	47.7	48.1	..
Life expectancy at birth, male (years)	45.8	46.0	46.3	46.5	46.8	47.1	47.4	47.8	..
Life expectancy at birth, total (years)	45.8	46.1	46.4	46.6	46.9	47.2	47.5	47.9	..
Proportion of seats held by women in nat'l parliaments (percent)	..	..	..	27.3	27.3	27.3	27.7	27.7	27.7
School enrollment, primary (percent gross)	63.6	85.7	95.9	89.9	93.8	92.1	94.8	92.4	97.1
School enrollment, primary, female (percent gross)	39.7	61.7	57.8	66.4	72.3	70.3	74.2	73.8	79.1
School enrollment, primary, male (percent gross)	85.8	108.2	131.5	111.8	113.9	112.4	114.1	109.8	113.9
Ratio of female to male primary enrollment (percent)	46.3	57.0	44.0	59.4	63.5	62.6	65.0	67.2	69.4
Ratio of female to male secondary enrollment (percent)	..	34.9	21.0	32.8	36.7	37.9	43.1	48.9	50.6

Source: Development Data Platform, World Bank, data as of March 27, 2012.

Note: .. = information not available.

Donor	2002	2003	2004	2005	2006	2007	2008	2009	2010	Average 2002–10	Cumulative 2002–10	Percentage of total disbursed 2002–10
All donors, total	1,309.8	1,593.7	2,311.5	2,837.6	2,961.7	4,964.9	4,875.1	6,235.3	6,374.0	3,718.2	33,463.4	100.0
DAC countries, total	990.7	1,220.8	1,722.6	2,175.4	2,406.7	2,995.3	3,954.8	5,089.3	5,416.3	2,885.8	25,971.8	77.6
United States	367.6	485.8	778.3	1,318.3	1,403.7	1,514.3	2,111.6	2,979.9	2,893.4	1,539.2	13,852.9	41.4
United Kingdom	130.8	98.6	224.0	219.9	246.5	268.7	322.3	324.4	234.8	230.0	2,070.1	6.2
Germany	92.6	82.1	75.1	99.2	118.0	217.2	294.0	337.3	469.8	198.4	1,785.3	5.3
Canada	35.8	73.1	56.2	89.5	140.3	345.4	207.9	232.6	267.1	160.9	1,447.9	4.3
Japan	31.7	134.4	172.5	71.1	107.4	101.0	208.0	335.9	745.7	212.0	1,907.7	5.7
Netherlands	88.3	77.4	90.3	79.1	87.3	88.8	112.0	147.9	59.2	92.3	830.3	2.5
Norway	60.9	68.8	67.7	60.0	69.7	94.4	129.1	115.9	120.2	87.4	786.6	2.4
Sweden	27.5	41.9	55.7	44.2	46.4	56.2	73.9	80.1	91.7	57.5	517.6	1.5
Italy	28.3	38.2	37.3	27.4	32.5	62.0	116.7	67.4	54.3	51.6	464.2	1.4
Turkey	0.4	0.7	8.7	28.6	57.7	71.6	142.0	96.5	107.6	57.0	513.4	1.5
Multilateral, total	290.5	362.8	550.4	603.9	473.2	851.7	703.6	953.4	786.2	619.5	5,575.8	16.7
EU Institutions	143.7	208.0	212.0	256.6	220.9	307.5	349.3	395.4	285.0	264.3	2,378.4	7.1
IDA	20.2	72.2	227.8	282.1	140.7	330.3	166.8	298.9	142.7	186.9	1,681.7	5.0
AsDB Special Funds	86.5	55.4	42.1	22.9	66.2	94.3	63.6	121.8	235.0	87.5	787.7	2.4
UNICEF	9.2	14.5	11.1	17.1	18.5	26.4	35.7	39.5	39.3	23.5	211.4	0.6
IMF	..	..	..	..	..	54.7	35.7	17.4	8.6	29.1	116.5	0.3

Table J.8 Total Net Disbursements of Official Development Assistance and Official Aid, 2002–10

Source: Source: Organisation for Economic Co-operation and Development (OECD) statistics as of 03/27/2012.

Note: .. = information not available.

Table J.9 — Afghanistan–World Bank IDA Credit by Sector Board, FY02–11 (number of projects and commitment amount)

Sector Board	FY02 No.	FY02 Amt	FY03 No.	FY03 Amt	FY04 No.	FY04 Amt	FY05 No.	FY05 Amt	FY06 No.	FY06 Amt
Agriculture and Rural Development					1	40				
Economic Policy							1	80		
Energy and Mining					1	105				
Financial and Private Sector Devt							1	5		
Global ICT					1	22				
Transport			2	128.4	1	31				
Urban Development							1	25		
TOTAL	0	0	2	128.4	4	198	3	110	0	0

Source: World Bank databases, July 2011 (includes Supplements).

Table J.10 — Afghanistan–World Bank IDA Grant by Sector Board, FY02–11 (number of projects and commitment amounts in US$ millions)

Sector Board	FY02 No.	FY02 Amt	FY03 No.	FY03 Amt	FY04 No.	FY04 Amt	FY05 No.	FY05 Amt	FY06 No.	FY06 Amt
Agriculture and Rural Devt					1	95.0	1	28.0	2	60.0
Economic Policy									1	80.0
Education	1	15.0					2	75.0		
Energy and Mining									1	30.0
Financial & Priv Sector Devt										
Financial Management										
Global ICT										
Health, Nutrition & Population			1	59.6					1	30.0
Public Sector Governance	1	10.0	1	8.4			1	27.0		
Social Development	1	42.0								
Social Protection										
Transport			1	18.8			1	45.0		
Water	1	33.0							1	40.0
TOTAL	4	100.0	3	86.8	1	95.0	5	175.0	6	240.0

Source: World Bank databases, July 2011 (includes Supplements).

	FY07		FY08		FY09		FY10		FY11		TOTAL	
	No.	Amt	No.	Amt	No.	Amt	No.	Amt	No.	Amt	No.	Amt
											1	40
											1	80
											1	105
											1	5
									1	0.5	2	22.5
											3	159.4
											1	25
	0	0	0	0	0	0	0	0	1	0.5	10	436.9

	FY07		FY08		FY09		FY10		FY11		TOTAL	
	No.	Amt	No.	Amt	No.	Amt	No.	Amt	No.	Amt	No.	Amt
	3	153.0	1	28.0	2	108.5	2	70.0	1	97.8	13	640.3
	1	80.0									2	160.0
			2	50.0			1	20.0			6	160.0
					1	10.0			1	52.0	3	92.0
	1	25.0	1	30.0	1	8.0			1	22.0	4	85.0
	1	33.4									1	33.4
									1	50.0	1	50.0
			2	30.0	1	30.0	1	49.0			6	198.6
	1	20.4			1	35.0					5	100.8
											1	42.0
							1	7.5			1	7.5
			1	112.0	1	6.8	1	50.5	1	40.0	6	273.1
											2	73.0
	7	311.8	7	250.0	7	198.3	6	197.0	5	261.8	51	1,915.7

| Table J.11 | Afghanistan: Trust Funds by Sector Board, FY02–11 (number of projects and commitment amounts in US$ millions) | | | | | | | | | |

Sector Board	FY02 No.	FY02 Amt	FY03 No.	FY03 Amt	FY04 No.	FY04 Amt	FY05 No.	FY05 Amt	FY06 No.	FY06 Amt
Agriculture & Rural Development[a]					1	195.4	1	0.3	1	34.3
Economic Policy							1	13.0		
Education							2	49.0		
Energy and Mining					2	27.4				
Financial and Private Sector Development[b]	1	4.6			2	185.0				
Financial Management	1	2,295.3			1	9.1				
Global ICT					1	6.1				
Health, Nutrition and Population			1	0.5						
Poverty Reduction			1	18.5						
Public Sector Governance			1	3.0						
Social Development	1	3.5								
Social Protection					1	2.8				
Transport			2	81.2	1	3.0				
Urban Development										
Water							1	41.0	1	7.7
TOTAL	3	2,303.3	5	103.3	9	428.9	5	103.3	2	42.0

Source: World Bank databases, July 2011 (includes Supplements).
a. Includes the NSP.
b. Only one project (FMBA Capacity Building, US$0.65Mln, FY04 under Financial and Private Sector Development) is JSDF funded; all others are ARTF projects.

| Table J.12 | Afghanistan Total Commitment Amount by Sector Board, World Bank IDA Credit, Grant, Trust Fund | | | | | | | | | | |

	FY02 Amt	FY03 Amt	FY04 Amt	FY05 Amt	FY06 Amt	FY07 Amt	FY08 Amt	FY09 Amt	FY10 Amt	FY11 Amt	TOTAL Amt
Agriculture and Rural Devt	0	0	330.4	28.3	94.3	621.9	28.9	116.5	336	139.8	1,696.1
Economic Policy	0	0	0	93	80	95	0	0	0	14	282
Education	15	0	0	124	0	0	144.1	0	20	0	303.1
Energy and Mining	0	0	132.4	0	30	0	57	70	0	52	341.4
Financial and Private Sector Devt	4.6	0	185	5	0	25	30	8	0	22	279.6
Financial Management	2,295.30	0.00	9.10	0.00	0.00	33.40	0.00	0.00	0.00	0.00	2,337.8
Global ICT	0	0	28.1	0	0	0	0	0	0	50.5	78.6
Health, Nutrition and Population	0	60.1	0	0	30	0	30	64	66.7	0	250.8
Poverty Reduction	0	18.5	0	0	0	0	0	0	0	0	18.5
Public Sector Governance	10	11.4	0	27	0	20.4	27.8	35	0	0	131.6
Social Development	45.5	0	0	0	0	0	0	0	0	0	45.5
Social Protection	0	0	2.8	0	0	0	0	0	7.5	0	10.3
Transport	0	228.4	34	45	0	0	192	24.8	50.5	40	614.7
Urban Development	0	0	0	25	0	0	5.6	0	0	0	30.6
Water	33	0	0	41	47.7	0	0	5.5	0	0	127.2
TOTAL	2403.4	318.4	721.8	388.3	282	795.7	515.4	323.8	480.7	318.3	6547.8

FY07		FY08		FY09		FY10		FY11		TOTAL	
No.	Amt	No.	Amt	No.	Amt	No.	Amt	No.	Amt	No.	Amt
2	468.9	3	0.9	1	8.0	2	266.0	1	42.0	12	1,015.8
1	15.0							1	14.0	3	42.0
		2	94.1							4	143.1
		1	57.0	1	60.0					4	144.4
										3	189.5
										2	2,304.4
										1	6.1
				1	34.0	1	17.7			3	52.2
										1	18.5
		1	27.8							2	30.8
										1	3.5
										1	2.8
		1	80.0	1	18.0					5	182.2
		1	5.6							1	5.6
				1	5.5					3	54.2
3	483.9	9	265.3	5	125.5	3	283.7	2	56.0	46	4,195.1

Table J.13	Project Ratings for Afghanistan and Comparators, Exit FY02–11									
	Total evaluated		Outcome (% moderately satisfactory or better)		Risks to Development Outcomes (% moderate or lower)		Institutional Development Impact (% substantial or higher)		Sustainability (% likely)	
	($M)	(No)	($)	(No)	($)	(No)	($)	(No)	($)	(No)
Afghanistan	926.4	22	96.6	86.4	14.7	10.5	91.6	66.7	100.0	100.0
Bangladesh	3,763.5	42	74.6	69.0	57.6	60.0	16.5	29.4	88.9	71.4
Haiti	120.1	7	58.4	42.9	9.6	20.0	-	-	-	-
Nepal	450.7	15	62.2	60.0	44.8	36.4	19.0	50.0	55.2	66.7
Pakistan	4,488.8	43	65.5	76.7	17.1	32.0	35.9	33.3	94.4	87.5
Tajikistan	169.9	14	80.7	78.6	18.1	11.1	6.7	20.0	80.4	60.0
Congo, Dem. Rep. of	823.5	5	65.1	60.0	-	-	7.5	33.3	73.0	66.7
South Asia Region	24,783.0	239	78.6	76.2	54.7	50.8	45.1	48.1	89.0	84.2
Overall result	152,194.8	2,381	82.4	76.3	71.0	60.9	56.5	52.3	82.3	77.1

Source: World Bank data as of April 4, 2012.

Note: - = information not available.

Exit FY	Project ID	Project name	Total evaluated ($M)	Total evaluated (number)
Table J.14		List of Projects Rated for Afghanistan, Exit FY02–11		
FY05	P077533	Emergency Community Empowerment Project	46.0	1
	P078618	AF - Programmatic Support for Inst. Bldg	79.6	1
FY06	P077417	1AF-Emergency Public Administration Project	11.5	1
	P077779	Emergency Infrastructure Reconstruction	36.2	1
	P077896	Emergency Education Rehab. & Dev.	17.4	1
	P090829	AF Program. Support for Inst. Bldg II	79.2	1
FY07	P082610	Second Emergency Public Admin Project	9.1	1
	P084329	Emergency National Solidarity Project	166.4	1
FY08	P082472	Nat'l Emergency Emp. Prog for Rural	41.6	1
	P102709	Program. Support for Inst. Bldg III	80.9	1
FY09	P078284	Emergency Transport Rehabilitation	155.3	1
	P078324	Afghanistan Health Sector Emergency Rehab	93.9	1
	P083964	Education Quality Improvement Program	31.0	1
	P084736	Public Admin Capacity Building Project	23.7	1
	P091036	ARTF - Nat. Emergency Employment Program	-	1
	P091060	ARTF- Improvement of Power Supply	-	1
FY10	P083720	AF: Emergency Communications Development	22.0	1
	P086228	AF: ARTF-Civil Service Capacity Building	-	1
	P091038	ARTF - RWSSP	-	1
	P100935	Avian Flu	0.5	1
	P107921	Strengthening Institutions DPG	-	1
FY11	P083906	Emergency Customs and Trade Facilitation	32.2	1
Result			926.4	22

Source: World Bank data as of April 4, 2012.

Note: - = information not available.

Table J.15 Project Ratings by IEG for Afghanistan, Exit FY02–11

Exit FY	Approval FY	Project ID		IEG outcome	IEG risk to development objective rating	IEG sustainability[a]	IEG institutional development impact
2005	2002	P077533	Emergency Community Empowerment Project	Satisfactory	#	Non-evaluable	Substantial
	2005	P078618	AF - Programmatic Support for Inst. Bldg	Satisfactory	#	Non-evaluable	Substantial
2006	2002	P077417	1AF-Emergency Public Administration Proj	Moderately satisfactory	#	Likely	Negligible
	2002	P077779	Emergency Infrastructure Reconstruction	Satisfactory	High	#	#
	2002	P077896	Emergency Education Rehab. & Dev.	Moderately satisfactory	High	#	#
	2006	P090829	AF Program. Support for Inst. Bldg II	Satisfactory	Significant	#	#
2007	2003	P082610	Second Emergency Public Admin Project	Moderately satisfactory	High	#	#
	2004	P084329	Emergency National Solidarity Project	Moderately satisfactory	Significant	#	#
2008	2003	P082472	Nat'l Emergency Emp. Prog for Rural	Satisfactory	Significant	#	#
	2007	P102709	Program. Support for Inst. Bldg III	Satisfactory	Significant	#	#
2009	2003	P078284	Emergency Transport Rehabilitation	Moderately satisfactory	High	#	#
	2003	P078324	Afghanistan Health Sector Emergency Rehab	Satisfactory	Moderate	#	#
	2005	P083964	Education Quality Improvement Program	Moderately unsatisfactory	High	#	#
	2005	P084736	Public Admin Capacity Building Project	Satisfactory	Significant	#	#
	2003	P091036	ARTF - Nat. Emergency Employment Pgm	Moderately satisfactory	Significant	#	#
	2004	P091060	ARTF- Improvement of Power Supply	Moderately satisfactory	High	#	#
2010	2004	P083720	AF: Emergency Communications Development	Moderately satisfactory	Moderate	#	#
	2005	P086228	AF: ARTF-Civil Service Capacity Building	Unsatisfactory	Significant	#	#
	2006	P091038	ARTF - RWSSP	Moderately satisfactory	Significant	#	#
	2007	P100935	Avian Flu	Unsatisfactory	High	#	#
	2009	P107921	Strengthening Institutions DPG	Moderately satisfactory	High	#	#
2011	2004	P083906	Emergency Customs and Trade Facilitation	Satisfactory	High	#	#

Source: World Bank data as of April 4, 2012.

Note: # = information not available.

a. Sustainability and institutional development impact were rated until around FY06; risk to development objective is rated in projects from FY07 onward.

Country	Indicator	Fiscal year									
		2002	2003	2004	2005	2006	2007	2008	2009	2010	2011
Afghanistan	Number of projects	4	8	13	17	17	21	22	23	23	23
	Net commitment amount	100	315	608	726	873	1,014	871	1,018	1,077	1,086
	Number of projects at risk	-	3	1	3	2	2	6	7	10	9
	Percent of projects at risk	-	38	8	18	12	10	27	30	43	39
	Commitments at risk	-	85	15	176	130	33	235	245	417	278
	Percent commitments at risk	-	27	2	24	15	3	27	24	39	26
Bangladesh	Number of projects	24	24	28	26	24	24	21	26	27	28
	Net commitment amount	2,266	2,142	2,530	2,318	2,044	1,966	1,997	2,767	3,562	4,975
	Number of projects at risk	4	6	5	3	7	6	3	1	5	3
	Percent of projects at risk	17	25	18	12	29	25	14	4	19	11
	Commitments at risk	355	710	598	325	782	464	339	16	741	166
	Percent commitments at risk	16	33	24	14	38	24	17	1	21	3
Congo, Dem. Rep. of	Number of projects	2	2	7	8	8	10	12	15	17	16
	Net commitment amount	500	504	1,240	1,332	1,407	1,737	1,956	2,310	2,179	2,023
	Number of projects at risk	-	-	-	2	3	6	7	7	10	11
	Percent of projects at risk	-	-	-	25	38	60	58	47	59	69
	Commitments at risk	-	-	-	160	262	1,171	1,444	909	1,444	1,718
	Percent commitments at risk	-	-	-	12	19	67	74	39	66	85
Haiti	Number of projects				3	5	10	12	16	15	15
	Net commitment amount				75	70	138	167	207	291	328
	Number of projects at risk				1	1	3	4	9	5	9
	Percent of projects at risk				33	20	30	33	56	33	60
	Commitments at risk				12	12	20	15	145	52	192
	Percent commitments at risk				16	17	14	9	70	18	59
Nepal	Number of projects	8	10	9	12	12	13	16	16	15	17
	Net commitment amount	226	303	302	424	422	470	823	858	1,079	1,259
	Number of projects at risk	2	2	1	1	3	4	4	5	11	7
	Percent of projects at risk	25	20	11	8	25	31	25	31	73	41
	Commitments at risk	126	78	76	76	145	139	163	304	753	558
	Percent commitments at risk	56	26	25	18	34	30	20	35	70	44

Table J.16 Afghanistan and Comparators—Portfolio Status Indicators, FY02–11

Country	Indicator	Fiscal year									
		2002	2003	2004	2005	2006	2007	2008	2009	2010	2011
Pakistan	Number of projects	10	13	16	14	17	18	20	24	21	24
	Net commitment amount	1,144	1,204	1,426	967	1,830	2,035	2,494	3,564	3,505	3,710
	Number of projects at risk	-	1	1	1	-	1	2	4	5	7
	Percent of projects at risk	-	8	6	7	-	6	10	17	24	29
	Commitments at risk	-	285	285	61	-	103	164	345	341	761
	Percent commitments at risk	-	24	20	6	-	5	7	10	10	21
Tajikistan	Number of projects	10	11	10	10	14	14	14	15	16	14
	Net commitment amount	151	171	127	143	164	175	161	174	226	192
	Number of projects at risk	4	1	2	-	-	1	3	4	3	1
	Percent of projects at risk	40	9	20	-	-	7	21	27	19	7
	Commitments at risk	29	20	24	-	-	10	37	54	54	5
	Percent commitments at risk	19	12	19	-	-	6	23	31	24	3
South Asia Region	Number of projects	129	142	149	156	145	161	160	171	183	193
	Net commitment amount	17,070	17,405	17,562	18,041	17,190	20,474	20,768	24,031	31,679	37,540
	Number of projects at risk	13	25	20	18	19	24	32	30	40	38
	Percent of projects at risk	10	18	13	12	13	15	20	18	22	20
	Commitments at risk	1,543	2,537	3,625	1,745	2,858	3,366	4,163	3,120	4,807	5,128
	Percent commitments at risk	9	15	21	10	17	16	20	13	15	14
Fragile and conflict-affected state[a]	Number of projects	104	108	110	123	122	141	162	178	184	194
	Net commitment amount	3,650	4,113	4,728	5,067	5,186	5,905	6,794	8,023	8,316	8,637
	Number of projects at risk	24	32	34	34	35	45	48	81	82	82
	Percent of projects at risk	23	30	31	28	29	32	30	46	45	42
	Commitments at risk	796	1,281	1,003	1,310	1,316	2,291	2,793	3,246	4,209	4,220
	Percent commitments at risk	22	31	21	26	25	39	41	40	51	49

Source: World Bank data as of April 11, 2012.

a. Fragile and conflict-affected states, IDA-Eligible Country List; no data available for Marshall Islands, Micronesia FS, Myanmar, Somalia, or Sudan.

- = information not available.

	Total	Project supervision	Lending	Analytical and Advisory Activities	Country program support	Client training	Impact evaluation
Cost structure (US$)							
Agriculture and rural development	10,298	6,276	3,174	629			218
Education	4,126	2,945	785	349		47	
Energy and mining	5,046	2,462	1,207	1,376			
Environment	690		67	623			
Economic policy	3,799	959	1,061	1,491	216	72	
Financial management	1,151	555	294	302			
Financial and private sector development (I)	4,531	1,267	1,397	1,640		227	
Financial systems practice	26		26				
Gender and development	604	(1)	21	559		25	
Global information/communications technology	1,725	690	287	747			
Health, nutrition and population	3,512	2,016	898	586		13	
Operational services	2				2		
Poverty reduction	2,338			2,324	1	13	
Procurement	33			33			
Public sector governance	8,037	2,354	1,478	4,121	27	58	
Social development	1,818	425	488	905			
Social protection	1,643	323	345	968		8	
Transport	4,781	3,149	1,299	269			65
Urban development	2,271	1,006	856	389			19
Water	3,195	2,104	1,039	51			
Sector board not applicable (I)	16			16			
Not assigned	16,892	4,031	1,223	4,770	6,868		
Overall result	76,535	30,561	15,947	22,148	7,113	464	302
Cost structure (percent)							
Agriculture and Rural Development	100	61	31	6	0	0	2
Education	100	71	19	8	0	1	0
Energy and mining	100	49	24	27	0	0	0
Environment	100	0	10	90	0	0	0
Economic policy	100	25	28	39	6	2	0
Financial management	100	48	26	26	0	0	0
Financial and private sector development (I)	100	28	31	36	0	5	0
Financial systems practice	100	0	100	0	0	0	0
Gender and development	100	0	3	93	0	4	0

	Total	Project supervision	Lending	Analytical and Advisory Activities	Country program support	Client training	Impact evaluation
Global information/communications technology	100	40	17	43	0	0	0
Health, nutrition and population	100	57	26	17	0	0	0
Operational services	100	0	0	0	100	0	0
Poverty reduction	100	0	0	99	0	1	0
Procurement	100	0	0	100	0	0	0
Public sector governance	100	29	18	51	0	1	0
Social development	100	23	27	50	0	0	0
Social protection	100	20	21	59	0	1	0
Transport	100	66	27	6	0	0	1
Urban development	100	44	38	17	0	0	1
Water	100	66	33	2	0	0	0
Sector board not applicable (I)	100	0	0	100	0	0	0
Not assigned	100	24	7	28	41	0	0
Overall result	100	40	21	29	9	1	0

Source: World Bank data as of October 28, 2011.

Table J.18	Public Financial Management Operations, FY02–11				
Name of project	Year approved	Project amount (US$ millions)	IDA funding (US$ millions)	IEG outcome rating
AF-Emergency Public Administration Proj	2002	11.62	10.0	MS
ARTF - Recurrent and Capital Costs	2002	[2,295.3]		S
Second Emergency Public Admin Project	2003	11.97(4.8)	8.4(4.8)	MS
ARTF - AF: Strengthening Fin. Capacity	2004	9.1		N/A
Public Admin Capacity Building Project	2005	27.4 (25.9)	27.4 (25.9)	S
AF - Programmatic Support for Inst. Bldg	2005	80.0 (23.2)	80.0 (23.2)	S
AF Program. Support for Inst. Bldg II	2006	80.0 (23.2)	80.0 (23.2)	S
Program. Support for Inst. Bldg III	2007	80.0 (23.2)	80.0 (23.2)	S
AF: Public Financial Management Reform	2007	33.4	33.4	N/A
Afg Strengthening Institutions DPG	2009	35.0 (11.7)	35.0 (11.7)	MS
Second Public Fin Management Reform Program	2011	73	0	N/A
Total excluding ARTF		441.49 (239.12)	354.2 (155.4)	

Note: Actual project costs for completed projects may be different due to exchange rate changes. Amounts in parentheses are components for public financial management.

Af = Afghanistan; ARTF = Afghanistan Reconstruction Trust Fund; DPG = Development Policy Grant; MS = mostly satisfactory; N/A = not applicable; S = satisfactory.

Table J.19	PAG Operations, FY02–11			
Name of project	Year approved	Project amount (US$ millions)	IDA funding (US$ millions)	IEG outcome rating
Second Emergency Public Admin Project	2003	11.97 (7.17)	8.4 (7.17)	MS
ARTF-Civil Service Capacity Building	2005	13.0		US
Public Admin Capacity Building Project	2005	27.4 (1.5)	27.4 (1.5)	S
ARTF-Management Capacity Program	2007	15.0		N/A
Civil Service Reform Project	2007	20.4	20.4	N/A
Afghanistan Judicial Reform Project	2008	27.8		N/A
AF - Programmatic Support for Inst. Bldg	2005	80.0 (34.4)	80.0 (34.4)	S
AF Program. Support for Inst. Bldg II	2006	80.0 (34.4)	80.0 (34.4)	S
Program. Support for Inst. Bldg III	2007	80.0 (34.4)	80.0 (34.4)	S
Afg Strengthening Institutions DPG	2009	35.0 (11.9)	35.0 (11.9)	MS
AF Strengthening Natl. Statistical System	2011	14.0		N/A

Note: Actual project costs for completed projects may be different due to exchange rate changes. Amounts in parentheses are components for public sector governance.

AF = Afghanistan; ARTF = Afghanistan Reconstuction Trust Fund; DPG = Development Policy Grant; MS = moderately satisfactory; N/A = not applicable; S = satisfactory; US = unsatisfactory.

Figure J.1 — Afghanistan: Governance Indicators

Comparison between, 2009, 2008, 2007, 2006, 2005, 2004, 2003, 2002, 2000, 1998, 1996 (top-bottom order)

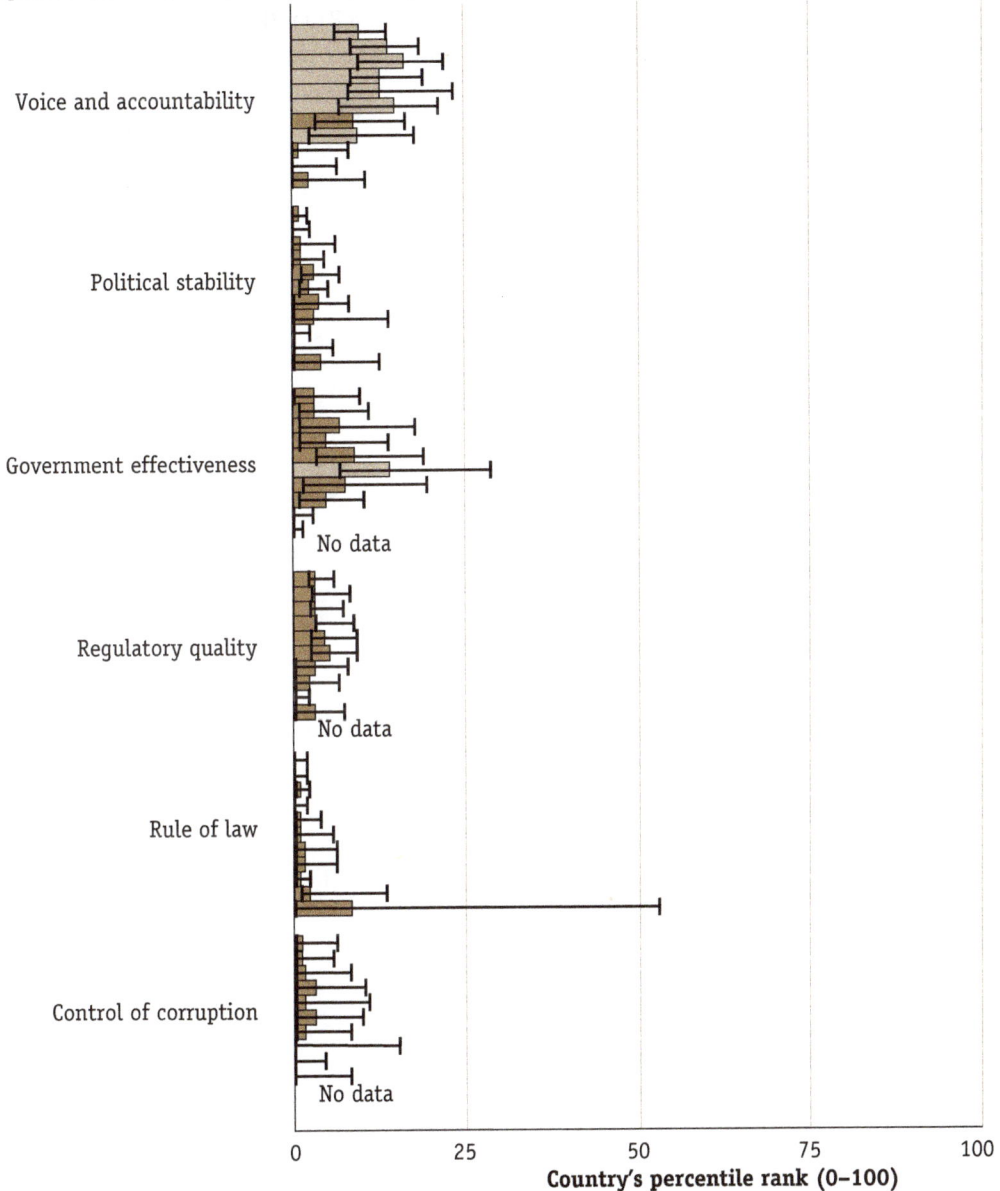

Voice and accountability

Political stability

Government effectiveness

No data

Regulatory quality

No data

Rule of law

Control of corruption

No data

Country's percentile rank (0–100)

Source: Kaufmann, D., A. Kraay, and M. Mastruzzi (2010), The Worldwide Governance Indicators: Methodology and Analytical Issues.

Note: The governance indicators presented here aggregate the views on the quality of governance provided by a large number of enterprises, citizens, and expert survey respondents in industrial and developing countries. These data are gathered from a number of survey institutes, think tanks, nongovernmental organizations, and international organizations. The WGI do not reflect the official views of the World Bank, its Executive Directors, or the countries they represent. The WGI are not used by the World Bank Group to allocate resources.

Reference

Kaufmann, D., A. Kray, and M. Mastruzzi. 2010. "The Worldwide Governance Indicators: Methodology and Analytical Issues." Policy Research Working Paper No. WPS 5430. World Bank, Washington, DC. Source data available at: www.govindicators.org.

Appendix K
List of AAA Panelists

Garg, Prem   Moderator

Breeding, Mary

Gopal, Gita

Hicks, Norman

Kang, Min Joo

Liebenthal, Andres

Markova, Svetlana

Martinez, Albert

McCarthy, Eugene

Nellis, John

Pellekaan, Jack W. van Holst

Penalver-Quesada, Manuel

Pirozzi, Stephen Francis

Schiavo-Campo, Salvatore

Stout, Susan

Wallich, Christine

Wescott Clay

Attachment
Comments from Government

Islamic Republic of Afghanistan
Ministry of Finance

June 26, 2012

Ali M. Khadr
Senior Manager Country, Corporate, and Global Evaluations
The World Bank
Dear Mr. Khadr,

Re: Afghanistan: Country Program Evaluation, 2002-2011

I am writing in reference to the Independent Evaluation Group's evaluation of the World Bank's Country program. I want to thank you and your team for carrying out the evaluation of the World Bank Group country program for 2002-2011 earlier and visiting Kabul again mid-June to present the draft evaluation report. The report has reflected our comments fully and I wanted to congratulate you and the team for the excellent report.

I believe that the participants from the government ministries provided comments during the presentation on June 16, 2012. Following are a few suggestions that we would like to convey to you for consideration as well;

1. The CPE, besides reflecting the comments from the Government, provides strong recommendations for improvement and therefore should not remain as a tool to only evaluate what has been achieved but the recommendations should be taken into consideration to improve operations in the future. Therefore taking into consideration the CPE recommendations in the design of CAS/ISN would be beneficial. Moreover, we believe that the CPEs should be conducted more frequently.

2. The donor contributions since Kabul Conference in 2010 have increased drastically considering the 50% on-budget principle, using ARTF mainly for that purpose. However the number of major IDA and ARTF programs has more or less remained the same and

the existing programs have grown in size rather than in number to fund more of the government priorities.

3. With the ARTF, the donor preferencing is an issue and does not allow appropriate and balanced funding to the government priorities. Some of the programs, like NSP, receive more funding than the program has the capacity for and cannot absorb any more funding. This results in a situation where a donor's favorite program has disproportionately large funding while other priorities remain underfunded or not funded at all.

4. Sustainability is another factor that has not been considered in some of the programs. NSP for example, and the modality of delivery are not very sustainability in the wake of decreased donor funding post transition. While the model of roads built through the rural roads program needs to adapt more to the geography and climate conditions of the country.

5. ARTF investment portfolio in particular, and the World Bank Group's overall portfolio in general need to be aligned with the national development strategy translated into the 22 National Priority Programs (NPPs) in the real and meaningful sense. Funding a component or subcomponent of the NPPs does not represent full alignment with the NPP and creates the problem of unequal funding of projects within the NPP.

6. Related to the above, shifts within the sectors should take place. (E.g. investing more in higher education or TVET rather than primary education via EQUIP)

7. With transition in sight the government of Afghanistan is planning for the transition and the decade after transition - the decade of transformation. In the government's medium-to-long term strategy, funding of Operation & Maintenance (O&M), Provincial Budgeting, Resource Corridor remain top priority for the Government of Afghanistan. Bank's operations need to acknowledge and focus on these areas.

8. The Government of Afghanistan supports the ARTF to channel funds to the government priorities. It provides the government with the vital funding of the national budget and at the same time provides the donors with the comfort of the fiduciary controls in place. With the funding increase through the ARTF and the demand to take on more projects,

there is a need for the World Bank to increase its footprint in the country including stationing more experts on the ground.

9. In relation with the ARTF, the World Bank needs to strike a balance between expectation of donors, parliament, Government, and the public. We believe there is rigidity and reluctance for new programs proposed by the Government compared to the programs proposed by donors.

10. One of the values that the World Bank brings is the quality of its analytical and advisory activities (AAA). Identifying areas to carry out such AAA's if carried out in consultation with the government, ensures their relevance to the needs and demands of the situation and will add more value.

11. With increased capacity and PFM strength, the Government can play a bigger role. Some of the responsibilities could be shifted to the government to expedite the process and avoid unnecessary delays.

12. While IBRD has had a very active portfolio in Afghanistan, IFC and MIGA need to be more proactive in seeking out new business opportunities in Afghanistan.

Thank you again for your assistance.

Sincerely

Dr. Omar Zakhilwal
Minister of Finance
Islamic Republic of Afghanistan

Bibliography

Afghan Public Health Institute, Ministry of Public Health (Afghanistan), Central Statistics Organization (Afghanistan), ICF Macro, Indian Institute of Health Management Research, and World Health Organization Regional Office for the Eastern Mediterranean. 2011. *Afghanistan Mortality Survey 2010*. Calverton, MD: APHI/MoPH, CSO, ICF Macro, IIHMR, and WHO/EMBRO.

BCEK-Interim_Estimates_of_Program_Impact_2010_07_25.pdf.

Bijlert, Martine van. 2010. "Imaginary Institutions: State Building in Afghanistan." In *Doing Good or Doing Better: Development Policies in a Globalizing World*, ed. Monique Kremer, Peter van Lieshout, and Robert Went. The Hague: Amsterdam University Press.

Böhnke, J., J. Koehler, and C. Zürcher. 2010. *Assessing the Impact of Development Cooperation in North East Afghanistan 2005-2009: Final Report*. Evaluation Reports 049. Bonn: Federal Ministry for Economic Cooperation and Development.

Chatain, Pierre-Laurent, John McDowell, Cedric Mousset, Paul Allen Schott, and Emile van der Does de Willebois. 2009. *Preventing Money Laundering and Terrorist Financing: A Practical Guide for Bank Supervisors*. Washington DC: World Bank.

CSO (Central Statistics Office, Afghanistan) and UNICEF (United Nations Children's Fund). 2004. *Moving Beyond Two Decades of War: Progress in the Provinces. Multiple Indicator Cluster Survey 2002*. Kabul: CSO and UNICEF. Economist Intelligence Unit. 2008. "Afghanistan Country Profile 2008."

FAOSTAT. Available at: faostat.fao.org.

ICON-INSTITUTE. 2008. *Using Knowledge to Improve Development Effectiveness: An Evaluation of World Bank Economic and Sector Work and Technical Assistance, 2000–2006*. Washington, DC: World Bank.

———. 2010. *Gender and Development: An Evaluation of World Bank Support, 2002–08*. Washington, DC: World Bank.

IMF (International Monetary Fund). 2007. Islamic Republic of Afghanistan: 2007 Article IV Consultation and Third Review Under the Three-Year Arrangement Under the Poverty Reduction and Growth Facility, and Request for Waiver of Performance Criterion; IMF Country Report 08/76; January 28, 2008. Washington, DC: IMF.

Islamic Republic of Afghanistan. 2007. "Afghanistan National Development Strategy." Kabul.

———. 2009. "National Agriculture Development Framework." Kabul.

Kremer, Monique, Peter van Lieshout, and Robert Went. 2010. *Doing Good or Doing Better: Development Policies in a Globalizing World*. The Hague: Amsterdam University Press.

Manning, Nick, Anne Evans, and Anne Tully with Yasin Osmani and Andrew Wilder. 2004. *Subnational Administration in Afghanistan: Assessment and Recommendations for Action*. Washington, DC: World Bank.

Ministry of Economy (Afghanistan) and the World Bank. 2010. Poverty Status in Afghanistan. Based on the National Risk and Vulnerability Assessment (NRVA (2007-2008). Available at: http://siteresources.worldbank.org/AFGHANI STANEXTN/Resources/305984-1326909014678/8376871-1334700522455/Poverty StatusLaunchPresentation.pdf.

OECD (Organisation for Economic Co-operation and Development). 2005. *The Challenge of Capacity Development: Working Towards Good Practice*. OECD/DAC Guidelines and Reference Series. Paris: OECD.

Pritchett, Lant, and Michael Woolcock. 2004. "Solutions When the Solution Is the Problem: Arraying the Disarray in Development." *World Development* 32(2): 191–212.

Scanteam. 2008. *Afghanistan Reconstruction Trust Fund: External Evaluation Final Report*. Prepared for the World Bank Office, Kabul. Oslo: Scanteam.

Scott, James. 1998. *Seeing Like a State: How Certain Schemes to Improve the Human Condition Have Failed*. New Haven: Yale University Press.

———. 2009. *The Art of Not Being Governed: An Anarchist History of Upland Southeast Asia*. Yale Agrarian Studies Series. New Haven: Yale University Press.

Tewari, Deepali. 2012. *Afghanistan - Kabul Urban Reconstruction Project : P083919 - Implementation Status Results Report : Sequence 18*. Washington, DC: World Bank. Available at: http://documents.worldbank.org/curated/en/2012/05/16260746/ afghanistan-kabul-urban-reconstruction-project-p083919-implementation-status-results-report-sequence-18.

UNFP (United Nations Population Fund), UNICEF (United Nations Children's Fund), WHO (World Health Organization), and World Bank. 2012. *Trends in Maternal Mortality 1990–2010*. Geneva: WHO.

UNODOC (United Nations Office of Drugs and Crime). 2011. "Afghanistan Opium Survey." Vienna, UNODOC.

Wong, Susan. 2012. "What Have Been the Impacts of World Bank CDD Programs? CDD Impact Evaluation Review and Operational and Research Implications." World Bank Social Development Department, Washington, DC.

World Bank. 2004. Afghanistan: State Building, Sustaining Growth and Reducing Poverty: A Country Economic Report. Poverty Reduction and Economic Management Sector Unit, South Asia Region, Report No. 29551-AF. Washington DC: World Bank. Available at: http://siteresources.worldbank.org/INTAFGHANISTAN/News%20and %20Events/20261395/AfghanistanEconomicReportfinalversion909.pdf.

———. 2005. *Afghanistan: National Reconstruction and Poverty Reduction—The Role of Women in Afghanistan's Future.* Washington, DC: World Bank.

———. 2006. "Service Delivery and Governance at the Sub-National Level in Afghanistan." South Asia Region, Washington, DC: World Bank.

———. 2008. "Afghanistan Public Financial Management Performance Assessment: Executive Summary." Washington, DC: World Bank.

———. 2010. *Scoping Strategic Options for Development of the Kabul River Basin: A Mulisectoral Decision Support System Approach.* Washington, DC: World Bank.

www.ingramcontent.com/pod-product-compliance
Lightning Source LLC
Chambersburg PA
CBHW081459200326
41518CB00015B/2316

* 9 7 8 0 8 2 1 3 9 8 7 2 2 *